D1259379

The Impact of the American Revolution Abroad

Library of Congress
Symposia on the American Revolution

The Impact
of the
American Revolution
Abroad

Papers presented at the fourth symposium, May 8 and 9, 1975

Library of Congress   Washington   1976

Library of Congress Cataloging in Publication Data

Library of Congress Symposia on the American
Revolution, 4th, 1975.
The impact of the American Revolution abroad.

1. United States—History—Revolution, 1775–1783—
Influences—Congresses. I. United States. Library of
Congress. II. Title.
E209.L52 1975   973.3   76-8163
ISBN 0-8444-0182-X

Advisory Committee

on the Library of Congress

American Revolution Bicentennial Program

Preface

Delivered at the fourth Library of Congress Symposium on the American Revolution, held in the Library's Coolidge Auditorium on May 8 and 9, 1975, the papers published here center on the Revolution in its relationship to other nations. Previous symposia have treated the establishment of independence largely from the American point of view: The Development of a Revolutionary Mentality (1972), Fundamental Testaments of the American Revolution (1973), and Leadership in the American Revolution (1974). In this volume, historians discuss the impact of the Revolution on France, Great Britain, Ireland, the Dutch Republic, the Russian Empire, and the Spanish- and Portuguese-speaking world. Comments by scholars from Germany, Mexico, and Japan follow the papers. The fifth in the series of symposia, to be held in May 1976, will center on the American Revolution as a continuing commitment.

The impact of the American Revolution abroad, as described in the papers and commentaries which follow, appears to have been greater than many have hitherto suspected. Although some scholars detect the influence of the American Revolution in the anticolonial struggles of our own day, the conventional notion has been that the American Revolution exerted a significant influence in Europe only until 1789, when its importance was eclipsed by that of the French Revolution. The view that emerges from the papers in this volume is that the influence of the American Revolution continued after 1789 and was discernible well into the 19th century in some European countries—Russia, for example, at the time of the Decembrist movement. In Latin America the influence of the Revolution appears to have persisted to an even later period.

Through the generosity and understanding of the Congress the Library is carrying on under the direction of the Assistant Librarian of Congress a broad program for the commemoration of the American Revolution. Among other activities, this program includes the preparation of guides to contemporary source materials in the Library, bibliographies, documentary and facsimile publications, musical programs, and exhibits. It also includes publication of letters of delegates to Congress, 1774–1789, in a multivolume edition, the first volumes of which are scheduled to appear in 1976.

The symposia on the American Revolution and the resulting publications are made possible through a grant from The Morris and Gwendolyn Cafritz Foundation, established by the late Mr. Cafritz, Washington realtor and philanthropist. Through this support the Cafritz Foundation, which fosters cultural, educational, and developmental activities in the District of Columbia, has made a lasting contribution to the understanding of the American Revolution.

We are also indebted to the United States Department of State, which enabled several foreign scholars to participate and which joined the Cafritz Foundation and the Library in welcoming all who attended this symposium at a reception in the Department's diplomatic rooms.

Elizabeth Hamer Kegan
Assistant Librarian of Congress

Contents

The Impact of the American Revolution Abroad

Richard B. Morris began his teaching career in 1927 as an instructor in history at the City College of New York, where he taught for 22 years. He joined the Columbia University faculty in 1949, served as chairman of the History Department, 1959–61, and in 1959 was named Gouverneur Morris Professor of History.

Professor Morris holds a B.A. degree from the City College of New York, M.A. and Ph.D. degrees from Columbia University, and an L.H.D. degree from Hebrew Union College. He has been a visiting professor and lecturer at many universities in the United States and abroad, including Princeton University, the University of Hawaii, and the Free University of Berlin. In 1961 he received an appointment as a Fulbright research scholar at the University of Paris.

Among Professor Morris' many publications are Government and Labor in Early America *(1946);* The American Revolution, a Short History *(1955);* The Spirit of 'Seventy-Six *(with Henry Steele Commager, 1958, 1967; Bicentennial edition, 1976);* The Peacemakers; the Great Powers and American Independence *(1965), awarded the Bancroft Prize in history;* The American Revolution Reconsidered *(1967);* The Emerging Nations and the American Revolution *(1970);* America, a History of the People *(with William Greenleaf and Robert H. Ferrell, 1971);* Seven Who Shaped Our Destiny *(1973, 1976), and* John Jay; the Making of a Revolutionary *(1975).*

Professor Morris is president of the American Historical Association, editor of The Papers of John Jay, *and a member of the Library of Congress American Revolution Bicentennial Program advisory committee.*

Introduction

RICHARD B. MORRIS

WRITING RETROSPECTIVELY about the American Revolution, Benjamin Franklin declared, "God grant that not only the love of liberty, but a thorough knowledge of the rights of man, may prevail in all the nations of the earth, so that a philosopher may set his foot anywhere on its surface and say, 'This is my country.'"

If Franklin's fervent prayer has not yet been fulfilled, it is not because Americans have not tried. And they did so beginning with the American Revolution.

In the three previous symposia sponsored by the Library of Congress through the generosity of the Morris and Gwendolyn Cafritz Foundation, we have probed the ideology of the Revolution, analyzed its great documents, and dissected its extraordinary leadership. It is seemingly most appropriate now that a symposium be devoted to the impact of the American Revolution abroad. At home, as our earlier symposia have richly developed, the American Revolution meant a victory for anticolonialism. It won for America independence and nationhood. It laid down novel constitutional principles defining the relation of the state to the people, and it touched off a series of far-reaching democratic reforms in the direction of social and economic equality.

What it meant to the rest of the world is the theme of these sessions. And, for an exposition of that theme, the Library of Congress has brought together a galaxy of superstars, many from abroad. Among them, but not formally listed on our program, are the following scholars: Professor Erich Angermann of Cologne, who continues to develop first-rate graduate talent in the area of American history; Professor Nagayo Homma of Japan; and Señor Ignacio Rubio Mañe of Mexico City.

I hope these gentlemen will have an opportunity to join the discussion of the papers at an appropriate time.

It is only suitable and proper—almost necessary, one might say—that the keynote address on the impact of the American Revolution abroad should be delivered by a formidable scholar who has made the "Era of the Democratic Revolution" (singular, not plural, by the way) a trademark which he has registered. No man in our generation has done more to explain the impact of the American and French Revolutions upon the movement of democratic upsurge and reform which swept wide areas of the world in the last quarter of the 18th century. Whether in Geneva or in Poland, in Italy or in Russia, the scholar whom we are about to hear has moved undaunted, with a range of erudition unrivaled in its scope and with an originality and profundity that have stamped his work as a pathmaking undertaking and have enlisted all the rest of us as his permanent debtors.

It is my pleasure to introduce Professor Robert R. Palmer of Yale University.

The Impact
of the American Revolution
Abroad

R. R. PALMER

It takes an effort of the imagination to see how people in Europe reacted to news of the American Revolution. Today, with our well-established Constitution, we say with satisfaction that we have the oldest government in the world. Then, the Americans were exciting to Europe because they were a new people—bold, innovative, and experimental. Today, we are of transcontinental dimensions, like the Soviet Union. Then, we were a fringe of colonies along a thousand miles of coast. Today, we are admired for scientific and technical excellence. In the 18th century the intellectuals of Europe hailed Benjamin Franklin as a scientific genius and took an exotic pleasure in election to the American Philosophical Society, but they knew very well that the sciences were in their infancy in America. No town in the 13 colonies in 1776 was as large as any of dozens of cities in Europe. Paris alone had about the same population as the whole of New England. The Americans, including the slaves, were about equal in numbers to the Dutch and Belgians. Only two or three thousand college graduates saw the birth of the United States. One could go on indefinitely to show how small, insignificant, and marginal the country then was.

Yet the shot fired at Lexington was indeed heard round the world, or at least in those parts of the world that were then looking at North America, which is to say Europe. The effects in Latin America became visible or audible somewhat later, after 1800. In Africa and Asia it is later still, toward 1900, that we find a consciousness of the American Revolution in movements of independence against colonial empires. But as time passed the influence of the American Revolution became diffused and merged with other influences, first with those of the greater revolution in France, and then with international economic and market forces, or Marxism, or the affirmation or reaffirmation of various national identities, whether in Europe or in the world beyond Europe.

The later the date the more difficult and unrealistic it becomes to try to identify any specific effects of the American Revolution.[1] That such effects continued for a long time is believable enough, but only in a general way, somewhat as one might say that the Protestant Reformation affected the moral ideas of our Victorian ancestors. The American Revolution could in the long run inspire distant peoples, giving them confidence in their own powers, reinforcing their own hopes, or at the very least providing points of reference for newspaper editorials or political speeches. Pursuing this line we would obtain an assemblage of quotations rather than a sober analysis of causes and effects. Wishing to say something tangible, I shall speak of the impact of the American Revolution only on the generation that was alive in 1776. With a few exceptions, it was the Europeans who felt this impact.

"Impact," like "influence," is an elusive concept. The impact of the sun and moon on the tides can be measured and predicted, with allowance made for a few local irregularities. The influences that arouse historical interest do not lend themselves to such scientific treatment. The evidence is always uncertain. The difficulty is that the "influence" or "impact" depends as much on the subjective state of those who receive it as on the object from which the influence supposedly emanates. The marquis de Lafayette and the count de Fersen were both officers in America during the War of Independence, which must have had some impact on both of them. But Lafayette admired what he saw and became a revolutionary leader in France. Fersen, the friend of Marie Antoinette, was less charmed by America and became one of the more picturesque figures of the counterrevolution in France and Europe. In general, people are influenced in ways to which they are already susceptible.

If questions of metaphysics and multiple causation are put aside, it may be said that the American Revolution had three kinds of impact outside the United States. Let us call them the impact of actions, of realities, and of ideas.

By actions I mean the simple fact of rebellion itself. Whatever the ideas of the Americans might have been, and whatever the consequences in the sphere of realities, the fact that the American insurgents took to arms, defied the British government, repudiated existing authority, and by their courage, sacrifice, and persistence established their independence made an impression on Europeans. The confrontation itself was dramatized. The British govern-ment, by its actions, cast itself in the role of a tyrant, or at least a bully, in eyes of liberal observers. For others, it began to be seen as the anchor of a reasonable conservatism which it became during the wars of the French Revolution. In any case the liberal European admiration for England and its constitution, the well-known Anglomania of the 18th century, was weakened. The fact of rebellion, or of successful rebellion, or what might nowadays be called the existential act, had a powerful impact in Europe and was also one of the longest lasting repercussions of the American Revolution. We are told that Ho Chi Minh asked the Americans arriving in Indochina in 1945 for a copy of the American Declaration of Independence. We may suppose that he was more interested in what the Americans did in 1776 than in what they had said or thought, especially since the 13 colonies had never been colonies at all in the sense in which Vietnam was "colonized" by the French.

By the impact of realities may be understood those states of affairs that followed from the American Revolution, without being intended by anyone, or even mediated through chains of conscious ideas. For example, one effect of French participation in the War of American Independence was to double the debts of the king of France, raising them from two billion to four billion francs and precipitating the French Revolution. This fact may have had more impact on Europe than all the actions and all the ideas of the Americans combined. Or to take another example, the founding of British Canada by American loyalists is surely an important real consequence of the American Revolution. One might multiply such thoughts indefinitely, especially by extending the time span into later years when a multiplicity of causes makes such speculations somewhat fanciful. It was independence from Britian which made it possible for Americans to establish banks in Philadelphia and New York, to engage in direct trade with Europe and China, and to build factories along the Brandywine and Merrimac rivers. If the British authority had remained, it is hard to see how the movement of population across the Alle-ghenies would have swollen so rapidly, or the Cotton Kingdom of the South become so potent, or black slavery been so long tolerated by the central government, or the native Indians been so unceremoniously displaced. We know nowadays that the liberty and equality of the American Revolution applied only to whites, with a few gradual modifications, and that Jeffersonian and Jacksonian democracy were in that respect like the white man's democracy that one finds in South Africa and Rhodesia, in both of which the British government has tried to restrain the whites. Whether it would have done so in the case of the Americans two centuries ago is admittedly uncertain. But we know that British attempts to protect Indian rights by the proclamation of 1763 and French Canadian Catholic rights by the Quebec Act of 1774 were considered in the 13 colonies to be serious grievances.

It is in the realm of ideas that the impact of the American Revolution can be most clearly seen and evidence most readily offered. Europeans immediately perceived that something big had happened in history. To them, as to the Americans when they put the words on their Great Seal, the New World now signified a novus ordo seclorum. There seemed to be a grand intercontinental readjustment of the balance of human forces. Books of large scope on America were eagerly read. The Frenchman Raynal's *Histoire philosophique et politique des Établissemens & du Commerce des Européens dans les deux Indes*, largely concerned with the "west" Indies or America, was translated into five languages. The Scotsman Robertson's *History of America* was translated into French, German, Dutch, Italian, Spanish, Swedish, Greek, and Armenian. He was rivaled by the German educational reformer Campe, whose book *Die Entdeckung von Amerika* appeared also in Danish and Serbo-Croatian.

Others cast their eyes into the future. It was common for Europeans to predict that the infant born in 1776 would become a giant. Roland de la Platière, a French official best remembered as the husband of Mme Roland of the French Revolution, wrote a paper in 1785 entitled "A View of the Causes Which May Make a Language Universal, and Observations on Which of the Modern Languages Is Tending the Most To Become So." At the very time when Rivarol was proclaiming the universality of French, Roland predicted that the language of the Americans would be the universal language of the future. Others, in vast geopolitical meditations, sensed the impending decline of Europe. A French merchant, Joseph Mandrillon, was of this school. "The New World," he said, "once our slave, but in large part peopled by our emigrants, will come in its turn to put us into chains. Its industry, strength and power will grow as ours diminish; the Old World will be subjugated by the New, and this conquering people, after equally undergoing the laws of revolution, will itself perish at the hands of some people that it has had the misfortune to discover." The Italian Melchiorre Gioja was more specific: All peoples are capable of liberty, he said; whether they achieve it depends on circumstances in historical time. In the cycle of human events the day might come when African Negroes would invade Europe to avenge themselves for European barbarities.[2]

When the Declaration of Independence submitted its self-evident truths to a candid world, the world whether candid or not was ready to listen. They were the ideas of the international Enlightenment, heightened by Jefferson's eloquence. It was not news in Europe in 1776 that men were created equal or were equal by nature, whatever differences might exist in the social order, or that they had a right to enjoy liberty or pursue happiness, or that just government should rest upon the consent of the governed. The right of revolution as claimed in the Declaration was more controversial; here we touch again on what the Americans did as well as what they thought. In any case, there were people in many countries who applied such ideas eagerly to their own situations. Let us make a quick tour of Europe with this in mind.

In Great Britain it was not Edmund Burke but the more advanced parliamentary reformers, the kind of people later called radicals, who were most sympathetic to the Americans, in whose cause they saw their own. In Ireland during the American war, battalions of armed and uniformed volunteers organized themselves against possible invasion by the French and also demanded reform of the Irish parliament and less control from England; they too looked to the example of the Americans, to whom many Presbyterian Irish were at this time related. In the United Provinces during the war, while John Adams was minister to The Hague, there arose the Dutch patriot movement against the House of Orange, a semirevolutionary effort that Adams enthusiastically praised, and which had begun when the city of Amsterdam recognized the American insurgents against the wishes of the stadtholder. In Belgium, then called the Austrian Netherlands, a revolution took place in 1789 against the Austrian emperor; the revolutionaries proclaimed the independent United Belgian States, talked of America, and set up articles of union whose language was taken in part from the American Articles of Confederation. A prize contest was held at the University of Copenhagen on the question of whether the discovery of America had had good or bad effects for the human race, and a work on the same question was published at the University of Upsala in Latin. In Italy there were translations of Benjamin Franklin's writings, and the grand duke of Tuscany, the future emperor Leopold II, contemplated the issuance of a constitution for Tuscany, for which purpose he had a copy of the new constitution of Virginia on his desk. One of the first Italian revolutionary secret societies called itself the *Filadelfia*. In Hungary a group of conspirators was known as the Red Lodge or American Lodge. In Russia, Catherine the Great said that Alexander Radishchev was especially dangerous because he talked about the Americans and read Benjamin Franklin. In Poland a great movement of political revival was in progress, designed to strengthen Poland against further partition by neighboring powers. It culminated in the Four Years Diet of 1788, in which American examples and American ideas were liberally cited. These have been recently studied by a Polish historian, Zofia Libiszowski, who has conveniently presented her findings in French.

In Germany, as indeed elsewhere, there was a mixed opinion. The professors at Göttingen, with its Hanoverian connection with England, generally regarded the Americans as rebels and supported the attempts of the British government to put them down. There was also in Germany, however, a large and literate middle-class reading public, which deplored the British use of German troops in America, objected to the parochial despotisms under which they lived, and hoped that somehow the American Revolution might portend a wave of the future. A huge recent study by a young German, Horst Dippel, done as a dissertation at the University of Cologne, has shown in great detail that there was more excitement in Germany about the American Revolution than had been supposed. An English translation of Dr. Dippel's study is scheduled for publication in 1976.[3]

It was in France that this international impact of the American Revolution had its most pronounced effects. Before turning to France, however, we may pick up a few stray strands from outside of Europe. Historians of South Africa note that the people of Cape Town talked of the American Revolution in protesting against the rule of the Dutch East India Company. A Dutch vessel stopping at the Cormoro Islands, in the Straits of Madagascar, reported that the islanders wanted to imitate the liberty of the Americans. In Latin America, where the real movement of independence was to come in Napoleon's time, a few earlier patriots made themselves known. One was the famous Miranda, who traveled in the United States in the 1780's; one was an unnamed Brazilian who consulted Jefferson in Paris; and one was a Spanish American Jesuit, Viscardo y Guzman, who said that "the valor with which the English colonists of America have fought for the liberty which they now enjoy covers our indolence with shame." [4]

It was France that intervened in the American Revolution, recognized the insurgents, signed an alliance with the Continental Congress, and sent a professional army and a fleet which enabled Washington to obtain the British surrender at Yorktown. These activities were sustained by some secret French government propaganda, by the ingenious efforts of Benjamin Franklin as American minister, and by a great deal of fashionable and literary excitement. France was especially well prepared to receive the American message. It was the center of the European Enlightenment. The Pennsylvania Quaker and the Huron Indian had already been celebrated by Voltaire. Rousseau had made his readers dream of the rural life away from cities. The parlements of the realm, the supreme high courts, only a few years before the American Revolution had raised the most serious constitutional issues concerning taxation, representative government, and the rights of the citizen. The word "citizen," in fact, was already common in ordinary language; it was no mere slogan of the French Revolution. The same can be said of "liberty" and "equality." French visitors to America, as well as those who only wrote or read about it at home, therefore felt the most intense curiosity. A few were also speculating in western lands, and some hoped to profit by the opening of American trade. A torrent of writing was let loose—books, pamphlets, periodical articles, encyclopedia articles, travel accounts, poetical compositions including at least one epic, along with epigrams, essays, epistles, papers written to win academic prizes, and polemics in which one author exposed another's misconceptions. Some of this writing was perceptive, some grossly misinformed, and some incredibly idealized and sentimental. An American "myth" was created, or what Durand Echeverria has called the "mirage in the West."

Some elements in this myth arouse an ironic sense of contrast between past and present. The Americans were supposed to be "natural," and this was a good thing. They were noted also for their unusual virtue. Their manners were unsophisticated and simple. They led exemplary personal lives. They knew nothing of luxury or corruption. In America reason prevailed, the natural and untutored reason of men free from the prejudices and impostures of the past. There were no social classes, and men were recognized and honored on the basis of talent, not social position. Persons of all religions were not only tolerated but welcomed. The small farmer owning his land paid nothing to a seigneur or tithe-collector, and taxes were almost nonexistent. Government was honest and pure, and there was no politics. To read some of these writers, one would suppose that a conclave of wise old men, sitting in the woods, had produced the American Revolution and the new American governments.

Perhaps in this "mirage" there was some small grain of truth, at least relatively and in comparison with the ancien régime in Europe. It is more certain that such myth-making was really a criticism of French life and society. It must be said, too, that even those who drew such glowing pictures did so with a worried expression, fearful that nothing so good could last. The philosopher Mably was one of those who harped most incessantly on American virtue, which he, like all philosophes, said was necessary to republics; but he thought too that there were forces in America that threatened it, and that unless the right steps were taken both the virtue and the republic would disappear. There was thus a refreshing note of realism in the myth itself. Many informed persons did not accept the myth at all. The marquis de Chastellux, who had been in America with Rochambeau's army, wrote a travel account in which he very sanely included the bad as well as the good. He drew an outraged reply from the future revolutionary Brissot, who accused him of aristocratic cynicism, and expressed some of the visionary overbelief that he was unfortunately to carry into the French Revolution.

But not all ideas about America were mythical, and not all arose only from fashionable literary excitement. There was a serious interest in the new American forms of government. It was not mainly an interest in the federal union, though most friends of America, like Lafayette, thought in the 1780's that the union should be made stronger. By the time of the federal Constitution, which went into effect in 1789 and so was simultaneous with revolutionary events in France, the attention of Europeans was engrossed by developments nearer home. There was, however, in the dozen years preceding the French Revolution, a period of maximum impact of American political ideas, and this impact came from the constitutions of the several American states. The state constitutions, often accompanied by the Declaration of Independence, were published in these years in French, German, Dutch, and Polish, and further search would probably reveal at least sporadic translations into other languages as well. In France they were published on at least five different occasions between 1776 and 1786.

The Americans were perceived as acting out in practice the theory of the social contract. They went far beyond the idea of government by consent, which, after all, even hereditary monarchs could reasonably claim. They began, as Patrick Henry once said, in "a state of nature." Freed from the past, they came together and produced a written constitution by agreement. They did not simply inherit their government; they planned it. They placed sovereignty not in the government but in the people. The constitutions were grants of power, made by the citizenry, and the powers of any office were temporary and delegated, as well as carefully limited and balanced against other powers. No public person exercised any authority by his own right. No class or kind of persons had any special access to government. All functioned simply as citizens, or as incumbents of offices which the citizens themselves had created. Law was not something mysterious and historic; it was made consciously by legislators, who were elected to office and who could fail of reelection. Law was also equal; all citizens had the same rights and stood in the same relation to the state. The constitution was above ordinary law; it was a brief written document, not to be modified by a legislature, as in England, and certainly more definite than the "fundamental laws" which the Parlement of Paris said made up the historic constitution of France. In addition, as a double guarantee that government would be kept within bounds, most of the American state constitutions were accompanied by declarations of rights. These ensured certain individual liberties against arbitrary taxation, confiscation, search, seizure, censorship, imprisonment, cruelty, unfair trials, official secrecy, and uncontrollable standing armies, such as were all too familiar in Europe.

Let me digress for a moment, to comment on the Library of Congress symposium held two years ago. The title of the symposium for 1973 was "Fundamental Testaments of the American Revolution." The testaments were Thomas Paine's *Common Sense*, the Declaration of Independence, the Articles of Confederation, and the treaty of 1783 which guaranteed American independence. Europeans of that time would have made a different selection. It was the French Revolution, not the American, which made Thomas Paine famous in Europe and caused translations of *Common Sense* to be made in France and Germany in the 1790's. Contemporaries in Europe seldom mentioned the Declaration of Independence, whose majestic beauty was perhaps less apparent outside the English language. It was the state constitutions with their accompanying declarations of rights that captured attention. These state constitutions, written from 1776 to 1782, have been overlaid by other symbols in the American national memory, but they deserve the honor of perpetuation as testaments.

Especially in France the constitutions and declarations had an overwhelming relevancy in the last years before the French Revolution. They clarified and formulated the very thoughts that the French themselves already entertained. They were therefore analyzed and written about by various notables, including Turgot, Condorcet, Mably, Mirabeau, and Dupont de Nemours. They were published and expounded in the *Encyclopédie méthodique*. They were generally commented on in travel books and other popular writing—a sign that a wide reading public was interested. The French Revolution began with a perhaps excessive belief in the urgent need for a written constitution, and possibly it would have been better if various structural changes had been attempted in a more piecemeal fashion. For this French insistence on a written constitution, which proved disappointing in practice, there were certainly many causes entirely indigenous to France. But the impact of the American Revolution must surely be added.

The American influence on the famous Declaration of the Rights of Man and the Citizen, as proclaimed by the French in 1789, has been debated since the days of Boutmy and Jellinek, about 1900, nor can much be added to what was said by the late Gilbert Chinard. There was more to it than the fact that Jefferson, when in Paris, talked with Lafayette about the Virginia Declaration of Rights. Members of the French National Assembly, in August 1789, were well informed on the declarations of rights in all the American state constitutions. Here again it was the action of the Americans, not their ideas, that was influential. The general notion of natural and civil rights was familiar in Europe. What the Americans did was to specify them and write them down as a numbered list on a well-publicized piece of paper attached to the Constitution itself. That the French did the same in 1789 may be plausibly ascribed to the American influence. The French also did more, making the statement of rights more concise and abstract, the ideas of national sovereignty and citizenship more clear cut, and the whole manifesto more universally addressed to mankind at large. With the combined strength of French and American precedent, assisted by Thomas Paine's book of 1791, the Rights of Man became the symbol, hallmark, talisman, and oriflamme of the 18th-century revolution. By 1799, with French victories, there were no fewer than six other revolutionary regimes in Europe, from Holland to Italy, each a republic, known as the Batavian, Helvetic, Cisalpine, Ligurian, Roman, and Neapolitan republics, as well as a similar proposal for the Greeks. Each of these had a written constitution, each proclaimed the sovereignty of the people, and each had a declaration of rights.

There were, however, two important American political ideas with which many Europeans, even friends of America, found it difficult to agree. One was the way in which the Americans understood the balance or separation of powers. The other was the American preference for a federal as distinct from a nationally centralized political system. The disagreement in both cases reflected real differences between the Old and the New Worlds, or the absence of what Louis Hartz once called the "feudal factor" from America and its presence in Europe.

In Europe any movement aiming at generally democratic objectives had to overcome the resistance of certain preestablished, privileged, and usually self-perpetuating bodies. These included nobility as a legally separate and superior class, the church as a strong institution with its own organs of public power, and law courts whose judges had inherited their own seats. There were also great provinces enjoying special advantages which others did not share, corporate towns with special immunities and their own exclusive local elites, and trade guilds and other occupational organizations which enjoyed rights that nonmembers did not have, not to mention various universities, academies, and chivalric orders. Civil equality and individual liberty could be advanced only if the strength of such bodies was reduced. Indeed, the main effect of the French Revolution was to wipe them out. In any case, they would yield only to a powerful central government deemed to represent none of these bodies individually but only the undifferentiated people as a whole. In Europe the democratic movement was centralizing and unitary.

The idea of checks and balances in America at this time turned mainly on the existence of a bicameral legislature and a strong executive who would be independent of legislative pressures. When Turgot and Condorcet read of these provisions in the American constitutions they were alarmed. In a two-chamber legislature, with a lower house and a senate, they saw the old European distinction between the common people and the privileged orders. In the strong executive, despite the reassurances of John Adams, who wrote a whole book against Turgot, they saw the everlasting menace of arbitrary government or despotism. They favored, therefore, a simple arrangement in which a single house of assembly controlled the whole machinery of state, to be checked itself only by frequent elections, enlightened opinion, the love of liberty, and declarations of rights. The same thought prevailed in the French National Assembly in 1789. It was not that this line of thinking was democratic in a later sense—those who upheld it generally limited the vote to property owners—but that voters were to vote as individual and presumably disinterested citizens, not as members of social classes or groups.

Nor did the American example quite fit the case of Poland. Here, in the Four Years' Diet of 1788, the problem of reformers wishing to strengthen the country was to do away with the old custom of election of the king by the nobles, which had repeatedly torn the country apart. The revolutionary and more-or-less democratic leaders wanted a stronger executive, such as a hereditary king would provide. It was the conservative Polish nobles, the most high-flying aristocratic magnates and their followers, who defended the idea of the elected executive—that is, an elected king—and who pointed to American revolutionary examples to strengthen their argument.

Similarly, in the federal principle, involving preservation of preexisting units while gathering them into a union for limited purposes, the European revolutionaries saw the same danger of merely protecting the privileged interests to which they were opposed. The French, in their constitution of 1789, simply abolished all provinces, estates, legal orders, and corporate entities. They reorganized the country into uniform departments, somewhat as Alexander Hamilton, to overcome the Virginia gentry, dreamed of abolishing the states and replacing them with territorial departments created by a national government. Nor were the French alone in this respect. In the Belgian revolution of 1789 it was the conservative wing of the anti-Austrian revolt— those who wished to maintain the position of the nobles, the clergy, and a few town notables after the Austrians were expelled—who admired the loose and decentralized union of the American Articles of Confederation. Loose confederation and states' rights, which in America were supposedly more popular and democratic, were reactionary in Belgium. There it was the Democrats, as the more advanced Belgian party explicitly called itself, that wanted a stronger central state with uniform rearrangement of subordinate parts. The Dutch faced the same problem in their Batavian republic of 1795, and divided along the same lines. Another example is offered by the Italian economist Melchiorre Gioja, in a book which he wrote at Milan in 1796, during the revolution brought on by the arrival of the French. His book is regarded as one of the first expressions of the Italian Risorgimento. It was entitled *Which of the Free Governments Is Best Suited to Italy?*[5] He took up three possibilities: an array of separate and merely adjacent independent republics; the American model of federation; and the republic "one and indivisible," as in France. He dismissed the first out of hand and rejected the American federal system after pointing out the conflicts and jealousies which it encouraged. Only a large, consolidated, unitary, all-Italian republic, he said, could overcome the special interests and privileges, the aristocracies and patriciates, that had so long comfortably nestled in the separate Italian states. A century and a half later, in finding that white supremacy could only be broken by a distant central power, the Americans may be said to have reached a similar conclusion.

In summary, the European idea of the American Revolution was more than a dream, or myth, or mirage. It was indeed partly a myth or moral story which, in rising above mere facts, could inspire action in Europe and in any case reflected the discontents of a class-ridden and overcomplicated society. But it was also a kind of laboratory for observations in political science. Europeans, then as now, could be intelligently critical of the United States. They were not all like Brissot, who said that human rights did not depend on the thermometer, meaning that they did not vary according to geography, as the followers of Montesquieu might say. More realistic observers knew that the rights that could be institutionalized and permanently enjoyed would depend upon circumstances, and that the difference in conditions in America and in Europe, conditions produced by history and by geography, meant that not everything in the American Revolution could be imitated in Europe. Tocqueville's *Democracy in America*, written 50 years later, was only the greatest in a long line of critical books on the subject, combining as it did a sense of the universal significance of what had happened in the United States with a keen appreciation of American differences.

The American Revolution was the opening signal, raised on a distant shore, for a revolutionary outburst which in the next 30 years was to sweep through the world of Western civilization. To call it the "cause" of anything would raise unanswerable questions. But it certainly contributed to a revolutionary spirit in France and elsewhere, and without it the French Revolution would not have been quite the same.

In revolutions not everybody agrees: revolutionaries dispute with each other, and conservatives, moderates, and reactionaries play their part as well as dreamers and hard-nosed committees of public safety. There were a variety of opinions about America, and the different lessons quite properly drawn from them only show the breadth of America's influence. Undoubtedly the main impact was to promote the demand for liberty and equality, for constitutional government and representative institutions, for the dignity of citizenship, religious freedom, and all that was then meant by the Rights of Man. The 200th anniversary of the American Revolution still deserves celebration.

Notes

Many source references for points in this paper, as well as more extended discussion, may be found in the author's book *The Age of the Democratic Revolution: A Political History of Europe and America* (2 vols.; Princeton: Princeton University Press, 1959–64), especially in volume 1., chapter 9, "Europe and the American Revolution." For France the indispensable work is Durand Echeverria's *Mirage in the West: The French Image of American Society to 1815* (Princeton: Princeton University Press, 1957). There is much on the same subject in Louis R. Gottschalk's volumes on Lafayette, especially *Lafayette Between the American and French Revolution (1783–89)* (Chicago: University of Chicago Press, 1950). There is also the older work of Bernard Faÿ, *L'esprit révolutionnaire en France et en Amérique . . .* (Paris: E. Champion, 1925), translated as *The Revolutionary Spirit in France and America . . .* (New York: Harcourt, Brace & Company, 1927).

European historians have not shown much interest in the impact of the American Revolution. Three recent works are known to the author, of which two are mentioned in the present paper: Horst Dippel's unpublished doctoral dissertation "Deutschland und die amerikanische Revolution: Sozialgeschichtliche Untersuchung zum politischen Bewusstsein im ausgehenden 18. Jahrhundert," (bound photocopy of typescript, 653 pp. plus 208 pp. of bibliography, "America Germanica, 1770–1800"; Köln, 1972); and a paper by Zofia Libiszowski of the University of Lodz entitled "L'opinion polonaise et la Révolution américaine au 18e siècle," published in *Revue d'histoire moderne et contemporaine* 17 (October-December 1970): 984–98, to which may be added her book in Polish with an English summary, *Opinia polska wobec Revolucji amerykanskiej w 18 wieku* (Lodz: 1962). The third is a doctoral thesis for the troisième cycle, completed at the University of Lille in 1973 by Gérard Defamie, "La mode des Etats-Unis et le voyage en Amérique pour les libéraux français à la veille de la Révolution" (typescript, 468 pp.).

The following references are given only for a few quotations and other specific points.

[1] But see Richard B. Morris, *The Emerging Nations and the American Revolution* (New York: Harper and Row, 1970), p. 220. Professor Morris has ventured upon a survey of the more distant forms of impact in time and space, from which the present author has more cautiously abstained.

[2] For Roland de la Platière, see Howard C. Rice, *Le Cultivateur américain; étude sur l'oeuvre de Saint-John de Crèvecoeur,* (Paris: H. Champion, 1933), p. 210. For Mandrillon, see his *Le Spectateur americain . . . ,* 2d. ed. (Amsterdam and Brussels: E. Flon, 1785), p. 489. For Gioja, *Dissertazione . . . sul problema . . . Quale dei governi liberi meglio convenga alla felicità*

dell'Italia? (Milan, 1797) and included in his *Opere minore*, vol. 4 (Lugano, 1833), pp. 99–311; see p. 167.

[3] To be published by the University of North Carolina Press and Franz Steiner Verlag under the sponsorship of the Institute of Early American History and Culture at Williamsburg and the Institut für Europäische Geschichte Mainz.

[4] For Viscardo y Guzman see Víctor Andrés Belaúnde, *Bolivar and the Political Thought of the Spanish American Revolution* (Baltimore: Johns Hopkins Press, 1938), pp. 83–85.

[5] Gioja's work is cited in note 2 above.

Robert R. Palmer joined the History Department at Princeton University in 1936. In 1952 he was named Dodge Professor of History at Princeton, a chair which he occupied until 1963, when he accepted a position as dean of the Faculty of Arts and Sciences at Washington University in St. Louis. He was appointed to his present position as professor of history at Yale University in 1969.

In addition to a bachelor's degree from the University of Chicago and a doctorate from Cornell University, Professor Palmer holds honorary degrees from Kenyon College, Washington University, the University of Chicago, and the University of Toulouse, France. He is a past president of the American Historical Association and the Society for French Historical Studies. His publications include A History of the Modern World *(with Joel Colton, 4th ed., 1971),* The Age of the Democratic Revolution *(1959–64),* The World of the French Revolution *(1971), and* The School of the French Revolution *(1975).*

Some of us who have had the opportunity to teach or lecture abroad have been impressed by the vigor of studies and research conducted in many European countries in the areas of American history and American studies, fashionable anti-Americanism notwithstanding. The two gentlemen who are going to address us this afternoon are playing key roles in their countries in graduate programs they are administering. The first speaker comes from the Sorbonne and has the special distinction of being the first recipient in France of a chair in American history. He is the author of a number of works on American history, both on contemporary themes and on minorities. I am honored to introduce my friend and colleague from Paris, Professor Claude R. Fohlen, who will speak on the impact of the American Revolution in France.

The Impact
of the American Revolution
on France

CLAUDE FOHLEN

AT FIRST GLANCE, it seems obvious that the American Revolution had a large impact on France. France was the first power to recognize the new state, to sign treaties of alliance and commerce with it (as early as 1778), and to send an expeditionary force to help fight the British. The anti-British sentiments deeply rooted in French governmental circles found a new outlet with the rebellion of the 13 colonies against the mother country. There had been a tradition of anglomania among the French intellectual elite represented by Montesquieu and Voltaire, but this tradition was weakened by the end of the 18th century as a result of increased economic competition with the British in France as well as on foreign markets and the reaction against an idealized image of British institutions which did not fit what actually existed on the other side of the channel. News of American independence was hailed with great enthusiasm in the political and intellectual circles of France, and to symbolize this enthusiasm, the street between the Ministry of Foreign Affairs, where the treaties of alliance and commerce were signed on February 6, 1778, and the Ministry of War, where the French expedition was prepared, received the name *Rue de l'Indépendance américaine*.

There has long existed an *image d'Epinal* about the impact of the American Revolution in France, the one describing the young Lafayette as eager to offer his services to the new republic and leaving France in secrecy, against the will of his family and of the government, reaching the land of liberty to fight under Washington, and bringing back to his country the spirit of liberty. The counterpart of this cliché is the famous "Lafayette, here we are," attributed to General Pershing, when he landed in France in 1917. These clichés are now disappearing, since recent French generations have not learned about the younger members of the nobility who left their country to fight for the liberty and independence of the insurgents. Liberty and independence are no longer the privilege of a small minority of affluent people but the universal aspirations of deprived and underdeveloped masses quite different from both the Americans and the French nobility. The image of Lafayette has also been modified by the patient research of Louis Gottschalk, who presents the young nobleman as having been converted to the idea of liberty by his American experience; concern over liberty played a relatively minor role in his leaving France. Like many young people of his time, Lafayette was seeking adventure, military glory, revenge on the British. When he returned to his country, he was hailed not only as a hero but also as the high priest of a new religion, namely the Enlightenment, which had taken root in the United States.

Gottschalk's views raise certain questions concerning the influence of the American Revolution on France. Were some Frenchmen really attracted to the American experience because of their ideas, and did they cross the ocean and fight with the insurgents to help their ideas to triumph? Or were they so impressed by what they experienced in the New World that they brought back a new *Weltanschauung* and tried to impose it in France? Actually, things were more complicated. One cannot dissociate the ideas from the exercise of politics. The French government was indeed the first one to become interested in what was going on in North America, but it considered its intervention as no more than a typical exercise in diplomacy and war, in the tradition of balance-of-power politics common in the 17th and 18th centuries. For Vergennes, it was more important to weaken the British and to gain some needed prestige for France than to foster the spread of revolutionary ideas in the kingdom.

The proximity between the American and French Revolutions—only 14 years elapsed between the battle of Lexington and the fall of the Bastille—poses a peculiar problem. Obviously, there is some common ground between the ideas behind the two revolutions. Obviously, we meet some of the same people in both, and Lafayette is only one of those who symbolize the ambivalence of the revolution. The question arises, then, of whether the French

Revolution is the child of the American or a revolution in its own right.

This question has been raised at various times but a satisfactory answer has yet to be given. It is only recently that historians have become more receptive to a comparative approach to their discipline, and many still refuse to accept evidence which contradicts their personal views. Much work remains to be done if we are to develop a better understanding of the hidden relationships between the two revolutions.

Aside from the contemporaries, the first historian to have been sensitive to this point seems to have been Tocqueville. In a written note which was never incorporated into his *L'Ancien régime et la révolution*, he asks: "Why have very similar principles and political theories driven the United States only to a change of government, and France to a total subversion of her society. Idea which could be very fruitful, although I don't know where to place it." [1] Actually Tocqueville never exploited his intuition because it did not fit his general explanation of the continuity between the ancien régime and the postrevolutionary era. For him, as for all his contemporaries, the revolution which took place in France was in all respects *French*; we can only regret that he did not pursue his intuition further.

Half a century later, during America's Centennial celebration, there was a renewal of interest in the origins of the United States, marked by a series of important publications. The historian Alphonse Aulard at the time raised the question of the direct connection between the two revolutions, mentioning a number of striking similarities. His statements stemmed from a political analysis of the events as well as from the testimonies of persons actually involved— Condorcet and Brissot, among others. For Condorcet, "the American Revolution was destined to extend soon in Europe, from the banks of the Neva to those of the Guadalquivir, but struck first the most enlightened and deprived country in the world" (i.e., France). For Brissot, "the American Revolution has been the mother of the French Revolution." [2] Aulard accepted, among other explanations, the idea of a direct relationship between the two revolutions. But his ideas were short lived, not only because they were limited to the political field, but also because they were challenged almost at once by two powerful figures who captured the attention of the younger generations, Jean Jaurès and Albert Mathiez. Together with Labrousse, they gave a new dimension to the French Revolution, adding the socioeconomic factors. In the field of ideas, they note some continuity, certain similarities, a measure of influence exerted by the events in America, but they conclude that the roots of the French Revolution were in the disruption of the French economy and the basic tensions of social relations. In other words, the crises in French agriculture, industry, and commerce, coupled with hostility against the so-, called feudal system, led to the outbreak of the French Revolution and determined its character. Ideas are subordinated to material and social factors in such an explanation, and the gap between the two revolutions is widened.

About 20 years ago two historians, Robert Palmer and Jacques Godechot, reexamined the nature of the revolutions we are concerned with, emphasizing their similarity not only to each other but also to the revolutions which occurred simultaneously in Geneva and the Austrian Netherlands and subsequently in the former colonies of ∘Spain in South America. Palmer and Godechot developed the idea of an "Atlantic Revolution," of which the American and French Revolutions were only two instances, albeit the most striking. The authors note the existence at the time of a common revolutionary spirit in what we now call the western world. Such an explanation is very tempting. There were many similarities in ideologies on both sides of the Atlantic, and colonization of the American shores by the French, British, and Spanish had in effect created the first common market, centered not on the land but on the ocean. This explanation was received with skepticism in France, however, because it contradicted certain basic assumptions of the historians. For the Marxists, who rallied under the authoritative banner of Georges Lefebvre and his spiritual heir Albert Soboul, it undermined the very foundation of their theories by eliminating the idea of class struggle and the materialistic view of the evolution of societies and denying the specificities of the French problems. For the non-Marxists, it deprived the French Revolution of its uniquely French origins, an unthinkable, almost criminal, offense. The most recent historians of the French Revolution do not deny the existence of areas of common ideological background on both sides of the Atlantic, although they do not emphasize the fact, but they do refer to what they call the "skid" of events which led to entirely different results in France and the United States.

No clear solution to this problem has been offered by French historians, a failure that results at least partially from their methodology, which focuses more on events than on ideas. We must therefore turn to other scholars who may be considered either historians or nonhistorians, depending upon one's concept of what history is. Gilbert Chinard, Bernard Fay, and Durand Echeverría, to mention only three, have all pointed out the influence that the ideas, institutions, and men involved in the American Revolution exerted in France, both before and after 1789. Even with their excellent contributions, however, the debate on the impact of the American Revolution on France remains open.

The special relationship between the American Revolution and France stems first from the direct participation of the French army on the side of the insurgents. The treaty signed between the king of France and the 13 American colonies did not provide for military and naval support, but some 8,000 troops, under the command of Rochambeau, were sent later on. It is important to note that Vergennes accepted an alliance with the newly created American republic primarily to wipe out the bad memories of the Seven Years' War. The alliance gave the French government an opportunity to reactivate a long and difficult struggle against the British.

Anti-British feelings, which were latent at least in the upper classes of French society, surged at once. The count of Ségur, who later joined the French expeditionary force, noted:

The insurgents' courageous audacity electrified everyone and excited general admiration, especially among the younger people, who were always in search of something new and eager for a war. . . . I was particularly struck to see such keen and universal sympathy for the revolt of a people against their king. The serious English card game whist was suddenly replaced in all the salons by a no less sober game which was christened "Boston." [3]

Among the 8,000 Frenchmen who participated in the war, there were about 700 commissioned officers, almost all nobles. Some of them are well known to us because they wrote memoirs or diaries relating their experiences in the war. Among them are such aristocrats as Broglie, Fersen, Lafayette, Lameth, La Pérouse, Rochambeau, Ségur, Pontgibaud, and Guillaume des Deux-Ponts. They had been sent to the New World by a monarchist government which had accepted some very limited reforms but was opposed to any basic transformation of institutions and society. As the story goes, many of these young nobles discovered in America a new spirit of liberty and the absence of privilege, and they returned to France as converts to the new ideas, eager to spread them. We cannot say for certain just how accurate this traditional image is. Actually, some of these nobles became liberals, following the example of Lafayette, and participated a few years later in the French Revolution. The reflections of the young count de Ségur, written in 1782, are characteristic: "The liberty for which I am going to fight inspires in me great enthusiasm, and I would like my own country to possess as much of it as is compatible with our monarchy, our status, and our customs." [4] But the majority of these nobles were not directly concerned with revolutionary ideas, and there was also a minority strongly hostile to the political and social changes they witnessed in America. Among this last group at least one—the count of Fersen—became an advocate of counter revolution.

We must not be misled by a few flamboyant and famous examples who were exceptions to the general rule. And even if we take for granted that these liberal nobles were converted to the new ideas during and because of their experience in the United States, they themselves exerted only a limited influence in France during the initial part of the Revolution, between 1789 and 1791. This influence faded rapidly because of the fundamental differences between the two countries. The viscount of Noailles, Lafayette's brother-in-law, who proposed the abolition of all hereditary privilege, was a liberal in the full meaning of the word as defined in 1789 but could not conceive of any form of government in France other than a monarchy. His American experience did him little good and he disappeared from the political scene, as did the other former nobles, between the end of 1789 and the fall of the king three years later. Some of them emigrated (Lafayette, for example), others were guillotined, and still others remained in France but concealed their identities. It would appear that experience gained in America was not transmissible to their native country.

Much more numerous in the French expeditionary force were the enlisted men and noncommissioned officers, who represented almost every part of the country and a variety of social classes, with a majority of peasants. The names and origins of these people were included in a list published in France and in the United States for the Centennial.[5] The data received relatively little attention, however, until 1951, when the American historian Forrest Mac-Donald published an article on the influence of the French veterans on the fall of feudalism.[6] The thesis is that "French armies, largely conscripted from the peasantry, served in America, where the soldiers were presented a clear picture of the missing concept [free land ownership] which they could not fail to appreciate." Once back in France, they spread the ideas they had acquired on American soil. And when, "in 1789, financial crisis, general discontent and the weakness of the monarchy combined to make revolutionary action possible in France, these veterans formed the dynamic element in a movement which guaranteed the completion of the Revolution by the destruction of economic feudalism." Thus according to MacDonald, French veterans of the American Revolution played a leading role in the revolutionary events which led to final suppression of the feudal system.

MacDonald's thesis rests on the geographical origins of the French veterans as recorded on the lists cited. He presents a map of France on which dots are used to show the location of peasants who returned from the American war. The dots are concentrated in areas in which there were agrarian riots in the summer of 1789—for instance, in Lorraine, Burgundy, and Franche-Comté in the east, in Normandy in the west, and in Guyenne and Gascony in the southwest. There is indeed a strange and striking coincidence between the number of veterans and the violence of the rural riots which preceded or followed the suppression of feudal rights. One is greatly tempted to conclude that there is a direct relationship between the two phenomena. Such a conclusion would seem to constitute a significant contribution in resolving the issue under discussion.

Actually MacDonald's demonstration is less convincing than it appears. For one thing, it would be too rational to link the location of the French veterans with the destruction of the feudal system—history is never that rational, even in the country of Descartes. Three other basic arguments against such an explantion may also be mentioned:

First, from what we know about the life and habits of French soldiers during their brief American experience, they had little contact with the realities of America. They stayed in military camps and brought their own equipment, armaments, and food. Contrary to well-established military tradition they did not "live off the land" and rarely met Americans. They did not speak English and therefore could not have communicated with the local population if they had wanted to. Their route of march extended from Newport, R.I., where they landed, to Yorktown, Va., where they ended their campaign, so they did see something of the country, albeit primarily from the main roads only. However, seeing the country did not tell them very much about the actual ownership of the land, which was not advertised. And it seems to me that the average French soldier of the late 18th century was less curious and certainly less openminded than MacDonald supposes.

Secondly, the French army of the ancien régime was made up not of draftees but of volunteers who came primarily from regions where it had become difficult to make a living, especially with the increase of population in rural areas in the 18th century. It was these same provinces that were shaken by the agrarian riots. Contrary to MacDonald's conclusion, however, the coincidence demonstrates only that the soldiers came primarily from the poorer areas, which seems quite normal. The picture could have been a little different, of course, if a number of units scheduled to join the expedition had not been detained in Brest owing to the lack of ships and the unexpected victory at Yorktown.

And finally, MacDonald's hypothesis is not supported by any extensive local research in the French archives. Were the veterans of the American Revolution among the people who attacked and burned the castles, destroyed the titles

of ownership, threatened the lives of the feudal owners, and even killed some
of them? We do not yet know. Further research is necessary before any final
conclusion can be drawn.

The debate remains open, and it is better at this point to admit our
ignorance. The American Revolution provided some French people of the
time with a unique opportunity to become acquainted with new ideas and to
introduce them in their country as a weapon against absolutism. So far, they
do not seem to have taken any definite advantage of their position.

To reject the direct influence of the men involved in the war does not mean
that there was no impact. Quite the contrary. Between 1776 and the beginning of the French Revolution, the French demonstrated tremendous interest in everything connected with America—books, periodicals, discussions,
clubs, travel, memoirs, and the like. This second discovery of the New World
had far-ranging consequences on the politics and social order of the country.

The initial rise in French curiosity concerning the new republic is reflected
in the sudden increase in the number of books published in France dealing
with British North America. Before 1775, the yearly average of such books
was insignificant—one or two each year, sometimes none. In 1776 the number
jumped to seven, all of them devoted to history and politics. Between 1776
and 1783 the yearly average remained at seven, with a peak of 10 in 1786
and a low of five in 1777. Throughout the period the majority of books
published were in the categories of politics and history, with only a few
pertaining to travel, geography, and literature in the broadest sense. Inter-
estingly, this curiosity did not decline with the return of peace: between 1784
and 1789, the average number of books on America reached a yearly level
of nine, with peaks of 13 in 1784 and 12 in 1787, the year of the Constitution.[7]
It is only in 1789, with the meeting of the States General, that the number
drops, and this decline needs no explanation.

Among the works on America published in France before 1789, several
were translations: Tom Paine's famous *Common Sense* and his letter to the
abbé Raynal, the major works of Franklin, who was the most popular American
in France, and pamphlets by John Adams, Jonathan Trumbull, Anthony
Benezet (on the Quakers), and others. Jefferson's *Observations on Virginia*,
in fact, was published in France before it appeared in the United States. Still
more works were published by Frenchmen, whose renewed interest in the
New World dated back to 1770, when the abbé Raynal published his famous

Histoire philosophique et politique ... des deux Indes. This book became the standard reference for those interested in the British colonies (the West Indies), and some authors even reproduced whole passages from it under their own names, as though it were an original piece of research based on their own experience. Antoine Hornot, for example, in his *Anecdotes américaines* (1776), reprints extensive passages of Raynal without mentioning the source. The abbé published two other books more directly connected with the American Revolution, *Révolution de l'Amérique* (1780) and *Considérations sur la paix* (1783). Raynal's books were among the bestsellers in France from 1770 to 1789—his *Histoire philosophique* went through 12 editions during that period, to say nothing of the numerous borrowings, digests, and later editions. Raynal was considered to be the great authority on the United States, although his documentation is very weak and almost entirely secondhand. These weaknesses, however, are characteristic of French interest in the new republic— readers were ready to accept their own images of America even if they did not fit reality. A number of other books were devoted to the political changes in the New World, including Dubuisson's *Abrégé de la révolution de l'Amérique anglaise* (1778) and Mably's *Observations sur le gouvernement et les lois des Etats-Unis.* The expression *American Revolution* is more common in the titles than *War of Independence*, a fact which indicates that contemporaries viewed the event as a true revolution and not just another war.

Travel narratives written by Frenchmen who had participated in the American Revolution were also highly popular. The first to be circulated (in very limited circles) described the voyage of Chastellux from Newport to Philadelphia (1781); a more comprehensive edition appeared in 1785. Abbé Robin, who had accompanied the French expeditionary force as a priest, published his *Nouveau-voyage dans l'Amérique septentrionale* in 1782. To his own memories of the experience he added many other anecdotes which had nothing to do with what he had seen and were simply borrowed from other travel books. The most successful publication in this category was St. John de Crèvecoeur's *Lettres d'un cultivateur américain* (1784), from which a generation of Frenchmen learned to know the United States. The new republic also inspired a number of epics which nobody reads anymore, among them Chavannes de la Giraudière's *L'Amérique délivrée*, whose title recalls Torquato Tasso's *Jerusalem Delivered* and Bourdon's *Voyage en Amérique, dialogue en vers.*

Many other monographs on the United States were published between the end of the war and the beginning of the French Revolution, the majority of them in the political field, but even more typical of the times are the numerous periodicals that devoted all or part of their coverage to American matters. *Les Affaires de l'Angleterre et de l'Amérique*, which first appeared in 1776, was

almost entirely devoted to America. Strangely enough, this periodical, which
lasted until 1779, was supported by money from the French Ministry of
Foreign Affairs. Part of its content was entirely documentary—the journal
published the basic texts of the new nation, including the Declaration of
Independence, the constitutions of the various states, and the declarations of
rights. Another part was devoted to political discussions on the responsibilities
of Great Britain in the conflict. The *Affaires* also published excerpts from
Paine's *Common Sense*. When it ceased publication, it was reprinted as a single
volume which became the standard reference work on America. In 1783
Vergennes asked the king's printer to publish a special edition of the constitutions of the 13 states, which had previously appeared in the *Affaires*.

A number of other periodicals covered events in the New World, although
the extent of this coverage varied considerably. The most conservative
journals, such as the traditional *Gazette de France*, showed little interest in
America, while the *Gazette de Leyde* and the *Mercure de France*, as well as the
Journal encyclopédique de Bouillon, provided extensive coverage. Some of
these periodicals were printed outside France, mainly in the Netherlands,
and smuggled into the country. It might also be pointed out that the Physiocrats, in their own periodicals, published technical and economic information
on America. It appears to be clear, then, that interest in the American Revolution was directly related to individual political leanings.

It is certain, in any case, that there was tremendous curiosity among the
French concerning what was going on in America. Part of the information
supplied to satisfy this curiosity was vague, unscrupulous, and outdated before
it was published. Such flaws were not limited to the subject of America, of
course: in those days it was quite common to reprint under one's own name
material written by others, for there was no copyright. And although the
considerable curiosity regarding the so-called Revolution of the New World
is obvious, we cannot determine just who the curious were. The question is
connected with what we now call public opinion, and to define public opinion
in 18th-century France is very difficult. It seems logical to suppose that the
readers of books and articles on America represented small circles of nobility,
clergymen, and upper-middle-class people and that the great majority of
French citizens were not touched by the changes taking place in North
America and, in fact, in most cases had not even heard about them. Consequently, no clear-cut conclusions may be reached regarding the ideological
impact of the American Revolution in France.

That there was, nonetheless, a real impact is obvious from a number of
special instances. A few provincial academies dominated local intellectual
life and each year awarded prizes for dissertations submitted on preselected

research topics. (Rousseau made himself famous with a dissertation submitted to the Académie de Dijon in 1750 under the title *Discours sur les sciences et les arts*.) Occasionally an academy chose the American Revolution as a topic for consideration. In 1784, for example, the Académie des Jeux Floraux in Toulouse chose the following as the theme for its annual competition: "On the Greatness and Importance of the Revolution Which Has Taken Place in Northern America." The winner was to receive 450 pounds, but Vergennes himself was so delighted with the topic that he added 750 pounds to the award. The winner was a 34-year-old lawyer named Jean Mailhe who later became representative of the Department of Haute-Garonne to the Legislative Assembly of 1791, was elected to the Convention the year after, and was author of the report on the prosecution of Louis XVI. His political career ended abruptly in 1795 because he had voted for the death of the king, although he lived on until 1835. His dissertation of 1784 is divided into two parts, the first devoted to the causes of the American Revolution and the second to its importance. Mailhe argued that the American Revolution was not limited in time and space and that its process was intended to extend to other countries: "It is going to influence the future of the human race, and forthcoming generations will share with you the benefits of this happy event." [8] It was the beginning of a new era, not only in politics but also in trade and industry. The United States was going to protect the weak and small nations against the larger ones and to defend liberty against the tyranny of the old kingdoms. There is something prophetic in Mailhe's views—whether they belong to him or reflect the mood of his time and city—and it is not surprising that he won the prize.

A grant from abbé Raynal made it possible for the academy in Lyons to present awards for original works on the New World. Each year from 1784 to 1789, the academy offered a prize for a paper on this subject. In 1786, a manuscript entitled *Influence de la révolution de l'Amérique* was submitted by a certain "Godard," a nom de plume used by the philosopher Condorcet. The next year two manuscripts were submitted, one by an abbé Genty, entitled *Influence de la découverte de l'Amérique sur le bonheur du genre humain*, and the other by an "M.P., vice-counsel at E.," whom some historians suspect to be Chastellux. Both were highly laudatory of the United States, expressing the opinion that the Americans would help redeem the human race.

All these works are theoretical and are not based on direct experience in America. With the possible exception of Chastellux, if he did indeed write the pamphlet referred to, the authors had no firsthand knowledge of the United States and had forged in their minds an ideal image of the country. For them the new nation possessed every virtue and was destined to serve as a guide for other nations. Strangely enough, there was no work that challenged these images, and the newly created United States thus became a model to be imitated, a paradise, an El Dorado, when compared to the decadent and corrupt societies of the Old World. The popularity of Crèvecoeur's book has something to do with this idealism. It contributed to building an image of the American farmer as plain, honest, simple, hard-working, protected against vice, the ideal citizen of a republic—a view reminiscent of certain of Rousseau's distortions.

Whatever the diffusion of these ideas among an elite—and we shall never know how large it was—there is one point which is of great interest in relation to the impact of the American Revolution in France, and that is the discussions centering around the Constitution and the balance of powers in the new state.

From John Locke on there had been general curiosity regarding constitutional matters in France, which happened to be, like other states of the time with the partial exception of England, without a constitution. The real question was: Who was the guardian of the traditions that replaced the constitution? Was it the king, as seemed normal in an absolute monarchy, or was it some intermediate body such as the French Parlements, which, taking advantage of the similarity of their name with the English Parliament and strengthened by their right to register the new laws on their books, tended to monopolize the opposition against the declining monarchy? This question had been discussed throughout the 18th century, by Montesquieu, Rousseau, Mably, and, just before the French Revolution, Condorcet. The American Revolution provided new arguments in favor of a constitution but also divided the so-called specialists over the question of whether one or two assemblies would be preferable and, if there were to be two, over the differences between the upper and the lower one.

We may recall the great interest on the part of the French elite in the constitutions of the different states before a federal constitution was drafted, as well as in the Declaration of Independence and the state declarations of rights. All these texts were translated and printed in France soon after their publication in the states and went through a number of French editions. According to Palmer, the state constitutions were published on at least five different occasions between 1776 and 1786.[9] France is the only country in which the American Constitution was discussed at great length, and the ideas expressed in it actually anticipated the debates of the various assemblies of the revolutionary period. Thanks to the American experience the French delegates were better prepared than those of any other country, although this preparedness did not guarantee success—quite the contrary, in fact. The different schemes adopted in France reflect the contradictions involved in all these discussions.

What they learned first from the Americans was the possibility of constituting a government "through the principle of the people as constituent power." [10] This was an entirely new exercise, and it must have been a fascinating one, if one bears in mind that people could for the first time witness the birth of a new state which had to build its new institutions by its own will. And this was also the first large state not to be a monarchy. There existed republics in Europe, in Switzerland, in the Netherlands, and in some parts of Italy, and the free cities of Germany were also republics, although they were included in the limits of the empire. In the 18th century all republics were supposed to be small, and Rousseau had cautioned against a large state's becoming a republic. How could it do so without crumbling? The United States provided the answer, in vivo.

Constitutional discussions had formerly made reference to Great Britain, but the American Revolution added a new and different view to the debate. The anglomania of the early 18th century turned to anglophobia, because of the continuing struggle between France and England and because the institutions did not prove to be as satisfactory as they had appeared to Montesquieu and Voltaire. The very fact that the mother country opposed the colonies showed that there was something wrong in the political system. Admiration for British institutions faded away and was replaced by great respect for what was going on in the New World.

Questions emerged at once, stemming from the discussions on the importance of intermediate bodies in the state and the desirability of a single assembly or of two. The opposing positions in France were represented by Turgot on the one hand and Mably on the other. In a letter written to Richard Price in 1778 but published only in 1784 in Price's *Observations on the Importance of the American Revolution*, Turgot criticized the multiplication of intermediate bodies and made it clear that his preferences were for a single body in which all legislative powers should be concentrated and which would defend the interest of the nation against the executive. Turgot understood that such a scheme was possible only in a new country, the traditions of the French monarchy being opposed to a weakening of the executive. In what may be considered a reply, the *Observations on the Government and the Laws of the United States of America* (1784), Mably approved the balance of powers established in some of the American states and expressed his preferences for the constitution of Massachusetts, inspired by his friend John Adams, over that of Pennsylvania, inspired by Benjamin Franklin. He liked the idea of a two-assembly legislature with a strong senate as the upper house and a lower house whose members were elected on a restricted basis. This was the case in Massachusetts, whose constitution was somewhat more aristocratic than Pennsylvania's, a fact which pleased Mably (although he is usually considered a democrat).

The opposition between these conflicting views cannot be separated from a question which had been raised in France at the same time: If there were two assemblies, did it necessarily mean that one had to accept some kind of aristocracy whose members would sit in the upper house according to British example? If so, how then could one reconcile the existence of an aristocracy with the realities of liberty, which was the basis of the new system of government? This point was made by Mirabeau in a pamphlet published in London in 1784, *Considerations on the Order of Cincinnatus*. According to recent authors, it seems clear that Mirabeau was directly inspired by Franklin, who, upon hearing that the Society of the Cincinnati had been established by former officers of the American and French armies, feared it to be the beginning of a new kind of hereditary order. Taking advantage of this opportunity, Mirabeau wrote a violent diatribe against aristocracy, assuming that such a body had its place in a monarchy but not in the American republic, because it violated the principles of the new state. This pamphlet had a special significance in France, as Mirabeau, an aristocrat himself, was questioning the very usefulness of an aristocracy.

Once again, we do not know what kind of people were exposed to these discussions and to what extent they influenced the opinion of the elite. It is at least interesting that they raised two basic points, equally important for France: one or two assemblies? an aristocracy or no aristocracy?

In the years just preceding the French Revolution, these discussions were exacerbated by the publication of three new works on the United States, written in reaction against those previously cited. In 1788 Jefferson's friend Philip Mazzei, who was Italian by birth and French by culture and who had established himself in Virginia in 1773, published his *Recherches historiques et politiques sur les Etats-Unis*, criticizing the views of Raynal and Mably in four thick volumes which, according to Bernard Fay, were the most serious work ever written on the United States. They were not taken as seriously as they deserved, unfortunately. At the same time, Brissot, one of the future leaders of the Girondins, published in London his *Examen critique des voyages de M. le Marquis de Chastellux*, which criticized the former officer of the French expeditionary force for not having given a nice enough image of the United States, which he considered as a model to be followed. And in 1789 a pamphlet by "a farmer of New Jersey" later identified as John Stevens was translated and published in France under the title *Examen du gouvernement d'Angleterre comparé à la Constitution des Etats-Unis* and helped reanimate the discussions on the Constitution, which were already in the forefront of French politics.

All this literature seems to have influenced some of the deputies to the Constituent Assembly when it replaced the States General. The Patriots, as they called themselves, as opposed to the Aristocrats, included participants in the American Revolution such as Lafayette, Noailles, Crèvecoeur, and Chastellux, others like Brissot, Condorcet, and Dupont de Nemours who had been involved in the controversies concerning government and the American model in the years just before 1789, and still others who sympathized with American ideals without having been connected with the Americans— Sieyès, Bailly, Mirabeau, Rabaut Saint-Etienne, Roederer, and Volney. What the Patriots wanted was to give France a constitution which would guarantee individual rights and destroy despotism once and for all. To do this, they had to contrast the French situation with that in America. The American Revolution was more or less present in the background of the Constituent Assembly.

The preparation of the Declaration of Rights was the first issue to be considered. Its origins are now well known, as the Constituents referred to American precedent. Rabaut Saint-Etienne declared during the discussion: "France has had for an example the States. But this does not mean that the Declaration must be the same, for circumstances are different." It had long been thought that the French declaration repeated more or less the American, which was in part an adaptation of the English Bill of Rights of 1689. Actually, if the French declaration was inspired by an American model it was Virginia's Declaration of Rights, although some articles were borrowed from the declarations of Massachusetts, Pennsylvania, Delaware, Maryland, and North Carolina as well.[11] The French declaration differed from the others primarily in that it claimed to be universal—good for everyone in the world. Before the bill was voted in the assembly, it was submitted by Lafayette to Jefferson, then near the end of his stay in France, who returned it with comments and approval.

The discussions on the Constitution also reflected the influence of the American Revolution. The main question, once again, was whether there should be one or two assemblies. Sieyès, in his popular pamphlet *Qu'est-ce-que le Tiers Etat*, referred to John Stevens' *Examen du gouvernement* to demonstrate the advantages of the American process whereas Mounier and Morellet, who knew the American Constitution, defended the opposite view. There were two serious obstacles against a second assembly: First, the aristocracy had been suppressed by the decrees of the fourth of August, which made all French people equal before the law. It would have been dangerous, then, to re-create some social body to play a political role in the upper assembly. Second, the

American model did not fit either, since France was a centralized state, the provinces had just been suppressed and replaced by departments, and federalism was alien to French minds. So the assembly decided for a one-assembly system, although this choice did not prove to be very successful.

Since that time, the debate between advocates of one- and two-assembly systems has never ceased. It has come to the forefront in every constitutional discussion from 1789 to 1969, when de Gaulle was defeated on his referendum on the suppression of the senate. Generally speaking, radicals have favored a single assembly and liberals and conservatives two assemblies, using the arguments inspired in Mirabeau by Franklin: An upper assembly does not express the will of the people and might become a kind of aristocracy; it is thus incongruous with democracy.

A few other influences might also be mentioned. The American Constitution had been framed by a special body called for this purpose, the Convention. Brissot was in the United States in 1787 and was so impressed by this experience that on returning to France he published a pamphlet contending that the States General had no right to draft a constitution, that it was necessary to summon a special assembly as had been done in the United States. He was not listened to at the time, but three years later, with the fall of the monarchy, the Legislative Assembly was dissolved and was superseded by a convention elected by universal suffrage to give France her new constitution.

Another discussion has centered on the origins of the National Guard, which was created in the summer of 1789. The idea seems to have come from Lafayette, who had been inspired by the militia he had known and admired in America. He organized the guard as a civil body different from the army in that its troops were not mercenaries and its officers were promoted for reasons of merit rather than of birth. This National Guard, under the leadership of Lafayette himself, was to give the revolution its guiding spirit and protect its conquests. The guard sank into oblivion under authoritarian regimes, reappeared under liberal regimes, and, eventually, was suppressed after the Commune.[12]

In the short run, no doubt, the impact of the American Revolution on France was tremendous, albeit difficult to assess. The American experience could have provided an example for curing the ills of the ancien régime. The extent to which it did so cannot be determined for certain, since the issues raised were very different in the two countries. France had to struggle against privileges deeply rooted in the so-called feudal regime, a problem almost unknown on the other side of the Atlantic. It is of interest to recall that Louis Hartz considered this absence of feudalism in the New World to be the primary difference between Europe and the United States. The United States thus could not provide any answer to what was then the basic issue in France. Another shortcoming of the American revolutionary experience was its complete silence on the future of the slaves held in bondage within the limits of the country. How could a democracy keep people in bondage and at the same time invoke individual liberty? Did it mean that there existed two categories of human beings? Jefferson was quite conscious of this basic contradiction and tried, without success, to resolve it throughout his long life. French people who, like the abbé Grégoire, devoted their lives to the freeing of Jews and slaves could not refer to an American precedent in this area. It becomes apparent, then, that the American Revolution did not and could not answer some of the fundamental questions the French people had to face.

Nonetheless, one cannot deny the far-reaching influence of the American Revolution in the field of ideas. For enlightened Frenchmen the American Revolution initiated the American dream. They had never questioned the virtues and simplicity of the inhabitants of the New World, but the Revolution added new dimensions of liberty, equality, and the pursuit of happiness. The United States became the land of opportunity, even the *only* land of opportunity in the world, and remained so for a century. People could contrast the stability of the new country with the political unrest and social turmoil of France. Thousands of Frenchmen could enjoy the amenities of the American political system while their countrymen were exposed to the hardships of war and revolution. There seemed to be something really exceptional in the American experience. No wonder, then, that it fell upon Tocqueville, an aristocrat of the same breed as those who had helped the Americans win their independence, to express such ideas in his *La Démocratie en Amérique*, which, though written a generation after the outbreak of the French and American revolutions, remains as everlasting evidence of the impact of the American Revolution on France.

Notes

1 Alexis de Tocqueville, *L'ancien régime et le révolution*, ed. J. P. Mayer, vol. 2 (Paris: Gallimard, 1967), p. 337.

2 Quoted from Francois Victor Alphonse Aulard, *La Société des Jacobins . . .*, 6 vols. (Paris: Librairie Jouanst, 1889–97), 2:622.

3 Louis Phillippe, comte de Ségur, *Mémoires, souvenirs et anecdotes* (Paris: Didot frères, 1859).

4 Thomas Balch, *Les Francais en Amérique pendant la Guerre de l'Indépendance des Etats-Unis, 1777–1783* (Paris: A. Sauton, 1872), p. 214.

5 Ministry of Foreign Affairs, *Les Combattants français de la Guerre d'indépendance, 1778–1873* (Paris, 1903). For the American edition, see Senate of the United States, 58th Congress, 2d Session, Document no. 77.

6 Forrest MacDonald, "The Relation of the French Peasant Veterans of the American Revolution to the Fall of Feudalism in France, 1789–1792," *Agricultural History* 25, no. 4 (October 1951): 151–61.

7 From the list given by Bernard Fay, *Bibliographie critique des ouvrages francais relatifs aux Etats-Unis* (1700–1800) (Paris: E. Champion, 1925). See also his *L'esprit révolutionnaire en France et aux Etats-Unis à la fin du XVIIIe siècle* (Paris: E. Champion, 1925).

8 On Jean Mailhe, very often mentioned by historians, see Jacques Godechot, "Les Toulousains et l'indépendance des Etats-Unis," *Caliban*, Annales publiées par la Faculté des Lettres et Sciences humaines de Toulouse 2, no. 1 (January 1966): 115–27.

9 Robert R. Palmer, *The Age of the Democratic Revolution*, 2 vols. (Princeton: Princeton University Press, 1959–64), 1:263.

10 Ibid., p. 266.

11 Gilbert Chinard, "Notes on the American Origins of the Déclaration des Droits de l'Homme," *Proceedings of the American Philosophical Society* 98, no. 6 (1954): 383–96. See also Chinard's *La Déclaration des Droits de l'Homme et du Citoyen et ses antécédents américains* (Washington: Institut français de Washington, 1945).

12 Jacques Godechot, *Les Institutions de la France sous la Révolution et l'Empire*, 2d ed. (Paris: Presses Universitaires de France, 1968), p. 125 ff. Louis Girard, *La Garde Nationale, 1814–1871* (Paris: Plon, 1964).

In 1967 Claude B. Fohlen became the first recipient of a newly established chair in American history at the Sorbonne, a position which he continues to hold today. He has also taught at Yale University, the University of Michigan, the University of California at Berkeley, and Stanford University. He completed his undergraduate studies at the universities of Bordeaux and Toulouse and was awarded a doctorat des lettres from the Sorbonne in 1954.

Professor Fohlen's publications include L'Industrie textile sous le Second Empire *(1956)*, L'Amérique anglo-saxonne de 1815 à nos jours *(2d ed., 1969)*, Les Noirs aux Etats-Unis *(5th ed., 1975)*, L'Agonie des Peaux-Rouges *(1970)*, Nous partons pour l'Amérique du Nord *(1969)*, *and* La Société américaine, 1865–1970 *(1973)*. He is currently working on a book to be entitled* The Times of FDR.

It is hardly necessary for me to say that, after France, no nation in the world contributed more in aid, in arms—whether by overt or illicit means—or in money to the American Revolutionary cause and to the development of the early American nation than the United Provinces, now known as the Netherlands. Even John Adams, whom the Dutch at times exasperated and who at almost all times exasperated almost anyone with whom he came in contact abroad, conceded the stout tradition of independence and republicanism so deeply entrenched among the Dutch. Here to treat the other side of the coin, the impact of the American Revolution on the Netherlands, is a scholar who has brilliantly explored various facets of American life, ranging from the 18th to the 20th century, and who at present is professor of American history at the University of Leiden, a center of significant studies in the field. It is my pleasure to introduce Professor J. W. Schulte Nordholt.

The Impact
of the American Revolution
on the Dutch Republic

J. W. SCHULTE NORDHOLT

Americanus sum, nec quidquam Americani a me alienum puto.

C. W. F. Dumas to John Adams
November 1, 1780.

It is one of the sweetest consolations I have found in Life, to see that while we have been contending for our own Liberties, we have given an opportunity to several other Nations for the Renovation of theirs. We have the satisfaction to reflect that we have set an example of political Liberty, religious Liberty and commercial Liberty before the Eyes of the present age.

John Adams to C. W. F. Dumas
May 16, 1783

I may yet bring my Family to the Hague and become a Dutchman.

John Adams to C. W. F. Dumas
September 10, 1783

"IN THIS OUR BLESSED COUNTRY the humblest laborer is as entirely king of his castle as is the most illustrious nobleman: the laws of the country are known to all and common property. ... Like a sovereign he disposes his children's destiny.... He settles in that area of the country which he judges will provide him with a livelihood." Thus reads a quotation from a book dated 1777. Compare a poetical description of the same happy scene: "There is no country where wealth is so unostentatious and poverty is so generously administered to and so charitably accepted. Where the peasant is so rich, . . . the sailor so beloved, . . . the merchant so respected, . . . the humblest servant even as merry as his master." [1] It would not be difficult to quote a whole series of similar eulogies, but the paradise they evoke is not, as one might have thought at the time, the New World of America. I do not quote Crèvecoeur here, or Freneau, or other laudatores mundi novi. No, the Old World of the Dutch Republic is the subject under discussion. The first quotation is taken from a book written by one of the most capable and conservative statesmen of that country, Laurens Pieter van de Spiegel, and the poet supporting his view is the author and historian Simon Stijl. What they both proclaimed, maybe a little too loudly, was their belief that their country's leading, outstanding characteristic was its stance as a bulwark of freedom and equality. Thus they aired what in their day was a general, albeit mythical, belief, quite common not only in their own country but all over Europe. Voltaire had already praised the Dutch for their freedom: "La grandeur d'un Batave est de vivre sans Maître." Mirabeau addressed them as "le plus ancien des peuples libres." [2] The well-read statesman John Adams, recently arrived in the Netherlands, expressed the same admiration: "I doubt much whether there is any Nation of Europe more estimable than the Dutch, in Proportion." [3]

The American envoy was to discover soon enough that the Dutch reality was quite different from the impression he had gained from his reading. Disappointment would even cause him to adopt virtually the opposite opinion, one which resembled more closely the actual situation but tended to develop into yet another myth—that of the total decline of the Dutch Republic— which survived considerably longer. In his recently published diary Drew Pearson recalls how he came to visit ex-President Truman, who was very glad to see him, played for him on both of his pianos, and then went on to teach him a history lesson in which the leitmotiv was the approaching fall of America. Truman discussed the "question of whether we would go the way of the Roman empire, the Greek cities, and the Dutch Republic. I didn't like to express my ignorance, but I asked him what happened to the Dutch Republic. He replied: They got too complacent, too fat, and too prosperous. We are in grave danger of being the same way." [4]

This is not the place to treat the complex problem of the relative or absolute decline of the Dutch state and society in the 18th century. Modern research has disclosed the relativity of absolute viewpoints. But we, on the other hand, cannot ignore the testimonies from the period itself, speaking as they do of an utterly gloomy situation; testimonies by such totally different personalities as James Harris, the English envoy, and his American counterpart, John Adams.

"Virtue," wrote Harris, "the main spring of a commonwealth, no longer sub-
sisted among the Dutch: the public was poor; the great riches of individuals
destroyed the equality necessary to a free state; . . . their government, their
administration, their consequence, their whole Republic, were in the last stage
of degradation, debasement and decay." And Adams confirmed his view:
"This country is indeed in a melancholy situation; sunk in ease, devoted to the
pursuits of gain, . . . incumbered with a complicated and perplexed constitution, divided among themselves in interest and sentiment, they seem afraid
of every thing." [5]

There is one aspect on which both contemporaries and historians agree:
the Dutch governmental system was completely out of date, did not function,
and was on the verge of collapse. And yet here too the myth had been kept
alive. Later, in 1775, the zealous reformer Pieter Paulus still defended the
Union of Utrecht as a perfect constitution, "which I never consider without
emotion and which I never read without experiencing the greatest admiration
of the surpassing wisdom and prudence of its authors." So excellent was this
constitution, it was said elsewhere, that it could not fail to serve as a model
for an American constitution. "It is surprising and to the credit of our fore-
bears that these inhabitants of another Continent, after a lapse of some two
centuries, adopted practically the same Measures and Arrangements as they
did when drafting the Union of Utrecht." Proudly Paulus himself quoted the
Articles of Confederation, "as passed and signed in the Philadelphia Congress
on the fourth of October 1776," and said that they "in some respects have
been formulated less haphazardly" but in other respects did not come up to the
Dutch model.[6]

Again, nothing but appearances. Those concerned knew better. James
Harris believed that no system that had ever been contrived in the way of
political arrangements appeared "to have been so weak and illiberal, so irregu-
lar and inaccurate, so preposterous and undefined as that of the Dutch."
John Adams, who gradually saw through the complicated system of this
fragmented sovereignty, complained bitterly about the devious and cumbrous
procedure: "These will deliberate and deliberate and deliberate, and probably
some will be for, and some against making a treaty." [7] Small wonder that the
man who may pass as the wisest Dutchman of his time, the philosopher
Hemsterhuis, advised the Americans "à ne jamais calquer le Gouvernement
de leur République sur celui de la nôtre."[8]

To add to that, the country was torn by party quarrels, quite complicated
in themselves. "Indeed, the views of all the parties are enveloped in clouds
and darkness," exclaimed the desperate Adams.[9] Seen in their historical
perspective, such quarrels are perhaps best accounted for as a struggle between

three groups—the "Regents," the Orangeists, and the Patriots—which by means of sundry cabals and factions fought each other, entered into alliances, and abused each other with new names coined in the Netherlands—Aristocrats and Democrats. Gradually the outsiders understood what it was all about. Thomas Jefferson, for instance, in several letters, particularly in one to John Jay dated August 6, 1787, made a clear and differentiated report: in the struggle between the three parties—Stadhoulderians, Aristocrats, and Democrats— the Aristocrats occupied a center position, the violent in their midst favored the prince, and the moderates would have preferred to join the Democrats, provided they did not become too radical.[10] This is the same picture as Gerrit Paape sketches in his "Unvarnished History of the Batavian Patriottismus," the same also that Johan Luzac paints in bolder strokes in a letter to J. Valckenaer: the aristocracy is the weather vane protruding above the house, "qui se renverse au moindre vent," but because of its pride and importance is more likely to join the Orangeists than the Democrats.[11]

In short, a complicated and ominous situation, boding ill for the future. In a cheerful mood, John Adams could well write home that "it is the United States of America that must save this republic from ruin,"[12] but even though the new nation in the west did indirectly play a comparatively important role in the course of Dutch events, the time when this nation might intervene directly and save us was still far away.

The factual history of the relation between the rebellious Americans and the Republic spans a mere seven years, 1775–82. The political troubles of the New World were not brought to our attention until the issue of the Scotch Brigade came up, and seven years later the United States was recognized as an independent nation. After that, interest waned again, we were overwhelmed by our own troubles, and, by way of a Prussian counterrevolution and a French revolution, our proud Republic was brought to an end and a new era was born.

What role did the American Revolution play in that whole complex of events? Apart from leading indirectly to the war with England, and thus to all subsequent difficulties and disasters, did it also directly influence the Dutch developments? Or must we resign ourselves to the conclusion which was the starting point of Pieter Jan van Winter's great work on the economic relations between Amsterdam and America, namely, that there was barely any interest on the part of the Dutch in the "spiritual process" of the Revolution.[13] It is my thesis in this essay that the American Revolution did indeed play an important part in the history of the United Provinces during the years around 1780, that in addition to the economic interest there definitely was a political and spiritual sympathy with the American cause, even a feeling of affinity.

First of all, it was the direct influence of American ideas which led to the great turmoil in our country in the eighties. The testimonies of contemporaries, whether or not they favored the American Revolution and the example it became, are unanimous on that score. Adriaan Kluit described "the evil of American freedom" as "the origin and beginning of all *subsequent* disasters, calamities and losses suffered by the Republic." Laurens Pieter van de Spiegel was of the same opinion: "The resulting Union of North America which was a pure democracy [note the pejorative use of these words in this context] turned many a head as if there were no freedom outside that Constitution." The English envoy James Harris affirmed that "the example of fortunate resistance in the British colonies in America had an influence on the tempers and sentiments of men all over Europe, but particularly in the United Provinces." [14] On the other side this opinion is corroborated, first, by Johan Derk van der Capellen, who, in his letters, frequently asserted that the great majority of his compatriots—he even mentioned the figure of four-fifths— were "friends and well-wishers" of the American cause.[15] This may sound somewhat exaggerated, but the opinion that "the political concepts postulated by the philosophers of this era . . . had been developed in no slight degree by the North American spirit of freedom" is a conclusion found even in the memoir of such a moderate Patriot as Herman Hendrik Vitringa.[16] As a matter of fact, the Revolution aroused not only popular excitement but also intellectual interest. The most enlightening testimony in this context is that of the French author and bookseller Joseph Mandrillon, who indicated quite accurately the way in which the American rebellion influenced our country: "But if one wishes to know the origin of the first fermentation amongst the inhabitants, I think one should ascribe it to the excellent works published in England on the subject of the American war and primarily to those by Doctor Price, which have been translated into Dutch and read with extraordinary eagerness by all ranks and classes of Burghers." [17]

Thus we come to the man who more than anyone else may be considered the leader of the Patriot party, Johan Derk van der Capellen himself, for it is he who translated the writings of Richard Price and who soon became the great champion of the American cause in the Netherlands; firstly, by his demonstrations against the sending of the Scotch Brigade and further, through his contacts with such leaders of the American Revolution as Jonathan Trumbull and William Livingston. It would lead us too far astray to deal with this controversial figure, so exalted by his supporters and so debunked by 19th-century historians. If it were possible to size him up by his ideological utterances we should rather view him with C. H. E. de Wit as a moderate conservative than with W. F. Wertheim and A. H. Wertheim-Gijse Weenink as a radical.[18] However, it is not his logic but his temperament that characterizes him, that makes him the best example in this country of what Caroline Robbins has called the "real Whigs," and that led him to so fervently take the side of the American rebellion.[19]

He and his friend Francois Adrian van der Kemp are indeed the heralds of what Kluit so disdainfully calls the evil of American Freedom. In their words and deeds they follow what they consider the shining example in the west; they want to ensure a similar freedom. Van der Capellen wrote to Benjamin Franklin that he would gladly give his blood for a united America, and he is indeed one of the very few who at least had the courage to stake his money—10,000 guilders—for a loan. Nervous and vulnerable as he knew himself to be, he believed—perhaps not without reason—that his siding with America had given his enemies, "those tyrants," the "arms with which to damage me," and that therein lay the real reason they should have barred him from the states of Overijssel. He recounted how a certain member had the nerve to say, in a public place, "when seeing extracts of my correspondence with Governor Livingston, *that as long as he had eyes in his head, he would not tolerate my being readmitted, because I had kept up a forbidden exchange of letters with the Americans."* [20]

Van der Kemp, the Mennonite minister from Leiden, was equally enthusiastic. He collected and published extracts and articles about America and from the pulpit proclaimed his political faith:

In America the sun of salvation has risen, which shall also shine upon us if we wish: only America can revive our Commerce, our Navigation: ... America can teach us how to fight the degeneration of the people's character, to stay moral corruption, to put an end to bribery, to smother the seeds of tyranny and to restore the health of our moribund freedom. America has been ordained by the Being of all beings to be The Netherlands' last preacher of penitence; America has been ordained to heal the flaws in the character of the Netherlands people, if they wish to follow in its footsteps.[21]

With such idealism, but with an eye on the merchants in his flock, did this preacher declare his American gospel.

The question that arises is, of course, how much these excited panegyrists actually knew about the New World. Was their exultation and that of others rooted only in eager credulity or also in sound information? The answer to this must be that in the Netherlands a stream of literature about the American rebellion was undoubtedly available; that a newspaper like the *Gazette de Leyde*, read all over Europe, gave very detailed news from America, that the works of writers like Raynal, de Pauw, William Robertson, Mandrillon, and even Paine were read and some were also published; and that, moreover, a good many were being translated—for instance, the famous itinerary of the English vicar Andrew Burnaby.[22] What kind of image a diligent and not too credulous reader received from such a mixture of contradictory information is difficult to say. Original Dutch works are scarce, the most important certainly being the collection of letters that the country squire Count van Nassau la Leck published in the years 1777–79. He tried to be objective but made conjectures and sometimes curious errors, adding a highly pessimistic prognosis for the future of a free, too unbridled America and an urgent plea for a stronger union than that established in the Articles of Confederation.[23]

The vague image already formed before 1780, the year the war broke out and also the year in which John Adams arrived in Amsterdam, was subsequently much clarified and enhanced by the dynamic zeal shown by that first American envoy. Struggling for recognition and rebuffed by the authorities, he sought refuge in publicity: "I had no way to come at them but by the press, because the president refused to receive my memorial." [24] To this zeal we owe not only his *Memorial* but also the 26 letters to Hendrik Calkoen, the Dutch edition of his *Novanglus Papers*, and his adaptation of Thomas Pownall's *Memorial to the Sovereigns of Europe*.[25] These nourished the enthusiasm of their public in the Netherlands, and it reciprocated with a spate of bad poetry and rhetoric, with further idealization of the image of America, and with intensified revolutionary sentiments.[26]

The essence of all this propagandistic image-building was the obvious and favorite comparison of the American with the Dutch rebellion, a pastime which, for that matter, was already in vogue in America itself at an early stage, as Pauline Maier documents, citing an example from 1772.[27] John Adams used it eagerly in his *Memorial*; other authors elaborated on it—like Cérisier in *Le Politique Hollandais*, in which he compared George III with Philip II of Spain, Thomas Hutchinson with Cardinal de Granvelle, Gen. Thomas Gage with the duke of Alva, Washington with William of Orange.[28] The propaganda reached its pinnacle in the glorification of George Washington, and we can judge its effectiveness from a series of utterances, not only of kindred spirits like Van der Capellen and of poets like Bellamy and Lucretia van Merken, but also of Gijsbert Karel van Hogendorp—a youngster educated in the Orangeistic tradition—who was so bitterly disappointed when he finally saw his hero face to face.[29] Others tremble with emotion at such encounters. The letters from travelers like Gerard Vogels and P. A. Godin are fascinating material for the hagiography of the great man:

And this day, this very day I saw the greatest Man who has ever appeared on the face of this Hemisphere ... then the Excellent Hero himself appeared mounted on an uncommonly beautiful horse that, seemingly proud of his burden, suggested to me Germanicus' horse, whilst we, elated at seeing the Hero, appeared to be in doubt whether we should wonder more at his simple yet impressively heroic bearing or at the graciousness of the greatest and best of all heroes. . . ." [30]

But everything was not always a bed of roses. With however much admiration people like Van der Capellen and his followers looked to the west, they were not totally uncritical. It must be pointed out that, from a distance, Johan Derk had already put his finger very accurately on the sore spot of American society. His deep repugnance for slavery, which had already led him to protest in his own country against the decision of the States-General not to emancipate the Negroes who had been brought by their owners to the home country, also caused him deep concern over the cruel system in America. To Price he wrote that he hoped that "les Américans, si tôt qu'ils se verront libres et en sureté, ne perdront pas de vue les interêts des pauvres nègres, qui gémissent encore sous le joug de l'Esclavage parmi eux." He admitted that it would be difficult to emancipate them all at the same time, but "perpetuer l'esclavage dans les 13 Etats serait une conduite, qui donnerait un démenti aux principes dont l'Amérique a toujours fait proféssion." [31]

That single note of sharp criticism is easily drowned out by the manifold expression of admiration, but the question of how much influence this high minded chorus has had on further developments in Holland can of course never be answered accurately. No Cliometry can help us gauge that emanation of a mood of exaltation. We have insufficient data. Let us summarize, cautiously, by saying that Van der Capellen, Van der Kemp, Luzac, and their circle prepared the field in which Adams could sow. It was due to his spirit of enterprise and self-assurance that the recognition of his country was in fact effectuated. Adams, who even before he had gained an official status furnished a stately mansion as an embassy, merits the gratitude of his country. His enemies were appalled. "Il est vrai et tristement singulier que le Mari d'Eve vient nb. d'acheter une belle maison au Burgwal, à la Haye," Nicolaas ten Hove wrote to Van Goens. [32]

Or do we seek the causes of the events too much with individuals, with persons? John Adams himself, with his customary bold assurance, really believed that with his *Memorial* he had sparked the train of events, mobilized the ramshackle cart of the Republic, and even advanced European politics. This is what he proudly wrote to Livingston in a long letter full of a vanity reminiscent of the immortal Mr. Toad in Kenneth Graham's tale *The Wind in the Willows* but also showing his inimitable heartwarming irony: "What a dust we raise, said the fly upon the chariot wheel." [33]

Propaganda and excitement created an atmosphere wherein recognition could be brought about. But first the canny Dutch merchants had to investigate the economic side of the affair. The years 1780–82 give evidence of discussions that seem entirely businesslike but which do not lack mythical factors—like most commercial considerations, for that matter. No, the Dutch would not dream of granting loans before the possibilities of a successful revolution seemed assured, as John Adams was very well aware; loans should be preceded by recognition, and in its turn this depended on the prospects of victory in the rebellion. But, nevertheless, all kinds of unrealistic hopes played a part in the discussions—dreams of an unlimited new market, no longer inaccessible as a result of English mercantilism, in a country that would remain agrarian for some decades to come and would consequently not compete with us. Such dreams were literally the echo of what Adams had whispered to Luzac and what the latter included in his introduction to the translation of Pownall's brochure.[34] The series of petitions directed by the Dutch merchants and cities in the early spring of 1782 to the states of their provinces, seeking the recognition of America, contained not businesslike prognoses but instead improbable illusions about an unlimited prosperity in commerce. Opposed to such optimism were the prudence, fear, and realism of others who warned against the possibility of a flourishing America that would most certainly become our competitor, especially in Asia. The wary suggested taking no action, as was so neatly formulated in a secret peace plan early in 1782: "neither to conclude [a treaty] at once nor to appear averse to it." But an atmosphere of excitement, not careful considerations, determined the course of events. To this Gijsbert Jan van Hardenbroek's diary bears clear witness: "feelings ran high. . . ." [35]

So we come to the pompous gaiety of April 1782—the official recognition, the reception of Adams as the first American envoy by Their High Mightinesses and even by the prince himself, the triumphal arches, the fireworks, the commemorative medals all over the country. Six months later the efforts were crowned with success by the signing of a Treaty of Friendship and Commerce in the Trèveshall in The Hague. John Adams might well be satisfied: "The standard of the United States waves and flies at The Hague in triumph, over Sir John Yorke's insolence and British pride. When I go to Heaven, I shall look down over the battlements with pleasure upon the stripes and stars wantoning in the wind at The Hague." [36]

From an economic point of view disappointment soon followed. Whoever had "considered the proceedings dispassionately and calmly might well have expected what actually happened, namely that all those magnificent chimeras envisioned in the first place by the notorious Knight Van der Capellen tot den Poll, have disappeared into thin air." [37] Thus wrote the burgomaster of Amsterdam, Joachim Rendorp, in his memoirs. And a patriotic work like the sequel to Jan Wagenaar's history confirms time and again that whatever illusions there had been were not realized, because "the enterprising character of the American merchants would not readily allow itself to be fenced in." [38]

Whatever had been stirred up by the American "Freedom systema" did not remain restricted to dreams and disappointment. A storm blew up that was not to abate for some time. What aspects of the initial American example were kept alive and were realized in the maelstrom of events? That question I shall endeavor to answer here.

Generally speaking, it is easy to say what direction the American influence was actually taking, that is, toward what an opponent like Adriaan Kluit called "an exaggerated people's government" [39] but what proponents preferred to call an extension of democracy. However, it is not so simple to pinpoint how and where that influence manifested itself. First it should be pointed out that in the Netherlands a certain democratic tradition already existed. But it was a cautious and veiled one, overshadowed by the appeal to the old Dutch freedoms that, as the Aristocrats were wont to say, implied everything one wished to understand by sovereignty of the people, representation, and imperium mixtum. The contention that it was solely owing to "American influence that the people's party no longer based itself on the restoration of the old but indefeasible rights of the people," as expressed in Robert J. Fruin's *History of the Dutch Public Institutions*, edited by Herman T. Colenbrander, may be incorrect, as De Wit asserts,[40] but to say that it lacks any element of truth is going too far.

The problem is that it is so difficult to discover a clearly defined line, a true Patriots' program. Their later critics may have judged them too harshly, no one more so than their old friend John Adams: "The Patriots in this country were little read in History less in Government; knew little of the human heart and still less of the World. They have therefore been the Dupes of Foreign Politicks, and their own undigested systems." [41] But Palmer's conclusion that their movement was "characterized by its lack of a developed ideology" [42] is not very far from the truth. In general, one could agree with the assertion of the 19th-century Dutch historian Willem Hendrik de Beaufort who wrote that the Democrats' ideal was "something vague that they could not or dared not define, but which would not be very far removed from our present constitutional monarchy." [43]

There is much to be said for this thesis, but the problem that our Dutch reformers had so few clear-cut constitutional ideas remains. The nearest attempt to constitutional thinking is found in the *Grondwettige Herstelling* [*Constitutional Restoration*],[44] that most interesting book which has suffered so many different interpretations. G. W. Vreede calls it the "political manual of the most ardent Patriots" and Pieter Geyl considers it the democratic Patriots' program. De Wit, however, describes it as a piece by the old or conservative Patriots, compiled by the literary hacks Cérisier and Swildens.[45] In any case, the work began the discussion about the necessity of a constitution, as the Union of Utrecht was no longer effective. Unlike the North Americans, the Dutch rebels had not "thought of compiling ... in the heat of war ... after careful consideration, a complete and fixed political codex." [46] This sounds progressive, but no proof followed; the authors were more inclined to further the restoration of the old freedoms than to allow themselves to be guided by new ideas from America.

It does not mean much in itself that the central theme of the book is the principle of the imperium mixtum. Mixed government is a basic tenet of all the available political literature of the period. There can be no good government without a balance between monarchy, aristocracy, and democracy. The Patriotic documents and declarations swear by this doctrine as solemnly as do those of their opponents. They are against "oligarchy," against "a Family-Government which smothers the reasonable and honorable Voice of the People," and also against "a total Democracy or People's Government without Representation"; all three of them are "highly pernicious." [47]

But the crux of the matter is this: how do we envision the possibility of the people influencing that mixed constellation? Does it mean that one persists, as does the *Grondwettige Herstelling*, in advocating the democratic foundation for an aristocratic form of government, and does one again revert to the old concepts of virtual representation? [48] Or should one venture to proceed one step further and give direct influence to the people? And if so, how?

There is, I believe, an evident—albeit somewhat illogical—development, by leaps and bounds, of a radical concept of representation. Indeed the entire evolution of Patriotism was not one of ideological clarity but of temperament and passion, fanned, as De Wit so aptly remarks, by the actions, or, if you will, reactions, of the opposition.[49] The beginnings of this development are to be found in the question of American recognition. The petitions pouring in from all cities to the states were actually the first example of the people's influence outside the traditional channels. Van der Capellen insisted on such petitions and considered them to be an example for further action.[50] The

Zuid-Hollandsche Courant deemed them proof that the voice of the people was the voice of God.[51] Mandrillon concluded that in them lay the beginning of everything and saw in these petitions "to request the independence of America ... the first instance of their interference in Government business; and this is, if you like, the origin of the Patriots."[52]

America was not only the cause but indeed also the model. The fact that already in 1781 a translation of all recently drafted constitutions of the 13 states of America had been published demonstrates the great political interest in the American system existing in our country.[53] Kluit's contention that the Democrats were out for "a so-called Representative People's Government, mostly along American lines,"[54] now begins to make sense. But again the question is how the people should acquire influence or what representation will mean. The people themselves, writes Van der Capellen, must not govern, but they must have influence, "by keeping their representatives under control," just as in America.[55] For this purpose the filing of petitions should be systematized. Committees from among the citizens are to assist the "Regents," but without the right to vote. Looking back, this does not sound so very radical; it sounds even less so when one reads that the foundation of such committees was to be the ancient guilds. But one should view these matters in the context of the time and not overemphasize the need for historical justification. Though the idea was traditional, it did open up possibilities of radicalization; and a leftwing historian like J. Romein was even able to see in the civil committees the precursors of the Raden or Soviet systems of modern times.[56]

But all this representation was still indirect, oblique. In the following years the Patriots went much further and soon called for true representation, for the election of the authorities by the people. This cause was furthered by a young, talented lawyer from the city of Deventer, Rutger Jan Schimmelpenninck. His thesis, *De Imperio Populare rite temperato*, defended in Leiden in 1785, was immediately translated and distributed.[57] A somewhat popular booklet for a thesis, it comprised only 84 pages. This booklet was, for the most part, inspired by the constitution of Massachusetts, drafted by John Adams, although it also had some more radical Rousseauistic aspects. It advocated a proper representation with free elections and the possibility of deposing governors; it pleaded for a system in which the best would go farthest as a result of their exemplariness and in which suffrage was given to all who were striving to uphold and promote the welfare of society, as did the ancient Roman who ploughed the field and reached for his sword. Age, property, independence, and expert knowledge were the conditions for suffrage.

Similar ideas soon emerged in the various declarations by the Patriots also.

Even though they adhered to the classic idea of mixed government, they placed more emphasis on the democratic element, and in the discussion with the oligarchy they loved to cite the American experiment as proof of the viability of a moderate democracy.[58] That was not radicalism; the accents had shifted. If the revered French ally, His Most Christian Majesty, were to be convinced, it could be done with the same argumentation. Moderate Amsterdam Patriots, including the banker Van Staphorst and Schimmelpenninck, sent a "Plan of an Aristo-Democratic Constitution" to France, "to prove to the Ministry of Versailles that by reforming and improving the Government of the Republic, specially in Holland, the good Citizens did not have any intention whatsoever to introduce a purely Democratic government." [59]

All this is seen in the light of later events to be no more than a relative radicalization. The American influence, like the whole American Revolution for that matter, was only partly radical. The moderate aspects had been clear from the start. There was only one point of real radicalization in which the American Revolution served as an example, and that was the proposal to arm the people. Again it was Van der Capellen who led the way, and his initial inspiration again came from the circles of the real Whigs in England. In 1774 he translated Andrew Fletcher's work *A Discourse of Government With Relation to Militia's*.[60] It was obvious that he would turn to his own Dutch tradition; the eighth article of the Union of Utrecht provided him with ample justification. But the American example was a convincing argument. In addition to the standing army, he wrote in his renowned pamphlet "To the Dutch People," "our burghers and farmers each should have a good musket and with that ... they must drill now and then ... especially on Sundays after church. That is how the Swiss and the Americans do it."[61]

Other proposals to arm the people followed the same line of reasoning. For instance, in the proposal by the radical district of Oostergo, the same area where the movement for the recognition of the United States had begun, "the respected, admirable, surprising North America" led the way.[62] In a discussion of this Frisian proposal by the *Post van den Neder-Rhijn*, an ardently Patriotic newspaper, the advantages of civil armament were summed up with arguments which would commend themselves to the most modern guerrilla theorists: an army of mercenaries is lost when defeated, but an army of "civilian warriors evades the danger by scattering themselves and becoming civilians again, ever ready to avail themselves of a better opportunity and to gird on the sword; of which the North Americans frequently gave proof in this war. ..." [63] This sounds dauntless, but the Dutch reality probably was not so impressive: much pomp and circumstance, many ranting songs, much drinking of health. Thus ran the description by Gerrit Paape, himself an ardent, but ironic and also disappointed, Patriot.[64]

There is yet another aspect, apart from the democratic one that emerges in this excitement about civilian armament. It is the national aspect. The American example was an incentive not only to more freedom but also to a belief in a Dutch regeneration, a new national pride. Even Colenbrander, who has little appreciation for the specifically Dutch character of the Patriot movement, mentions the national reunions of the delegates of the local volunteer corps as the first national organizations since the Dordrecht Synod.[65] The more detailed national profession of faith that he thinks is missing is definitely found in the various accompanying speeches, articles, and slogans voiced in this connection.[66] What is also striking is a certain Puritan emphasis, a protest against luxury and effeminacy; but it would be wrong to detect in this only a heritage of Dutch Calvinism. The similarities to a debate on the virtue and evil of luxury, so typical for the late 18th century, are evident. Our Dutch Patriots were not so far removed from an American revolutionary like Samuel Adams, dreaming of a "Christian Sparta." [67]

Until their very last days the Patriots remained inspired by American examples. In the summer of 1787, just before the start of the Prussian invasion smothered the entire revolution, there was some talk of negotiations about the Dutch situation taking place in Paris between the interested powers. The Civilian Corps conceived the plan to send delegates on behalf of the Patriot party in the same way that the Americans had sent Franklin and Adams to Europe before the recognition of their country was even being considered. [68] The whole plan miscarried, and soon all the democratic dreams were shattered by the Prussian occupation. The counterrevolution triumphed. There followed a period of stagnation and disillusion in the Netherlands or exile in France for the Patriots.

When another opportunity arose in 1795, everything had changed. Revolutionary America had consolidated itself by way of a centralizing constitution, but in France the ancien régime had been drowned under the torrent of revolution that now also flooded our country. What happened in France provided a compelling and overwhelming new example to supplant the old, somewhat utopian American model. Thus, for conservative minds an inevitable development from bad to worse appeared to be in process. This is how an intelligent man like R. M. van Goens saw it:

I do not hesitate to say it, because I know it is pointing out a great truth. It is not in France, it is in Holland, and originally in America that the French revolution is to be studied ... whatever horrors were committed in France, on a large scale, had been plotted in miniature and tried in dumb shew in Holland. It is in Holland and ultimately in America, that the Demon of Revolution has served his prenticeship.[69]

But that is an extreme viewpoint not shared by moderate conservatives. On the contrary, when a difference of opinion arose in the Batavian Republic and the vague complex of Patriotic thought led to party quarrels between conservatives and progressives, Federalists and Unitarians, the former appealed to the American example. Since its adoption, the 1787 Constitution had become quite acceptable to them. Ex-Patriots and Orangeists were one in their joint admiration for that document. The learned town clerk of the city of Deventer, Gerhard Dumbar, elucidated the U. S. Constitution in three volumes, and he gave in this work extensive extracts from *The Federalist*. The institutions of the French Revolution, he wrote, are beacons indicating rocks, but the Constitution of the United States has been "built on that real foundation on which the freedom, tranquility, prosperity and independence of a nation should and can be built." [70] Equally enthusiastic was the man who was one day to become the founder of the Kingdom of the Netherlands, Gijsbert Karel van Hogendorp. As a young man of 20 he went to America to study the birth of a nation, but he returned disillusioned: "In America itself I have learned to see America with other eyes. . . . The freedom of America has had a bad influence on ours. This is what I have learned and that is preferable to having seen a heaven on earth there." [71] Thus spoke the archrealist who became a leader of the counterrevolution of 1787, forgetting his earlier friendship with Thomas Jefferson. In 1793, however, the same Van Hogendorp, appalled by the terror of the French Revolution, began to write a number of essays on concepts such as freedom and equality, partly as a reaction to Pieter Paulus' book on that issue. In those essays America is crown witness against what he called false equality. There was a new Constitution there, which had put an end to revolutionary chaos and divided the government; and thus we return to the classic trias politica, "between the inhabitants in general, the well-to-do in particular, and the wisdom and virtue of a single person." [72]

The speech given by Johan Luzac, professor of Greek at Leiden University, when handing over the rectorship in 1795, breathes the same spirit. There spoke the old-fashioned Patriot, great propagandist of the American Revolution, editor of the *Gazette de Leyde*. Soon he was to be unseated by Batavian revolutionaries, including friends and even relatives, because he was considered too conservative. In his discourse, "Socrates Seen as a Citizen," he supported the balance in state government as was now being realized in America, "where the laws so beneficially tempering the State, safeguard the freedom of the people, simultaneously restraining it." [73] It was no accident that the discourse was dedicated to his old friend John Adams, who reacted gratefully. The third in this bond of friendship, the most ardent François Adrian van der Kemp, now emigrated to America, wrote in full agreement from his home, far away in Oldenbarneveld, N. Y., how much he admired Luzac's idea that a mixed form of government was always necessary for a powerful or rich nation.[74]

In the discussions held in the Batavian Republic, especially in the National Assembly, struggling so desperately and vainly to formulate a constitution, the same phenomenon was seen. The American example had not yet been forgotten. At the opening of the National Assembly a civil celebration was organized, with all kinds of allegorical manifestations, including three heralds holding the Batavian, French, and American flags joined by ribbons bearing the national colors.[75] But this example had been relegated to the background. When the committee of 21 presented its draft constitution, its chairman, the historian Simon Stijl, moved its adoption, even if opinions differed on certain minor points, "following the example of the great Franklin, who put his seal to the whole, although not everyone agreed on all details." [76] But in reality French examples and, more important still, French pressure were determining our governmental system. Moderates and Unitarians rejected a comparison with the American federation, so eagerly advocated by the Dutch Federalists, who really meant confederalism according to their own tradition rather than the unitarian federalism envisioned by the authors of the American Constitution. There was, the Unitarians and Moderates asserted, "a world of difference between the American system and the rightly abhorred Federalismus of the United Netherlands because there the regional government is purely domestic and can never fetter the decisions of the National Assembly." [77]

Only on minor details did the Federalists manage to suggest alternatives and to cite meaningful American examples. The Federalist Vitringa praised the system of impeachment in America,[78] and the man of the center Pieter Leonard van de Kasteele asked whether the principle of judicial review, adopted in America, should also be applied in our country.[79] The Frisian Federalist Meinardus Siderius warned against too strong an executive power to be elected by the people, for, after all, we had no Washington and what was possible in the wide open spaces was not possible here: "I do not think that the Americans will fail to have a capable man placed at the head of the executive branch." [80] Egbert Jan Greve, also from Friesland, saw in those same American wide open spaces the reason why people were less vulnerable over there and had more opportunity to make mistakes. (He had, however, only a vague notion of American polity, as is apparent from his remarks about the president of Congress.) [81]

The American example was of essential importance for the question of "the Separation of Powers," on which Burger de Rhoer presented a report in March 1797, warning against a dominating position of the legislative branch, and appealing to Jefferson's *Notes on the State of Virginia*. He further argued that, to use a modern expression, the so-called balance of power should follow not the conflict model but the harmony model, since "the idea of weights and counterweights" might easily lead to "struggles, clashes, opposition." For the heavier body would repel the lighter and thus "the entire Power of the State is overruled by the heavier body." The latest American constitutions were therefore more prudent and only wanted separation "inasmuch as a free commonwealth allows this, and insofar as such separation is compatible with the unity and the harmony, which should unite the entire Body of the Constitution." [82]

Another important discussion into which America was drawn was the issue of slavery. Bitter words were spoken about "the vile greed of some American cantons," but the sincere radical Pieter Vreede had the courage to recall the Dutch contribution to this disgrace: "If only our wretched African brothers deported by Batavian violence to America, doomed to eternal slavery, could find consolation in the compassion of your hearts." In his passionate discourse he appealed to Raynal: "whoever defends slavery, merits the philosopher's deep contempt and a stab by a Negro's dagger. . . . Even if America has betrayed its sworn principles . . . would that justify our being injust?" No, better to model ourselves on "the tranquil dwellings of the peace-loving Quakers in America. There you would have seen the fields of these humanitarian Friends, tilled by black hired hands whom they have granted their freedom and who since then work voluntarily for a wage." A sizable majority were not moved by such idyllic pictures but kept their feet firmly on the ground, believing the Negroes to be children and not yet ready for freedom, "because," as J. J. Rousseau says somewhere, "freedom is a heavy meal and requires a strong stomach." [83]

Thus, time and again, the American example was used for all kinds of issues. But, in general, it was the party of the conservative Federalists who clung to it and used it as a shield for their defense, whereas the radicals dismissed a constitution after the American pattern, as was apparent from their weekly *De Democraten*.[84] They swore by France. They believed as much in the antithesis between the American and the French revolutions as their conservative opponents. In the National Assembly the Rotterdam wine merchant J. H. Midderigh, a staunch Democrat, declared: "The one party is sincerely disposed to . . . make the people not seemingly but really free and happy; the other party wishes as much as possible to cling to the old values, swears only by Roman law, the Union of Utrecht, or moves heaven and earth to make the American Constitution more appetizing than the French one." [85] Actually there was not much choice, America was far away and France nearby, but the irony, or, if you wish, the tragedy, of history was that the Batavians, craving freedom, soon were compelled to follow the French models of Directoire and Consulat.

Protest against this growing French influence was vague and in vain. It easily clad itself, not surprisingly in a Calvinist country, in a religious garb. And here again, America could be of use. Against what was considered the atheism of the French Revolution, an appeal was made to a religious affinity with the Americans. With much pathos the Reverend IJsbrand van Hamelsveld, a respected member of the National Assembly, gave expression to his feelings: "Yes, Citizens, Representatives, I declare publicly that, with the Americans, I consider religion as one of the first rights and obligations of man and citizen." [86] Such proclamations were of little avail against a compelling reality, yet they gave expression to a feeling of a certain spiritual affinity. Not much more was left of American sympathies for the time being than this kind of vague sentiment. A friendship from afar was all that remained of a relationship whose beginnings were so promising, so enthusiastic. It would be a long time before Dutch people would again bless the ties that bound them to America and tune in to the voice of liberty coming from the west. I could point to the immigrants of the 1840's, seeking freedom in the wilderness of Michigan —"We have turned our eyes towards the United States." I could even mention—if you allow me a personal recollection—my own generation, listening in the darkness of war and occupation to the voice of Franklin D. Roosevelt. Such moments are rare in history, but, thank God, they do occur, even if they are seldom so emphatically expressed as they were two hundred years ago, by, for instance, the first chargé d'affairs of the United States in the Netherlands, a Dutchman of Swiss origin, Charles Willem Frederik Dumas. That is why his words, written in a letter to John Adams, have been chosen as a motto at the heading of this talk, with the warm response they received from Adams in several letters. Words in which, with a variation on a classical saying, America stands for all humanity. These words state: I am an American and I deem nothing American alien to me.

Notes

First of all I wish to express my gratitude to Dr. E. H. Kossmann of the University of Groningen, Drs. A. Lammers of the University of Leiden, and Dr. C. H. E. de Wit of Oirsbeek (L.), all of whom have read the manuscript of this paper in its Dutch or English version and through their invaluable comments have been of great help to me. Of course, all responsibility for opinions and errors is entirely my own.

[1] Pieter Geyl, *Geschiedenis van de Nederlandse Stam*, 6 vols. (Amsterdam and Antwerp: Wereldbibliotheek, 1961–62), 5:1205–6.

[2] François Marie Arouet de Voltaire, *Oeuvres,* 9 vols. (Amsterdam: Et. Ledet, 1738–56), 6:190; Honoré Gabriel Riquetti de Mirabeau, *Aux Bataves sur le Stathoudérat* (London, 1788), p. 3.

[3] Lyman H. Butterfield et al., eds., *Adams Family Correspondence,* 4 vols. (Cambridge: Harvard University Press, Belknap Press, 1965–73), 3:414.

[4] Drew Pearson, *Diaries, 1949–1959,* ed. Tyler Abell (London: Jonathan Cape, 1974), pp. 507–8.

[5] James Harris, *An Introduction to the History of the Dutch Republic for the last ten years, reckoning from the year 1777* (London: G. Kearsley, 1788), pp. 108–9; John Adams to the President of Congress, May 16, 1781, in John Adams, *The Works of John Adams . . . ,* ed. Charles Francis Adams, 10 vols. (Boston: Little, Brown and Co., 1850–56), 7:418–19.

[6] Pieter Paulus, *Verklaring der Unie van Utrecht,* 3 vols. (Utrecht: J. van Schoonhoven en Co., 1775–78), 1: Dedication; *Vaderlandsche Historie vervattende de Geschiedenissen der Vereenigde Nederlanden zints den aanvang der Noord-Americaansche Onlusten etc., ten vervolge van Wagenaars Vaderlandsche Historie,* 48 vols. (Amsterdam: Johannes Allart, 1788–1811), 1:62–63; Paulus, *Verklaring,* 3:240–54; cf. W. H. Riker, "Dutch and American Federalism," in *Journal of the History of Ideas* 18, no. 4 (October 1957): 495–521.

[7] Harris, *Introduction,* p. 122; John Adams to the President of Congress, March 19, 1781, in Adams, *Works,* 7:381.

[8] Franciscus Hemsterhuis, *Oeuvres Philosophiques de Francois Hemsterhuis,* ed. L. S. P. Meyboom, 3 vols. (Leeuwarden: W. Eekhoff, 1846–50), 3:100.

[9] John Adams to Secretary Livingston, February 19, 1782, in Adams, *Works,* 7:513.

[10] Thomas Jefferson to John Jay, August 6, 1787, in Thomas Jefferson, *The Papers of Thomas Jefferson,* ed. Julian P. Boyd et al. (Princeton: Princeton University Press, 1950–), 11:695–96. In note no. 7, annexed to this letter, the editor has wrongly corrected Jefferson, who wrote about "the states of [the province] Utrecht [meeting] at Amersfo[o]rt" (because the city of Utrecht was in the hands of the Democrats).

[11] Gerrit Paape, *De Onverbloemde Geschiedenis van het Bataafsche Patriottismus van deszelfs begin tot op den 12 Junij 1798 toe* (Delft: M. Roelofswaart, 1789), pp. 44–50; J. Luzac to J. Valckenaer, August 7, 1789, Arch. Collection Dumont-Pigalle, MMMM, Algemeen Rijksarchief, The Hague.

[12] John Adams to Secretary Livingston, February 19, 1782, in Adams, *Works,* 7:517.

[13] Pieter Jan van Winter, *Het Aandeel van den Amsterdamschen Handel aan den Opbouw van het Amerikaansche Gemeenebest,* 2 vols. (The Hague: M. Nijhoff, 1927–33), 1:1–2.

[14] Adriaan Kluit, *Iets over den laatsten Engelschen oorlog met de Republiek, . . .* (Amsterdam: Wouter Brave, 1794), pp. 145, 49–51; George W. Vreede, ed., *Mr. Laurens Pieter van de Spiegel en zijne Tijdgenooten (1737–1800),* 4 vols. (Middelburg: J. C. & W. Altorffer, 1874–77), 2:82; Harris, *Introduction,* p. 286.

[15] Joan Derk van der Capellen tot den Pol, *Brieven van en aan Joan Derck van der Capellen van de Poll,* ed. Willem Hendrik de Beaufort (Utrecht: Kemink & Zoon, 1879), pp. 114, 211, 249, 284, 342 (hereafter cited as Capellen, *Brieven*).

[16] Campegius Lambertus Vitringa, *Gedenkschrift . . . ,* 4 vols. (Arnhem: I.A. Nijhoff en Zoon, 1857–64), 1:100.

[17] Joseph Mandrillon, *Gedenkschriften betrekkelijk tot de Omwenteling in de Vereenigde Nederlanden in 1787* (Dunkirk: Van Schelle & Co., 1792), p. 96.

[18] Cornelis Henricus Eligius de Wit, *De Nederlandse Revolutie van de Achttiende Eeuw 1780–1787: oligarchie en proletariaat* (Oirsbeek, Drukkerij Lindelauf, 1974), pp. 27–28; W. F. Wertheim and A. H. Wertheim-Gijse Weenink, eds., *Joan Derk Baron van der Capellen tot den Pol, Aan het Volk van Nederland, het Democratisch Manifest, 1781* (Amsterdam: J. M. Meulenhoff, 1966), Introduction; Murk de Jong Hendrikszoon, *Joan Derk van der Capellen, Staatkundig Levensbeeld uit de Wordingstijd van de moderne Demokratie in Nederland* (Groningen-The Hague: J. B. Wolters, 1922), pp. 215–19.

[19] Caroline Robbins, *The Eighteenth Century Commonwealthman; Studies in the Transmission, Development, and Circumstance of English Liberal Thought From the Restoration of Charles II Until the War With the Thirteen Colonies* (Cambridge: Harvard University Press, 1959).

[20] Capellen to Benjamin Franklin, April 28, 1778, Capellen, *Brieven*, p. 64; de Jong, *Joan Derk van der Capellen*, p. 359; Van Winter, *Het Aandeel*, 1:35–36; Francis Adrian van der Kemp, *Francis Adrian van der Kemp, an Autobiography, Together With Extracts From His Correspondence*, ed. Helen L. Fairchild (New York: G. P. Putnam's Sons, 1903), pp. 67–70 and facsim. opp. p. 70; Capellen to Valk, April 23, 1782, Capellen, *Brieven*, pp. 287–88.

[21] Francis Adrian van der Kemp, *Elftal Kerkelijke Redevoeringen* (Leiden: L. Herdingh, 1782), pp. 239–40 (through a misprint there are two pages 239 and 240 in this book).

[22] Andrew Burnaby, *Beknopte en Zakelyke Beschryving der voornaamste Engelsche Volkplantingen in Noord-America* ... (Amsterdam: Petrus Conradi, 1776). Added to this translation are pamphlets by Josiah Tucker, Richard Price, and the Jewish merchant Isaak de Pinto, who was a paid British agent in Holland. The editor evidently tried to give the views of both sides in the conflict, but leaned heavily toward the English viewpoint.

[23] Lodewijk Theodorus Grave van Nassau la Leck, *Brieven over de Noord-Americaansche Onlusten* ... , 18 letters (Utrecht: G. T. van Paddenburg, 1777–79); Francis Adrian van der Kemp, *Verzameling van Stukken tot de Dertien Vereenigde Staeten van Noord-America betrekkelijk* (Leiden: L. Herdingh, 1781), pp. xvi–xvii.

[24] John Adams to Secretary Livingston, February 19, 1782, in Adams, *Works*, p. 516.

[25] John Adams, *Memorie aan Hunne Hoog-Mogenden, de Staaten-Generaal der Vereenigde Nederlanden* (Knuttel, catalog of pamphlets, no. 19507), *Twenty-Six Letters upon Interesting Subjects respecting the Revolution of America* ... (New York: John Fenno, 1789), *Geschiedenis van het Geschil tusschen Groot Brittannië en Amerika* ... (Amsterdam: W. Holtrop, 1782, Knuttel, no. 19958), and *Pensées sur la Révolution de l'Amérique Unie* (Amsterdam: Harreveld, etc., 1781).

[26] *Lierzang op de Verklaarde Onafhanglijkheid* (Knuttel no. 19771); *Eerkroon voor de Beschermers van Noord-Amerika* (Knuttel no. 19770); *Eerkroon op de Hoofden der Doorluchtige Staatsmannen*, 2 vols. (Dordrecht: A. Blussé & Zoon, 1782–83).

[27] Pauline Maier, *From Resistance to Revolution: Colonial Radicals and the Development of American Opposition to Britain, 1765–1776* (New York: Alfred A. Knopf, 1973), pp. 217, 263–64.

[28] Antoine Marie Cérisier, *Le Politique Hollandais* (Amsterdam: J. A. Crajenschot, 1781–82), pp. 118–41.

[29] Capellen to Gillon, October 16, 1780, Capellen, *Brieven*, pp. 190–91; J. Aleida Nijland,

Leven en Werken van Jacobus Bellamy, 2 vols. (Leiden: E. J. Brill, 1917), 1:285–86; H. A. Höweler, "Lucretia Wilhelmina van Merken en George Washington," *Tijdschrift voor Nederlandsche Taal—en Letterkunde* 52 (1933): pp. 70–77; G. K. van Hogendorp, *Brieven en Gedenkschriften van Gijsbert Karel van Hogendorp,* 7 vols. (The Hague: M. Nijhoff, 1866–1903), 1:350–51, 354–55.

[30] Letter of Gerard Vogels, December 13, 1783, Six-archief, Amsterdam; letters of P. A. Godin, in Rijksarchief Utrecht, Archief Slot Zuylen, no. 920.

[31] Capellen to Richard Price, July 1, 1779, Capellen, *Brieven,* p. 105.

[32] R. M. van Goens, *Brieven aan R. M. van Goens,* ed. Willem Hendrik de Beaufort, 3 vols. (The Hague: N. Nijhoff, 1884), 3:117.

[33] John Adams to Secretary Livingston, February 21, 1782, in Adams, *Works,* 7:521–30.

[34] John Adams to J. Luzac, September 15, 1780, in Adams, *Works,* 7:255; Cérisier, *Le Politique Hollandais,* pp. 171–72; *Memorie wegens het commercieële Belang deezer Republicq in het Sluiten van een Tractaat van Commercie met de Vereenigde Staaten van Noord-Amerika* (1781, Knuttel no. 19511).

[35] Gijsbert Jan van Hardenbroek, *Gedenkschriften van Gijsbert Jan van Hardenbroek,* ed. F. J. L. Krämer and A. J. van der Meulen, 4 vols. (Amsterdam: Joh. Müller, 1901–15), 3:268, cf. 2:145.

[36] Lyman H. Butterfield, ed. *John Adams and the Beginnings of Netherlands-American Friendship, 1780–1788* (Boston: G. K. Hall & Co., 1959), p. 43.

[37] Joachim Rendorp, *Memorien dienende tot Opheldering van het Gebeurde gedurende den laatsten Engelschen Oorlog,* 2 vols. (Amsterdam: Johannes Allart, 1792), 2:169.

[38] *Vaderlandsche Historie,* 14:29; cf. 13:33–35, 9:187–89.

[39] Kluit, *Iets,* p. 145.

[40] Cornelis Henricus Eligius de Wit, *De Strijd tussen Aristocratie en Democratie in Nederland, 1780–1848 . . .* (Heerlen: N. V. Uitgeverij Winants, 1965) p. 42.

[41] John Adams to Abigail Adams, March 14, 1788, quoted in Harry F. Jackson, *Scholar in the Wilderness, Francis Adrian van der Kemp* (Syracuse: Syracuse University Press, 1963), p. 56.

[42] Robert R. Palmer, *The Age of the Democratic Revolution: A Political History of Europe and America, 1760–1800,* 2 vols. (Princeton: Princeton University Press, 1959–64), 1:339, n22.

[43] Willem Hendrik de Beaufort, *Geschiedkundige Opstellen,* 2 vols. (Amsterdam: P. N. van Kampen & Zoon, 1893), 2:5.

[44] *Grondwettige Herstelling van Nederlands Staatswezen,* 2 vols. (Amsterdam: Johannes Allart, 1784–86).

[45] Vreede, *van de Spiegel,* 2:47; Pieter Geyl, *De Patriottenbeweging 1780–1787* (Amsterdam: P. N. van Kampen, 1947), p. 113; de Wit, *Nederlandse Revolutie,* pp. 61–62.

[46] *Grondwettige Herstelling,* 1:71.

[47] Verklaring van 79 leden der regering, August 8, 1786, Arch. Collection Dumont-Pigalle, GGGG, Algemeen Rijksarchief, The Hague.

[48] *Grondwettige Herstelling,* 1:159–67; cf. P. W. A. Immink, "Beschouwingen over de ontwikkeling van de begrippen volk en volksvertegenwoordiging," in *Publiekrechterlijke Opstellen*

aangeboden aan Prof. Mr. Dr. C. W. van der Pot (Zwolle: W. E. J. Tjeenk Willink, 1950), pp. 114–41.

[49] De Wit, *Nederlandse Revolutie*, pp. 41.

[50] Capellen to Valk, March 13, 1782, Capellen, *Brieven*, pp. 272–75; August 16, 1783; Arch. Collection Dumont-Pigalle, GGGG, Algemeen Rijksarchief, The Hague.

[51] *Zuid-Hollandsche Courant*, March 25, 1782, Arch. Collection Dumont-Pigalle, GGGG, Algemeen Rijksarchief, The Hague.

[52] J. Mandrillon, *Gedenkschriften*, p. 102.

[53] *Verzameling van de Constitutien der Vereenigde Onafhankelijke Staaten van Amerika* ... (Dordrecht: Fred. Wanner 1781–82).

[54] A. Kluit, *Iets*, p. 215.

[55] Capellen to Ruckenfelder, December 30, 1782, Capellen, *Brieven*, p. 464.

[56] J. Romein and A. Romein-Verschoor, *Erflaters van onze Beschaving*, 4 vols. (Amsterdam: Em. Querido, 1938–40) 3:165.

[57] Rutger Jan Schimmelpenninck, *Verhandeling over eene Wel-ingerichte Volksregeering* (Leiden: Frans de Does, 1785).

[58] De Wit, *Nederlandse Revolutie*, pp. 157–58.

[59] Arch. Collection Dumont-Pigalle, GGGG, Algemeen Rijksarchief, The Hague.

[60] Andrew Fletcher, *Staatkundige Verhandeling over de Noodzakelijkheid eener Welingerigte Burger-Land-Militie van den Heere Andrew Fletcher, Schildknaap*, trans. Joan Derk van der Capellen tot den Pol (Amsterdam: C. N. Guerin, 1774).

[61] Wertheim, and Wertheim-Gijse Weenink, *Capellen ... Aan het Volk van Nederland*, p. 64, cf. p. 131.

[62] *Post van den Neder-Rhijn* (Utrecht: Gisbert Timon van Paddenburg), no. 102, 1782, pp. 881–88.

[63] Ibid., no. 103, pp. 897–904.

[64] Paape, *De Onverbloemde Geschiedenis*, pp. 56–59.

[65] Herman Theodoor Colenbrander, *De Patriottentijd, Hoofdzakelijk naar Buitenlandsche Bescheiden*, 3 vols. (The Hague: M. Nijhoff, 1897–99), 1:279.

[66] Arch. Collection Dumont-Pigalle, QQQQ, Algemeen Rijksarchief, The Hague.

[67] Gordon S. Wood, *The Creation of the American Republic, 1776–1787* (Chapel Hill: Published for the Institute of Early American History and Culture at Williamsburg, Va., by the University of North Carolina Press, 1969), p. 119.

[68] Arch. Collection Dumont-Pigalle, GGGG, Algemeen Rijksarchief, The Hague.

[69] Van Goens, *Brieven*, 1:91.

[70] Gerhard Dumbar, *De oude en nieuwe Constitutie der Vereenigde Staten van Amerika, uit de beste Schriften in haare Gronden ontvouwd*, 3 vols. (Amsterdam: J. A. Crajenschot, 1793–96), 3:iv–v.

[71] Van Hogendorp, *Brieven*, June 22, 1786, 1:418–20.

[72] Arch. Collection G. K. van Hogendorp 71: "Gelijkheid der Menschen (door Pieter Paulus) weerlegd," and "Omwendingen," Algemeen Rijksarchief, The Hague.

[73] Johan Luzac, *Socrates als Burger Beschouwd*, door Mr. Johan Luzac, in eene plechtige redevoering, uitgesproken op den 21 February 1795, bij het nederleggen van 't Rectoraat der Hollandsche Universiteit. Door denzelven uit het Latijn vertaald . . . (Leiden: A. en J. Honkoop, 1796).

[74] Arch. J. Luzac, June 1, 1800, Westerse Handschriften, Bibliotheek der Rijksuniversiteit, Leiden. Univ.

[75] Corn. Rogge, *Geschiedenis der Staatsregeling voor het Bataafsche Volk* (Amsterdam: Johannes Allart, 1799), p. 29.

[76] *Vaderlandsche Historie* 37:103.

[77] *Dagverhaal der Handelingen van de Nationale Vergadering*, January 18, 1797, 9 vols. (The Hague: Swart & Co., 1796–98), 4:544.

[78] Ibid., February 8, 1797, 4:834.

[79] Ibid., February 3, 1797, 4:835.

[80] Ibid., February 14, 1797, 4:936, 941–42.

[81] Ibid., February 21, 1797, 4:1023.

[82] Ibid., March 6, 1797, 5:59–64.

[83] Ibid., April 22, 1797, 5:727–33; May 12, 1797, 6:10–14.

[84] De Wit, *Strijd*, p. 141.

[85] *Dagverhaal*, June 2, 1796, 2:43.

[86] Ibid., January 27, 1797, 4:611–62.

Jan Willem Schulte Nordholt has been professor of American history at the University of Leiden since 1966. He has also taught at Brooklyn College and, under a grant from the American Council of Learned Societies, lectured at various universities in Japan, Australia, New Zealand, and the United States in 1972. He holds a Ph.D. degree from the University of Amsterdam.

Several of Professor Schulte Nordholt's many publications have been translated into English. These include The People That Walk in Darkness; a History of the Negro in America *(1960), and "The Civil War Letters of the Dutch Ambassador" (Journal of the Illinois State Historical Society, vol. 54, no. 4, 1961). He is currently completing a study of the image and influence of America in the Netherlands in the 18th century.*

The scholar who will treat a subject which, understandably, is still not popular in his own country—the impact of the American Revolution on Great Britain as a world power—comes to us with superlative qualifications. Just as Robert Palmer has a monopoly on world revolutions, so the first speaker this morning has a stranglehold on England in the 18th century, and on much more than that. A distinguished editor and interpreter of modern civilization, which he has made comprehensible to a wide nonacademic readership, he has by the wit and literary grace which stamp his writings demonstrated convincingly that history is a branch of belles lettres, cliometricians notwithstanding. It is a pleasure to introduce Professor J. H. Plumb of Christ's College, Cambridge.

The Impact
of the American Revolution
on Great Britain

J. H. PLUMB

IN AUGUST 1775 a great coach lumbered into the courtyard of the military governor of Metz, the comte de Broglie, who was waiting to receive an unlikely yet extremely distinguished guest—H. R. H. the Duke of Gloucester, and younger brother of George III, who was traveling with his wife to winter in Rome. Gloucester was, as royal brothers often were in 18th-century England, something of a problem. He had imprudently married the illegitimate daughter of Sir Edward Walpole, the son of the former Prime Minister, an action which, naturally enough, had shocked the aristocratic world and outraged his brother. As young princes were wont to do, he had contracted huge debts, living extravagantly beyond his means. Black marks enough, but there was worse. He had become a supporter, first, of the radical John Wilkes, whose slogan "Wilkes and Liberty" had goaded George III and his ministers for years. Indeed, the king had taken a fierce personal dislike to Wilkes. Subsequently Gloucester had developed an ardent sympathy for the cause of America, which naturally infuriated the king even more. Although ostensibly Gloucester had left England because of his debts and his marriage, the king and his ministers were relieved to be rid of a liberal-minded prince. It was his opinions, particularly his antipathy to his brother's American policy, which interested de Broglie. And so it was in Metz that one of the most remarkable dinner parties of the 18th century took place. Remarkable not only for the prince's presence or de Broglie's, or even that of de Kalb, a professional soldier who had already reconnoitered the situation in the American colonies for the French, but because of the presence of a young captain—Lafayette.[1]

Decades later Lafayette recalled that dinner party, for it fired his imagination about those Americans struggling for their freedom, and he mentioned how persistently he cross-examined Gloucester on the state of England. Nothing is more unlikely. Lafayette was, in 1775, only 18 years old and very immature-looking for his age—a junior officer, at the dinner party solely because of his family relationship with de Broglie.[2]

Yet even if Lafayette did not cross-examine Gloucester, de Broglie most certainly did. He passionately wanted to know the strength of the opposition toward George III's American policy; how deeply it was dividing British society and what chance there might be of the opposition leading either to the downfall of Lord North's government or to the outbreak of civil riots and commotion. Gloucester, little different from most men of affairs, is likely to have interpreted the situation generously in favor of his own opinions. The opposition, he most probably said, was powerful, the public enraged, North's position precarious, and civil tumult likely. Sweet words for de Broglie, inspirational to Lafayette, and significant to the historian of the impact of the Revolution on Britain.

The American problem was beginning to affect most acutely British power relationships in Europe and the wider world. No longer could the conflict be contained between the British government and its insubordinate subjects in America. De Broglie was not alone in seeing the potentiality in the situation that might be exploited in favor of France and so reduce the overwhelming power of Britain, not only in the West but also in the East. Neither was Lafayette the first to be carried away by the idealistic slogans of the Americans, or to consider them as the defenders not only of their own rights but also of the fundamental rights of mankind.[3]

Since the early days of the American dispute the French government had been fascinated by the prospects of George III's difficulties, for they felt bitterly the defeat of the Seven Years War and the humiliations of the Treaty of Paris in 1763. As well as relying on their ambassadors, they had also supported two agents worthy of the imagination of Howard Hunt—the Chevalier d'Eon, who dressed and lived with such success as a woman that his sex remained a matter of speculation until the autopsy which followed his death, and Beaumarchais, the creator of *Figaro*, a man whose capacity for imaginative fantasy was as great in politics as it was in literature. Nevertheless, Beaumarchais' English contacts were complex and far ranging and, quite obviously, d'Eon was both cunning and astute.[4] But as agents will, they exaggerated the evidence which seemed to support the policy which they felt their masters wished to pursue. Even though they failed to convince Louis XV, who in any case was becoming less and less effective and more and more besotted with his adolescent seraglio at the Parc aux Cerfs, or, indeed, Louis' more cautious ministers, they were heady wine for men of the stamp of de Broglie who longed to take their revenge on the British. After all, de Broglie had drawn up a detailed plan for the invasion of England; a plan whose secrets were known only to d'Eon.

Nevertheless, it required the optimism of an agent or the strong antipathy of a sibling to discover grave fissures in the fabric of British political society in 1774, or even the early months of 1775. Indeed, the friends of the American cause seemed in disarray and without strong popular support. The sympathy so especially powerful at the time of the Stamp Act appeared to be evaporating fast. Important voices, it is true, still spoke vociferously for America. After all, some of the most popular pamphlets read by Americans between 1773 and 1775 were by distinguished Englishmen writing for their own countrymen. And Horace Walpole was railing as hard as ever against North in his letters to Horace Mann.[5] Alderman Frederick Bull, whose political base was the strong dissenting party in the City of London, continued to denounce British soldiers in Boston, referring to them as "brutes that have too long been suffered to live there."[6] Indeed, the City was still powerfully radical even though torn by squabbles over the irrepressible Wilkes, but the strong alliance with the opposition in Parliament which had been such a marked feature of the agitation against the Stamp Act had broken down. As Edmund Burke wrote to the General Assembly of New York on April 6, 1774:

The popular current, both within doors and without, at present sets strongly against America. There were not, indeed, wanting some few persons in the House of Commons, who disapproved of the Bill, and who expressed their disapprobation in the strongest and most explicit Terms. But their Arguments upon this point made so little impression that it was not thought advisable to divide the House.

Indeed, Burke said that they spoke to discharge their own consciences and did not hope either to gain support or even keep that of "those who had formerly concurred in the same general Line of Policy with regard to the Colonies."[7] Part of the trouble lay in the absence of a coherent policy; some followers of both Rockingham and Chatham approved measures against Boston and voted for the government. Indeed, the highest vote that the opposition could muster was 64 against the Massachusetts Bay Regulating Act on May 2, 1774, but by May 6 only 24 went into the lobby against the government. The position in the House of Lords was worse. On May 18, for example, Rockingham could only secure eight signatures to the Protest which he entered into the House of Lords Journals.[8] Only one bishop, Jonathan Shipley, bishop of St.

Asaph, gave Rockingham consistent support. He had been radicalized by the British policy on taxation not in the American colonies but in Bengal. Nevertheless, his pamphlets in support of the American colonists enjoyed great success in America as well as in England.[9]

The decay of support for the American cause in the middle seventies has been attributed to the changed attitude of the commercial classes. The years which immediately followed the Stamp Act witnessed the flowering of a powerful radical movement not only in the City of London but also in the major trading towns and seaports of Britain, ardent support for John Wilkes, and a demand for parliamentary reform under the slogan "Annual Parliaments, Equal Representation, Place and Pension Bill." A sense that liberty was in danger in Britain as well as in America pervaded the commercial classes and the principles of government were debated in newly formed clubs in London and the provinces.[10] But the ardor seemed to fade, the close relationship between the Rockingham Whigs and the City of London broke down, and it required great efforts on Burke's part to secure a reference to American affairs in the City of London's petition in 1774.[11] The cause commonly given for this decline of support for America is the change which came over British trading relations in the early 1770's. Indeed, this aspect was strongly stressed by Richard Champion, Burke's merchant friend at Bristol. He maintained that the opposition to the Stamp Act had arisen because of the deleterious repercussions it was expected to have on British commerce, whereas the events of 1774–75 had very little effect on British trade. As Champion wrote in March 1775, "The trade of Yorkshire, Manchester, Norwich and the clothing countries near this Town [i.e., Bristol] continues very brisk, even Birmingham is not greatly affected." [12] And Champion's views have been vindicated by modern statistical research. Although exports to the American mainland fell by 25 percent between 1771 and 1775, they rose spectacularly to most European countries, as well as to Africa and Canada.[13]

With Chatham and Rockingham divided about policy, the radicals at loggerheads, and popular support languishing, there could be no strong opposition to the coercive policy of North that was to lead inexorably to Lexington and Concord. Furthermore, once the guns barked, the shadow of France lengthened and darkened over England, a factor of which a friend of America as ardent as Josiah Wedgwood was fully aware. No man had been a stronger supporter of the colonists' claims. He was fully conscious of what he felt to be the justice of their cause and of the failures of British policy. He remained absolutely steadfast to his beliefs, giving full support to the Americans whom he refused to call rebels, right up to 1778, but America's alliance with France chilled even his ardor and created a sense of doubt about the wisdom of his continuing support. True, he survived these doubts, but then Wedgwood was a man of rugged principle and obstinate temperament.[14] Many others fell by the wayside, putting patriotism above political principle. After 1776, in spite of the revival of opposition in the City of London, and the gradual strengthening of the Rockingham party, the support for America was never widespread in the English political establishment, and opposition to the war after 1780 certainly did not imply conversion to the principles of the Declaration of Independence. In consequence many historians, both American and English, have belittled the impact which the Revolution had on British politics and underestimated the sympathy which was felt in England for the plight of the American colonies even though that sympathy was somewhat inhibited by the course of war between 1776 and 1782.[15]

Once the dispute became a general global war, as it did in 1778, and so brought about a revival of that conflict in which France and England had been locked for the best part of a hundred years, patriotism overrode radical sympathy. As I have pointed out elsewhere, in America patriotism strengthened radical sympathies; in England the reverse process took place.[16] Indeed, the war changed the nature of the impact of the American Revolution upon Britain. Up to that point, the conflict had stimulated radical causes in a most fundamental way. And that stimulus was not stifled by the war, only partially submerged. Once the war was over, or rather lost, that new radicalism gained even greater public support for issues that were essentially those raised by the revolt of the American colonies.

Yet vital though these effects were, the war itself had a far profounder impact on Britain's destiny, for not only did it change power relationships with the rest of the world, but it also altered the very nature of the British Empire. The impact, therefore, was both internal and external. Firstly, the former.

From the 1730's, England had developed a political nation, alive to issues of every kind: the Jewish Naturalisation Bill, the hire of Hessian troops, the cider tax, even the question of the National Debt. This political nation, however, was not commensurate with the electorate, with those who might from time to time take conventional political action by voting. It was largely serviced by a relatively free press of pamphlets, newspapers, broadsheets, and political prints. Although the political nation was most clearly to be perceived in London, both the old trading cities, such as Bristol and Norwich, and the new, such as Birmingham, Manchester, Leeds, and Sheffield, possessed many politically minded inhabitants who, excluded from formal politics, organized themselves in clubs and debating societies and provided a responsive audience to every kind of political propaganda.[17] This was the market which

Wilkes and his supporters exploited so skillfully, not only with pamphlets, letters, addresses, and petitions but with Wilkes badges, buttons, pins, mugs, and statuettes. Indeed, politics had become commercialized. There was now profit in radical propaganda. It was in this political nation, so much of it excluded from formal politics, that the clarion call of 'Wilkes and Liberty' resonated most deeply. But it was also the audience which Otis, Lee, and others were eager to address in their pamphlets, because they knew that many of the frustrations felt by the colonists struck a responsive chord in this political nation. Or if they did not, their publishers certainly did.

One of the arguments constantly employed by ministerial apologists was that of virtual representation, that is, that although the inhabitants of Birmingham were not directly represented in the House of Commons they were virtually through the representatives for the county of Warwickshire. But the double-edged nature of this argument was quickly stressed by James Otis, who wrote in *Considerations on Behalf of the Colonists* in 1765: "To what purpose is it to ring everlasting changes to the colonists in the cases of Manchester, Birmingham, and Sheffield, who return no Members? If these now so considerable places are not represented, they ought to be." [18] Nearly a decade later, John Cartwright was making the same point with equal vigor in his *American Independence, the Interest and Glory of Great Britain*, which was widely read in both America and Britain.[19] In 1766 Wilkes himself had attempted to introduce a bill for a comprehensive reform of Parliament, and the years between 1765 and 1780 witnessed an ever more vociferous debate on both the principles of representation and the corrupt nature of the House of Commons, a debate which derived a great deal of strength from the issues raised by Americans.[20] Indeed, it is no exaggeration to say that the first strong movement for parliamentary reform was sired by the American Revolution. Before the 1770's and 1780's, the discussion of Parliament had centered on the position of placemen and pensioners or on the duration of Parliaments, not the reform of the representative system as a whole. But during those decades the question of franchise and of the redistribution of representation came to the fore. This reform movement also gained from America's success, which strengthened the argument that the British Parliament was not responsive to the nation's will or even competent to carry out a policy, no matter how wrongheaded. Parliament, it was argued, was not only corrupt and unrepresentative but, perhaps worse, a failure. Although badly battered by the French Revolution and the Napoleonic wars, the movement for parliamentary reform was never crushed, nor did the debate on representation stop. And if the old system was slow to crumble, in the end it did. By then the origins of the reform movement were long forgotten, but to us they are clear enough.

The unrepresentative nature of the House of Commons was scarcely questioned in the 18th century until the issue was raised in the 1760's by Wilkes and by Americans.

Important though the American Revolution was for the growth of radicalism and parliamentary reform, its influence was far greater in the world of power. England's most important colony was not in America, nor in the West Indies, nor in the East; it was in the British Isles, namely Ireland, and the repercussions on the Irish question of the American Revolution were profound. Up to the 1770's, apart from the fracas caused by the *Drapier Letters*, Ireland had known a longer period of peace in relation to England than ever before in its history. Prosperity had increased. Some Anglo-Irish, later known as the Patriots, had acquired a keen sense of identity with Ireland. The tensions vis à vis the Catholics had somewhat eased. The American Revolution came at a curiously critical period of Ireland's development. The Anglo-Irish Protestant leadership, resentful of the amount of patronage and power dispensed by Whitehall, was poised to do battle for reform. In consequence, the majority of them took up the American cause. As Franklin wrote in 1771, after a visit to Dublin, "I found them disposed to be friends of America, in which I endeavoured to confirm them, with the expectation that our growing weight might, in time, be thrown into their scale, and by joining our interests with others, a more equitable treatment from this nation [i.e., the English] might be obtained for them as well as us." [21]

Ironically, the major support for British policy in America came from the Catholics. Dire poverty made mercenary service attractive to both the landlord, who got rid of paupers, and the peasants, who escaped destitution. Catholic regiments were dispatched to America, much to the bitter fury of the Protestants, who howled in the press that "Irish Papists were being permitted to murder American Protestants." [22] Later the Quebec Act and the Irish Catholic Relief Act of 1778 further strengthened this seemingly unholy alliance between Westminster and the Irish Catholics. But war quickly put the British government at a disadvantage and strengthened the Protestant leadership, which was able to use the threat of French invasion to mobilize its own forces in the Volunteer movement. North's government was horrified by the hotheaded talk about separation from Britain, although no serious Irish politician even entertained the idea. Nevertheless, the threat was potent enough for the Patriots to secure a rapid series of reforms that began to change the relationship between Ireland and Britain. At the same time, the Catholics secured greater relief, this time through the exertions of the Patriots, who wished to create an Irish nation and realized that they could not do so as long as the gulf between the two societies, Protestant and Catholic, was not bridged.

In the end they did, but only to lose their own power and see the political leadership of Ireland become increasingly Catholic and increasingly bent on independence. Furthermore, although some Catholics might volunteer for service in the British army in America, more emigrated; indeed the stream of Irish emigration grew into a river after 1782. As the *Dublin Evening Post* wrote in August 1783, "America stands with outstretched arms ready to receive the injured and oppressed sons of Liberty." [23] And the long-term effects of the American Revolution on Ireland were to prove as grievous for England as the short-term were beneficial to Ireland. The events of 1778–82 were but the first stage in a long struggle—Anglo-Irish relations never again recovered the stability which they had enjoyed between 1700 and 1775. As we know, English policy toward Ireland was always too little and too late. Throughout the 19th century the most bitter, violent, and desperate elements of Irish politics could always look across the Atlantic for help in money or in arms, or in both. A situation, alas, that still continues. Perhaps the last two centuries of strife in Ireland were inevitable. Maybe so, but certainly the American Revolution helped to precipitate that terrible conflict.

The gains made by the Patriots were due not to the farsighted benevolence of Lord North and his ministers but to the strategic dangers implicit in the Irish conflict. Any turbulence in Ireland could only be to the advantage of France, and in 1778 France, not the American colonies, was Britain's chief enemy. By 1780 the war had become global, stretching from southern India to Gibraltar to the Caribbean and involving, in addition to the French, Spaniards and, finally, the Dutch. For most of the war the luck ran France's way. Armaments and an army were shipped across the Atlantic without undue hindrance, the Franco-Spanish fleet under de Grasse dominated the Caribbean, and Suffren inflicted grievous losses on the British in India. And there was the miracle of Yorktown: two French fleets three thousand miles apart made a rendezvous with a Franco-American army within a narrow margin of time, almost inconceivable in a world of sailing ships and marching armies. But after Yorktown France's luck ran out. An attack on Jamaica was crushingly defeated by Rodney at the Battle of the Saints, and Britain's naval dominance in the Western Atlantic was thereby restored. Gibraltar withstood its siege and a desperate situation for Britain in Southern India was saved by the signing of the Preliminaries of Peace.[24]

Without the American Revolution, there would have been no such war. Without French aid, the American Revolution might not have succeeded. True, as an aide-de-camp of Rochambeau said, "America was unconquerable," [25] that is, by British troops and their mercenaries, no matter how decisive any individual battle might have been. But Britain was fighting not to establish a military hegemony in the American colonies but to reestablish in power those loyal and neutral Americans whose numbers have usually been underestimated. But the American Revolution succeeded, and in so doing it changed the nature of the British Empire and the context of its rivalry with France.

America and the Atlantic shores, and to a lesser extent the Mediterranean, had been for over a century the battleground of Europe. France in possession of Canada had always posed a threat of a Mississippian empire linked with Spain in the Gulf of Mexico. No matter how improbable that may seem 200 years later, it was a fundamental factor in Anglo-French rivalry. So was the Caribbean and the trade with Spanish America; so, too, was the West African coast, and its endless supplies of slaves upon which Britain's sugar islands, above all Jamaica, depended. The retention of Canada by Britain, combined with the independence of America, which could only mean that the West would be hers, and the reassertion of British power in the West Indies, ended the French threat in America for ever. It did not, however, end Anglo-French imperial rivalry. What had formerly been a subsidiary battleground—India and the Indian Ocean—became the major one, a development which also increased the strategic role of the Mediterranean. Long before the Suez Canal was cut, the Mediterranean route to the East was, as Napoleon realized, of vital consequence to the British in India.

Before 1784 Britain's involvement in India was partly influenced by commercial rivalry with France in southern India, where the Mogul power was very weak. The rivalry had led to a large increase in both European and native troops under the command of the British East India Company. Although the troops were not successful in throwing the French out of India, they succeeded all too well in wringing political and trading concessions from native rulers or, as at Plassey, inflicting upon the rulers defeats so decisive that their power collapsed. By 1784, certainly, Britain was politically as well as commercially involved in India and, although officially Britain was still concerned to trade rather than rule, the two had become inseparable, particularly in Bengal. Already Englishmen were taking over sugar, indigo, and jute plantations and making a considerable profit.[26] New and vast sources of commercial profit, based on a growing imperialism, had been tapped in the 1760's and 1770's. India would have become far more important to Britain whether the American Revolution had taken place or not, but the loss of America and the resultant ending of the Anglo-French rivalry in the Atlantic certainly helped to make India the fulcrum of empire, with consequences that were immense.

As David Brion Davis has demonstrated, the growing exploitation of Bengal

sugar weakened the economic base of the British West Indian planters at a
time when the strategic importance of the Caribbean for Britain declined.
As a result, the slave trade, and indeed slavery itself, diminished rapidly in
importance in the eyes of British politicians. Although some voices had been
raised against slavery in the 1760's, the great surge in antislavery activity
came in the 1780's [27] with the British West Indian islands becoming strategi-
cally and economically of less and less importance; in consequence, the opposition to the anti-slavery movement weakened too. Also, when Britain outlawed
the slave trade, there was great military and naval advantage in her policing
the coasts of Africa, particularly the East Coast with its routes to Europe.[28]
Indeed, the success of the antislavery movement in Britain only makes sense
in the immediate context of the American Revolution and the larger context
of Britain's new focus of empire.

The loss of America affected the growth of the British Empire in other
ways—particularly the settlement of Australia, a necessary dumping ground
for convicts now that America was free and Georgia unavailable. And the
possession of Australia naturally raised the strategic importance of the Malacca
Straits, leading to the foundation of Singapore. Nor could the French in New
Zealand be tolerated. Perhaps at this point the impact of the American Revolution may seem tenuous, but though the consequences may appear remote
they stem from the collapse of the first British Empire, which was Atlantically
based, to the second, whose center was undeniably India. And that change of
focus developed from the loss of the American colonies, although not directly
or simply. The involvement in India was acquiring its own momentum before
the American Revolution, but that involvement was bound to intensify once
America was lost. And the consequences for British society, let alone British
Imperialism, were profound. Increasingly Britain had to find rulers rather than
traders. To govern millions of people with complex and sophisticated cultures
required a ruling class educated, in a totally different way, to the needs of a
growing industrialized society. The educational system of the English upper
classes changed dramatically—the public school (i.e., private boarding school),
with its emphasis on the classics and muscular Christianity and its rejection
of science and technology, became all-pervasive. Proconsuls, not engineers,
were needed. By 1840 England was losing her leadership of the Industrial
Revolution. The acquisition of India and the loss of America both helped to
strengthen the class system in Britain; the former made status more numinous,
the latter made middle-class radicalism unpatriotic.

However, it would be wrong to think of the impact of the American Revolution purely in terms of imperial strategy or of its inhibiting effects on the
growth on the one hand of industrial society and on the other of middle class

radicalism. Although Lord Carmarthen or the duke of Dorset might regard the fledgling American republic with ill-disguised contempt, smile at the weakness of Congress,[29] and see little future for America, for many Englishmen, Irishmen, and Scots the image of America was refulgent—America for them was still the home of liberty, equality, and economic opportunity. As William Turner of Wakefield wrote to his son in the 1780's,

Through the folly and wickedness of the present, you of the rising generation have indeed a dark prospect before you. . . . Your best way will be to gather as fast as you can a good stock of the arts and sciences of this country; and if you find the might of despotism and wretchedness overwhelm this hemisphere, follow the course of the sun to that country where freedom has already fixed her standard and is creating her throne; where the sciences and arts, wealth and power will soon gather around her; assist and strengthen her empire there.[30]

The Carmarthens and the Dorsets were proved wrong by time, the unknown William Turner right. What the English aristocracy could not believe was that America had engendered social hope to the needy craftsman as well as the poor peasant. In the 1790's William Pitt's government was already attempting to curb the flow of skilled workers to America.[31] As von Bülow wrote from Philadelphia in 1791, "Robust farmers and sturdy mechanics find a very easy market." Indeed, it required personal incompetance of a high order for a skilled immigrant to fail. But the greatest appeal was to the poor and to the dispossessed. Each year that the republic strengthened, social hope gleamed more strongly in Europe. The gradual opening up of the huge resources of continental America provoked a migration of ordinary men and women of an extent unprecedented in human history. The intensity of social hope generated by the new America can be judged by the appalling conditions which immigrants were prepared to tolerate for generation after generation. The conditions were the worst in ships sailing from England and Ireland: one in six passengers died, those that survived were usually riddled with sickness. In the 1850's, one in five immigrant passengers arrived from London with cholera.[32] Conditions in the 1790's were no better, possibly worse. That men and women and children should endure such horrors might be used to underline the squalor and wretchedness of their lives in the British Isles. That is true. And often they exchanged one hopeless scene for another. Yet it is also true from the letters we have—some from very humble immigrants who could scarcely write, let alone spell—that America was to these people more than a refuge. Austerity, hard work, near poverty might be their lot, but these could be endured because there was hope. And it should be stressed that tens upon tens of thousands found a better life, free from the petty tyrannies, free from the arrogance of landlords and masters that so often was the experience of those left

behind. For a generation of scholars highly conscious that the United States, ●
since its inception, has sanctioned deprivation and tolerated destitution, that
for generations it deprived a fifth of its people of the common necessities of
social life, let alone political freedom, it is hard to grasp that for the Irish,
the Scots, and hundreds of thousands of Englishmen in the 19th century it
was the land that William Turner described to his son—a land of liberty and
opportunity. That liberty and that opportunity were not created by the
American Revolution, but only a very blinkered historian could deny that
they were strengthened by it.

The impact of the American Revolution on Britain, which at first sight
seemed to many English politicians of little or no concern, proved to be one
of the great turning points in its history. It helped very greatly to consolidate
a new focus of empire, and an empire that was markedly different from that
which had gone before. It helped to change England's relations with Ireland.
Few would deny that while inspiring some radical or at least some liberal
causes such as the abolition of the slave trade and the reform of parliament,
it did far more to strengthen the conservative forces in Britain—its hierarchical
aristocratic structure.

On the other hand, the expansionist forces released by the Revolution
worked, surprisingly, for the benefit of Britain. The growth of the American
economy made for the vastly increased profit of Britain and enabled her to
sustain a long and expensive war against France and Napoleon. At the same
time the expansionist drives of American society, so much more vigorous
after 1789, demanded labor, skilled and unskilled, and so produced both a
refuge and hope for the laboring classes of Great Britain, its peasantry and its
workers. Indeed, there is no aspect of English life after 1782—imperial,
political, economic or social—upon which the impact of the American Revolution is not writ large.

Notes

[1] Henri Doniol, *Histoire de la Participation de la France à l'Etablissement des Etats-Unis
d'Amérique*, 5 vols. (Paris: Imprimerie Nationale, 1886–92), 1:98, 642–43.

[2] Louis Gottschalk, *Lafayette Comes to America* (Chicago: University of Chicago Press,
1935), pp. 49–51. Gottschalk writes "Lafayette said nothing but was greatly affected" (ibid.,
p. 50). The origin of the story that Lafayette cross-examined Gloucester derives from Lafayette
himself, not in his memoirs but in a conversation with Jared Sparks in 1828, when the latter
was working on his *Life of George Washington*. According to Lafayette, Gloucester had received dispatches relative to American affairs and made them the topic of conversation at

dinner. This is most improbable: Gloucester would not have been the recipient of any official dispatches. Also Lafayette wrongly dates the dinner, placing it in 1776, whereas Gloucester visited France in July and August 1775. See Doniol, *Histoire de la Participation de la France*, 1:642–43. Also George Washington, *The Writings of George Washington*, ed. Jared Sparks, 12 vols. (Boston: F. Andrews, 1838–39), 10:445.

[3] Vergennes, for example, was well aware of the opportunities the situation was creating for France. See also J. H. Plumb, "British Attitudes to the American Revolution," in *In the Light of History* (London: Allen Lane, 1972), pp. 70–87.

[4] For Chevalier d'Eon, see Edna Nixon, *Royal Spy: The Strange Case of the Chevalier d'Eon* ... (New York: Reynal, 1965); also Frédéric Gaillardet, *The Memoirs of the Chevalier d'Eon*, trans. Antonia White, with an introduction by Robert Baldick (London: Corgi, 1972). For Beaumarchais, see René Pomeau, *Beaumarchais, l'Homme et l'Oeuvre* (Paris, 1956).

[5] Horace Walpole, *Horace Walpole's Correspondence*, ed. Wilmarth S. Lewis, vol. 24 (New Haven and London: Yale University Press, 1967), p. 124.

[6] Charles R. Ritcheson, *British Politics and the American Revolution* (Norman: University of Oklahoma Press, 1954), p. 157. For Bull's dissenting support, see Edmund Burke, *The Correspondence of Edmund Burke, July 1768-June 1774*, ed. Lucy S. Sutherland, vol. 2 (Cambridge: Cambridge University Press, 1960), p. 492.

[7] Ibid., p. 528.

[8] Bernard Donoughue, *British Politics and the American Revolution: The Path to War, 1773–75* (London: Macmillan, 1964), pp. 135–45.

[9] For Jonathan Shipley, see *Dictionary of National Biograrhy*. Also Paul Smith, comp., *English Defenders of American Freedoms, 1774–1778* (Washington: Library of Congress, 1972), pp. 9–13, 31–32 for Shipley's concern for Bengal.

[10] Plumb, *In the Light of History*, pp. 78–85.

[11] Donoughue, *British Politics*, pp. 154–55.

[12] George H. Guttridge, ed., "The American Correspondence of a Bristol Merchant, 1766–1776: Letters of Richard Champion," *University of California Publications in History* 22, no. 1 (Berkeley, 1934): 51.

[13] Elizabeth B. Schumpeter, *English Overseas Trade Statistics, 1697–1808* (Oxford: Clarendon Press, 1960), pp. 16–17.

[14] Plumb, *In the Light of History*, pp. 81–83.

[15] See John C. Miller, *Origins of the American Revolution* (Boston: Little, Brown, 1943), p. 145; Eric Robson, *The American Revolution in its Political and Military Aspects, 1763–1783* (London: Batchworth Press, 1955), pp. 36, 80.

[16] Plumb, *In the Light of History*, pp. 85–87.

[17] J. H. Plumb, "Political Man," in *Man Versus Society in Eighteenth Century Britain*, ed. James L. Clifford (London: Cambridge University Press, 1968), pp. 10–14.

[18] Charles F. Mullett, ed., "Some Political Writings of James Otis," *University of Missouri Studies* 4, no. 3 (Columbia, 1929): 110.

[19] John Cartwright, "American Independence, the Interest and Glory of Great Britain," in Smith, *English Defenders*, p. 166.

[20] For the reform movement, see George S. Veitch, *The Genesis of Parliamentary Reform* (London: Constable & Co., 1913); Eugene C. Black, *The Association: British Extra-Parliamentary Political Organization, 1769–93* (Cambridge: Harvard University Press, 1963).

[21] Maurice R. O'Connell, *Irish Politics and Social Conflict in the Age of the American Revolution* (Philadelphia: University of Pennsylvania Press, 1965), pp. 25–26.

[22] Ibid., p. 35.

[23] Ibid., p. 30. The majority of Irish emigrants to America before 1775 were Protestant and came from Ulster. Emigration during the peak years—the early 1770's—was caused by the decline of the linen trade and rack-renting. See R. J. Dickson, *Ulster Emigration to Colonial America, 1718–1775* (London: Routledge & Kegan Paul, 1966), pp. 60–81. The bulk of Catholic emigration came after the Revolution.

[24] Piers Mackesy, *The War for America 1775–1783* (Cambridge: Harvard University Press, 1964), pp. 458, 482–84, 494–500.

[25] Ibid., p. 510.

[26] P. J. Marshall, "British Expansion in India in the Eighteenth Century," *History* 60 (February 1975): 39.

[27] David Brion Davis, *The Problem of Slavery in the Age of Revolution, 1770–1823* (Ithaca and London: Cornell University Press, 1975), pp. 60–64.

[28] See J. H. Plumb, *Men and Places* (London: Cresset Press, 1963), pp. 193–94.

[29] Charles R. Ritcheson, *Aftermath of Revolution: British Policy Toward the United States, 1783–1795* (Dallas: Southern Methodist University Press, 1969), pp. 40–42.

[30] Plumb, *In the Light of History*, p. 73.

[31] See also H. J. Habakkuk, *American and British Technology in the Nineteenth Century* (Cambridge: Cambridge University Press, 1962), pp. 15, 17, for higher wages paid to American skilled workers. For the rapidity with which American technology outstripped Britain in agricultural machinery, see Robert F. Dalzell, Jr., *American Participation in the Great Exhibition of 1851* (Amherst: Amherst College Press, 1960).

[32] Quoted by Mary Cable, "Damned Plague Ships and Swimming Coffins," *American Heritage* 11 (August 1960): 76.

[33] Ibid., p. 80.

In 1939 J. H. Plumb was elected Ehrman Research Fellow at King's College, Cambridge. Becoming a fellow of Christ's College in 1946, a position which he continues to hold, he was appointed a tutor in 1950 and vice-master in 1964. A lecturer in history at the University of Cambridge from 1946 to 1962, when he was appointed a reader in modern English history, Mr. Plumb was named professor of modern English history in 1966 and was chairman of the history faculty from 1966 to 1968.

Mr. Plumb has served as visiting professor and lecturer at several universities, among them Columbia University in 1960, as Ford's Lecturer at Oxford University in 1966, and as Distinguished Visiting Professor at the City University of New York in 1971 and 1976. A contributor of articles to professional journals, a book review editor, and a historical adviser to several publishing houses, Mr. Plumb is also an editor of a series of books on European history. Among his published works are England in the Eighteenth Century *(2d ed., 1968),* Sir Robert Walpole *(2d ed., 2 vols., 1960),* The First Four Georges *(3d ed., 1975),* Men and Places *(1963),* Crisis in the Humanities *(1964),* The Growth of Political Stability in England, 1675–1725 *(1967),* The Death of the Past *(1970),* In the Light of History *(1972), and* The Commercialization of Leisure *(1974).*

It has been my privilege to have personally known the next speaker for quite a number of years. I have followed his meticulously scholarly studies on Russian-American relations between 1775 and 1832, and he has turned up some extraordinarily significant documents both on the diplomacy of the mediation during the American Revolution and on the role of the Russian press. I was honored last spring by an invitation to lecture in Moscow at the Institute of General History of the Academy of Sciences USSR, and I can attest at first hand to the serious interest in American history and culture which he and his colleagues are generating in Moscow. When the Russian liberal A. N. Radishchev wrote his stirring Journey From St. Petersburg to Moscow, *in which he praised the reforms instituted in America in the Revolutionary era, Catherine II responded by having him exiled to Siberia. The present speaker has just made a journey from Moscow to Washington, and I am sure, from this audience at least, a pleasanter fate awaits him.*

It is my genuine pleasure to introduce my good friend Dr. N. N. Bolkhovitinov from the Institute of General History of the Soviet Academy of Sciences.

The American Revolution
and the Russian Empire

N. N. BOLKHOVITINOV

THE AMERICAN WAR OF INDEPENDENCE, in the words of Karl Marx, "sounded
the tocsin for the European middle class." In the course of this war there
arose in America "the idea of an indivisible great democratic republic and the
first impulse was given to the European revolution of the 18th century." [1]

Of course, the Russia of the second half of the 18th century was not a pre-
revolutionary France, an industrially developed England, or a bourgeois
Holland (the republic of the United Provinces). The capitalist system was
only beginning to take shape and le tiers état as such was still nonexistent.
Therefore, to speak of a direct and immediate influence of the American War
of Independence on the revolutionary movement in Russia would be an
obvious exaggeration. But it would also be profoundly wrong to believe that
the development of Russia followed its own totally exclusive and special course
off the high road of world progress, that in general Russia did not belong to
the region of "Western civilization." In fact, Russian society was not completely isolated from the influence of European culture and the Enlightenment. News of the events in America reached the Russian public not only in
the capital—St. Petersburg—and Moscow but even in far-off Siberia. I will
cite just one example, the reports of the American traveler John Ledyard.

In his letter from Irkutsk dated August 20, 1787, Ledyard wrote that he
found himself "in a circle as gay, rich, polite and scientific as at Petersburg."
He mentioned proudly that he drank "French and Spanish wines" and went

on "philosophic walks" with the disciples of the famous Swedish naturalist Carolus Linnaeus, and, what is still more important to us, he pointed out: "In Russia I am treated as an American with politeness and respect and on my account the health of Dr. Franklin and General Washington has been drunk at the tables of two governors; and at Irkutsk the name of Adams has found its way." [2] Ledyard's evidence is rather noteworthy, especially if we consider the fact that it referred to a remote Siberian town on the shores of the Angara River, near Lake Baikal. The Siberian educated public was also influenced by the ideas of the Enlightenment, as indicated in particular by the publication in Tobolsk in 1790 by T. Voskresenskiy of Condorcet's speech which gave an exceptionally high appraisal of the services of Franklin and Leonhard Euler. (Though the names of the two scientists were not mentioned in the speech, it left no doubt whatsoever whom the speaker meant.) [3]

All this may appear incredible at first sight. In Irkutsk in the 18th century people knew not only about Washington but also about John Adams. A journal appearing in faraway Tobolsk published Condorcet's speeches and glorified Franklin.

To gain an understanding of why the news of the American Revolution of the 18th century and its leaders could spread at all in the Russian Empire, we should bear in mind that, owing to a number of favorable circumstances, the course of the American War of Independence received much more objective coverage in the Russian press than the events of the Great French Revolution of 1789–94. In principle, of course, the revolutionary war for American independence and the revolution in France, being events of a similar type, were bound to evoke a sharply negative reaction on the part of the Russian ruling circles. But this is only in principle. In practice, the events in America above all affected the interests of England. For Russia, they were occurring far across the ocean and, it seemed, did not present any real danger to the existing system. As Engels said, the very origin of the American colonies was bourgeois in character [4] and their development proceeded mainly already after the English revolution of the 17th century. As a result, the revolution in America belonged to the intra-formation type: it occurred within bourgeois society and its maturing was accelerated by the national—or rather the national-liberation—factor. The American Revolution was above all a colonial revolution, a struggle of colonies in revolt against the mother country, a war of American independence. By contrast, the formidable events of 1789–94 in France, apart from their being more radical than those in America, were directed first of all against the ancien régime, against absolutism, and were taking place not in some far-off lands but in the center of Europe, creating, in the eyes of the European monarchs, a direct threat to the existing order.

It is not surprising, therefore, that Catherine II viewed the revolt of the British subjects in North America rather calmly and, as a rule, did not go beyond sarcastic remarks, which occasionally showed her perspicacity and even censured the shortsighted policy of George III and his ministers. The czarina emphatically refused to send a Russian corps to America and later declined all attempts of the British cabinet to induce Russia to sign a treaty of alliance. It was felt in St. Petersburg that the genuine "state of the English court and ministry was not such as to inspire national or outside trust towards them." From this secret report of the College of Foreign Affairs, submitted to Catherine II on July 31 (August 11), 1779, it can be seen that the Russian government not only considered the separation of the colonies from the mother country an accomplished fact but also held that the separation came about "through the very fault" of the English cabinet.[5]

In 1780–81 N. I. Panin, head of the College of Foreign Affairs, favorably disposed toward the United States, and, incidentally, influenced by constitutional ideas,[6] advanced proposals for a peaceful settlement of the conflict. The Russian plan provided for the signing of an armistice following which America would have "complete liberty to decide its own fate."[7] As can be seen from a note of the College of Foreign Affairs which was approved by Catherine on January 22 (February 2), 1781, the Russian government envisioned that the "American settlements" should "negotiate with the English crown and conclude treaties with it either wholly or partially by provinces," while France could subsequently be satisfied by "guarantees of the pacts concluded between England and the American colonies and such trade advantages as would be granted to her."[8]

To understand the reasons for the more or less objective evaluation of the events of the American Revolution in the Russian press, we should also take into account the fact that in the 1770's and 1780's Catherine still retained some vestiges of "liberalism," trying thereby to cover up the odious forms of serfdom in Russia. Extending patronage to the European philosophes, Catherine hoped to consolidate her position inside the country and, even more, to raise her prestige abroad. Voltaire, "the sovereign of the minds and fashion," conducted regular correspondence with the empress up to his death in 1778. Still more lively and prolonged (till 1796) was Catherine's correspondence with Baron Melchior von Grimm, a French critic who belonged to the circle of the Encyclopedists. He was not only a regular correspondent but also a confidant and agent of the empress abroad. Catherine sought Grimm's counsel on the most varied problems and, moreover, supported him materially.[9]

The highest Russian aristocrats were eager not to lag behind the "enlightened" czarina. While Catherine called Diderot and d'Alembert to

St. Petersburg, G. Orlov and K. Razumovskiy invited the exiled philosopher Rousseau. The czarina avidly read Montesquieu's *L'Esprit des Lois*, Count P. S. Potemkin translated Rousseau and Princess E. R. Dashkova published extracts from Helvétius' *De l'Esprit* in the journal *Nevinnyye uprazhneniya*. While in Paris, the princess was not averse to getting acquainted with Franklin, having breakfast with the abbé Raynal, and entertaining, of an evening, a "whole circle," including Diderot.[10] Last but not least, Prince M. M. Shcherbatov even declared to the French charge d'affaires in Russia that he was a republican and a resolute advocate of America's independence.[11]

Though we should not make too much of the extent to which Russian educated society was informed about the American War of Independence, still a study of the Russian press of the last third of the 18th century permits one to conclude that Russia's educated circles possessed extensive and rather varied information about the situation in North America and the events taking place there. The Russian reader had at his disposal translations of books about America by foreign authors, numerous magazine articles, and, finally, the extensive and varied material about the course of the War of Independence which regularly appeared in the St. Petersburg and Moscow newspapers.[12]

Special mention should be made here of the services rendered by N. I. Novikov, whose name is associated with the genuine flourishing of *Moskovskiye vedomosti* and the Moscow press in general. As noted by N. M. Karamzin, with Novikov's arrival (i.e., after 1779), the newspaper became "much richer in content" and its circulation rose from 600 to 4,000 copies.[13] Among the extensive and varied articles on foreign affairs provided by the newspaper, most prominent were reports associated in one way or another with the war which England was waging, first against its former colonies in America and then also against France and Spain. We could mention, for example, a series of short biographies of "famous men of the current century" which contained "notes" on Washington, Adams, Franklin, Raynal, and Lafayette. A laudatory article on Washington was also published in 1784 in a supplement to *Moskovskiye vedomosti*. In the opinion of the author of that article, outstanding heroes of the past could not compare with Washington, for "he founded a republic that is likely to become a refuge of freedom banished from Europe by luxury and depravity." [14] Supplements were published by Novikov for two years only (1783–84) but even during that brief period the journal carried a series of articles specially devoted to America.[15]

Although, due to censorship, many documentary records and books on America (e.g., the famous work of abbé Raynal) could not appear in Russian translation, the educated section of Russian society was rather well informed about their content, chiefly through French and, to a lesser extent, Dutch editions. In some cases original American materials could be acquired. Thus, in the autumn of 1781 the *St. Peterburgskiye vedomosti* published the following important announcement:

It has been reported from Philadelphia on July 28 that by a decision of the American Congress a collection of its various acts was recently published in the city related to the new government of the 13 United American Provinces, viz.: 1. Constitutions of various independent states in America. 2. Declarations of Independence of the said states. 3. The Articles of Confederation among these states. 4. Treaties concluded between His Majesty the King of France and the United American States. This collection comprises 226 pages in octavo and those who want it can order the collection from Holland.[16]

It is noteworthy that 1783, the year when the American War of Independence ended, saw the publication in St. Petersburg of the first book by a Russian author especially devoted to the new nation. This small reference work by D. M. Ladygin included a general outline of the history of colonization in America and an account of the contemporary situation in the former English settlements that had proclaimed their independence.[17] It is significant that in the very title of the book its author reflected the new designation of the state which arose in place of the former English colonies in North America —the "United Provinces." It is also to the credit of the author that he favored establishing and promoting trade relations between Russia and the new nation in America.

That same year saw the publication in Riga of a book by the rector of the local gymnasium, K. Snell, which was entitled *Von den Handlungsvortheilen, welche aus der Unabhängigkeit der Vereinigten Staaten von Nord-Amerika für das russische Reich entspringen.* A detailed review of the book appeared later on in *Yezhenedel'nyye izvestiya vol'nogo ekonomicheskogo obshchestva 1788 goda.*[18] Snell pointed out that the peace treaty which proclaimed the independence of North America was "one of the most important events" of the 18th century and that it would "result in great revolutions in both the political and commercial worlds." [19] The book described the United States of North America as "a well organised and comparatively populated state" which was almost as big as Europe and which boasted rich natural resources. No wonder that Snell predicted "a rapid growth of this happy state" and pointed out that it would take "no more than one generation to see it in all its imposing grandeur." And since this state would base its future might "mainly on trade, for which Nature has endowed it with the most desirable gifts, commercial ties all over the world will acquire a new image and a new direction." [20]

The events of the American Revolution of the 18th century had a direct influence on F. V. Karzhavin, who came from "a family of free thinkers" and was one of the few representatives of the "third estate" in Russia. During his stay in the United States Karzhavin had the opportunity of acquainting himself with American reality in a detailed and profound way. He wrote that he got to know "this huge country, and to know it well." The circle of his Virginian friends included such well-known personalities as future President James Madison, one of the most educated representatives of the American Enlightenment Prof. George Wythe of the College of William and Mary, Carlo Bellini, and others. Karzhavin's correspondence with Bellini continued after he left the United States.[21] Regretably, his book on his American travels never appeared. At the same time, his numerous publications contained many quite unexpected and often very interesting observations directly connected with his stay in North America. Thus, among study materials the reader could find a general characterization of his American journey:

One of our compatriots, an inquiring and knowledgeable man, sets out across the Atlantic Ocean in 1776 and, making his way to the South-West, steps on the shore in the West-Indies . . . From there he proceeds to mainland America and returns to his native country not earlier than 1788. . . . This Russian is the first of our people who has spent twelve years in those distant countries and who must have seen them with keen eyes. . . .[22]

Also indicative is the fact that Karzhavin signed the preface to one of his books "A Russian American." [23]

Of special interest is Karzhavin's strong condemnation of Negro slavery, an attitude characteristic of advanced representatives of Russian society at the time. In the same book, whose subject seems to be far removed from politics and which was characterized by the author as "an innocent exercise of bored people who do not want to do anything better," one encounters angry lines directed against slavery and its supporters: "All the African and American shores are moaning from the inhumanity with which sugar manufacturers treat the black-skinned peoples." [24] Karzhavin's democratic feelings and sympathy for the Negroes and the oppressed Indians of America were vividly manifested in his characterization of the so-called "savage" peoples:

For twelve years I have lived in various regions of America, both cold and warm. All in all, I have spent 28 years abroad . . . I have seen many peoples who live differently from us and other Europeans; I have seen both intelligent and stupid people; I have seen human beings everywhere, but I have not met a savage, and I admit that I have not come across a man who would have been more savage than myself.[25]

The most important work rich in content touching upon the events and ideas of the American Revolution was the famous ode "Vol'nost' " [Freedom] by A. N. Radishchev, which he included in the text of his *Journey From Petersburg to Moscow*. In reading the ode one is struck by the exceptional profundity of its content as a whole and in its separate details. Radishchev not only grasped many characteristic features of the American Revolution but also showed their essence in an imaginative, concise, and expressive manner. With exceptional perspicacity he discerned, for example, the just nature of the American War of Independence and the advantages of a new, popular army over the old, "subjugated" army of the feudal states. As an illustration let me cite here the famous 34th stanza of the ode:

> Gaze on the boundless field,
> Where the host of brutality stands effaced:
> They are not cattle driven there against their will.
> It is not a chance that brings courage,
> Nor the crowd—
> Each soldier feels himself a leader.
> He seeks a glorious end.
> O steadfast soldier,
> Thou art and wert unconquerable,
> Your leader—freedom, Washington.[26]

Let us also turn special attention to the line "They are not cattle driven there against their will." How much contempt for the old army, with its organization based on subjugation, and for militarism in general is conveyed in these few stark words! And consider the line: "Each soldier feels himself a leader," which in itself shows how clearly and correctly Radishchev perceived the main characteristic of an American army founded on altogether different principles of organization, principles which were progressive for their time.

It was precisely the analysis of the 34th stanza that led V. P. Semennikov to draw the conclusion that the ode was written around 1781–83, since it speaks of the War of Independence as a current or at any rate contemporary event and Washington appears as the leader of the army.[27]

Radishchev indeed writes about the American War of Independence in the present tense, as if it were just taking place. However, V. P. Semennikov and many other scholars after him paid insufficient attention to the next stanza, the 35th, which in all probability also refers to America and which depicts the triumph of a republic gaining its freedom:

> The temple of the two-faced god has been closed;
> Violence is discarded,
> The god of triumph appeared amid us
> And blew the horn of festivities.

Let us recall that in keeping with established custom the temple of the two-faced Janus was open in wartime and closed once peace had been restored.

Thus in the 35th stanza "the temple of the two-faced god has been closed" means that the war has ended. "Violence is discarded" and the time has come for rejoicing as "the god of triumph appeared amid us." Finally, in his well-known address to the "glorious country" (the 46th stanza) Radishchev exclaimed, "Thou rejoiceth now" (i.e., the United States is rejoicing). It is obvious, therefore, that the ode (or at least the stanzas quoted here) was written not during the War of Independence but after it ended, most likely immediately after reports of the American victory were published in Russian newspapers.[28] This assumption is confirmed by the unusual freshness of impressions made by the events described, which have not yet been overshadowed by subsequent occurrences. And since George Washington appears in the ode also as a commander in chief, the "leader" of the revolutionary army, it definitely could not have been written in the 1790's, after he had already become President of the new state. Moreover, in the 1790's the events of the American War of Independence were pushed into the background by the French Revolution of 1789, which Radishchev almost certainly would have mentioned had he been writing the ode in 1790 or later. Lastly, in the 18th-century vocabulary the very term *vol'nost'* connoted primarily independence or political freedom; that is, it differed semantically to some extent from the word *svoboda*, "freedom." This difference in meaning also points to a link between the ode and the liberation struggle of the United States against England.

Thus a textual analysis of the ode "Vol'nost'," with due consideration for the events and ideas of the American Revolution, proves to be rather fruitful, as we have seen, and makes it possible to define more correctly the date when this remarkable work was written.

Radishchev repeatedly turned to American themes in his *Journey From Petersburg to Moscow*, revealing in each case that he was well informed and had a clear understanding of the essence of the matter. He dealt most thoroughly with the question of freedom of the press. "The American governments adopted freedom of the press among the very first statutes confirming civic liberty," he wrote, providing pertinent extracts from the constitutions of Pennsylvania, Delaware, Maryland, and Virginia to support this statement. Typical of his constitutional citations were the following: "The people have a right to freedom of speech and of writing and publishing their sentiments; therefore freedom of the press ought not to be restrained" (Pennsylvania Constitution of 1776, section 12 of the Declaration of Rights), and "The freedom of the press is the greatest protection of freedom of the state" (Constitution of Virginia, article 14).[29]

As a practical example illustrating the democratic pattern of society in

America, Radishchev quotes the case of a prominent participant in the War of Independence, John Dickinson of Pennsylvania, who came forward with an open refutation of unjust criticism directed at him. "The first town governor of the province [Pennsylvania]," Radishchev wrote, "descended to the jousting ring, issued a defence of himself, justified himself, refuted the arguments of all his opponents, and put them to shame. . . . This is an example to follow of how to avenge oneself by means of the printed word when someone accuses another person publicly." [30]

While praising political freedom in the United States, Radishchev at the same time indignantly rejected Negro slavery and the annihilation of the Indians:

Once having slaughtered the Indians, the wicked Europeans, preachers of love of peace in the name of God's truth, teachers of meekness and love of humanity, graft upon the root of violent murder of conquest the cold-blooded murder of enslavement through the acquisition of slaves by purchase. These unhappy victims from the sun-drenched shores of the Niger and the Senegal . . . work the bountiful cornfields of America, which disdain their labor. And we call a country of devastation blissful because its fields are not overgrown with thorns and its cornfields abound with a variety of plants. We call that country blissful where a hundred proud citizens roll in luxury while thousands have neither reliable subsistence nor their own shelter from the burning sun and the frost.[31]

It would be no exaggeration to say that for their depth of analysis of the events and ideas of the American Revolution, the richness of thoughts and brilliance of exposition, the appropriate passages in the ode "Vol'nost'" and the book *Journey From Petersburg to Moscow* may be qualified as the most conspicuous responses of the contemporary world literature to the American Revolution of the 18th century. Noteworthy too is the fact that on the major questions of the liberation movement Radishchev took up a thoroughly consistent position—an advanced position for the time—and was, so to speak, in the vanguard of world revolutionary progress.

To be sure, the voice of Radishchev could not be heard by broad masses of the Russian people in the 18th century. Frightened by the formidable events of the revolution in France, Catherine II incarcerated him in a fortress and then exiled him to Siberia. The czarina declared "with fervor and deep feeling" that Radishchev was a "rebel worse than Pugachev" and pointed out to her secretary A. V. Khrapovitskiy a place in the end of the book where he praised "Franklin as the initiator and presented himself as such." [32] However, history has its own laws, which were outside the control of Catherine and her servitors. And today, almost 200 years later, the important thing is not what the "great" empress said or wrote and what was faithfully executed by a host of her staff and supernumerary officials but what our first revolutionary poet and writer, Alexander Nikolayevich Radishchev, thought, wrote, and dreamed of.

The extracts from the constitutions of Pennsylvania, Delaware, Maryland, and Virginia quoted by Radishchev in the *Journey* were the first and perhaps the only American constitutional materials to appear in the Russian language in the 18th century. It was only 30 years later, in 1820, that the journal *Dukh zhurnalov* [Spirit of the Journals], published by G. M. Yatsenkov, gave a detailed exposition of the Constitution and sociopolitical organization of the United States.[33] It should be noted that in general American subjects occupied a special place in this journal. Never before had any Russian periodical published such wide-ranging and informative materials on various aspects of life in the United States, its state system, economic development, etc. These materials, among which was the introductory note to the "State Calendar of the American United States," were used by the tsarist authorities as a pretext for closing down *Dukh zhurnalov* in the autumn of 1820.

Having studied the numerous articles dealing with America in *Dukh zhurnalov*, we have been able to reappraise this important periodical, which for the first time ventured to raise a number of the most acute political problems relating to such issues as constitutional rule, civil liberties, and freedom of the press.[34]

In general, the events and ideas of the American Revolution attracted the attention not only of contemporaries such as N. I. Novikov, F. V. Karzhavin, and A. N. Radishchev but also of several generations of Russian men of letters and revolutionaries of the 19th century, including the Decembrists, A. I. Herzen, N. G. Chernyshevskiy, and others.[35]

The participants in the Decembrist movement, and in particular the Decembrist republicans, more than once referred to the revolutionary experience in France and America. They were filled with admiration for Washington and Franklin and were in close touch with the developments on the European and American scene. In his letter to General Levashov of February 24 (March 8), 1826, P. G. Kakhovskiy wrote:

The latter half of the last century and the events of this century are so crowded with various government upheavals that we need not refer to more distant epochs. We witness great happenings. The product of the New World, the North American States have by their formation induced Europe to emulate. They will also serve as an example for many generations to come. The name of Washington, the friend and benefactor of the people, will pass from generation to generation. Recollections of him will fill the souls of citizens with love for the good and for the fatherland. ... The revolution in France severely shook the thrones of Europe and exercised a still greater influence on its government and peoples than the formation of the United States.[36]

V. D. Vol'khovskiy, a former lyceum pupil and a close friend of V. K. Kyukhel'beker and I. I. Pushchin, wrote in March 1823, "My beloved hero, Franklin, a printer's son, himself was an ordinary workman. . . ." [37] In the words of V. F. Rayevskiy, "Bonaparte did not make the revolution: he merely took advantage of it to gratify his lust for power . . . . Washington and Franklin liberated people from slavery." [38]

The Decembrists admired the activities of Washington and Franklin not in a purely speculative and abstract way but as the groundwork for their own revolutionary endeavors. As documented by M. Murav'yev-Apostol, P. I. Pestel made a case for establishing a provisional government by invoking the example of the United States, whose cause was successful due to the existence during the war of a centralized government concentrated "in the person of Washington, who was America's military and civil head." [39]

In the list of Nikita Murav'yev's books given in N. M. Druzhinin's monograph, we can see, along with the works of outstanding 18th-century French philosophers (Voltaire, Montesquieu, Rousseau) and English economists (Adam Smith, David Ricardo), the works of leading political figures in the United States—a three-volume work by John Adams in defense of the American state system and a manual on parliamentary practice by Thomas Jefferson. [40] Historical writings include a well-known work on the American Revolution by D. Ramsay, a supporter of federalist views, as well as a French translation of H. M. Brackenridge's book on the Anglo-American war of 1812. [41]

A lengthy quotation from Ramsay's book, transcribed by N. Murav'yev in the early 1820's, attested to the sympathy which the Decembrists had for the insurgent Americans: The colonist, Ramsay noted, had never heard of the Magna Carta, the Great Charter. His political faith was simple but very rich in content. He believed that God had made all men equal from birth and had vested them with the rights of life, property, and freedom to an extent harmonizing with the rights of others. He believed that the government, a political institution between naturally equal people, existed not to exalt one or a few persons but to ensure the happiness of the whole fatherland. [42]

It is well known that N. Murav'yev's constitutional project was influenced by the federal constitution of 1787 and the constitutions of individual American states. Like the U.S. Congress, Murav'yev's popular *veche* (assembly) consisted of two chambers—the Supreme Council and the Chamber of Representatives—and was to be convened at least once a year, "on the first Tuesday of December, unless otherwise fixed by law." Moreover, the text of the oath given by the Russian emperor repeated almost word for word the oath of the U.S. President, and there were to be four *prikazy* corresponding to the four original U.S. departments. [43]

As Academician N. M. Druzhinin pointed out, Muravev was acquainted with the constitutions of all 23 North American states and understood perfectly "the distinctive character of Anglo-Saxon law in its American interpretation." In drafting his constitution he made extensive use of the most diverse sources, including American ones,

> but the form of this use was independent and rather varied: comparatively seldom did he incorporate separate articles of the foreign text, confining himself to a literal and precise reproduction; more often he interpreted the content of a juridical norm, lending a particular tint to it; not infrequently he altered its content, giving a new interpretation to the principle borrowed; very often he discarded unnecessary material and introduced his own additions, in accordance with Russian law and his own theoretical ideas. . . .

"In this sense," Druzhinin concluded, "his constitution is no less an independent work than the French constitutional acts or drafts of Russian political reformers." [44] We can add that the text of the constitution was written in conformity with the Russian national tradition, with broad use of such terms as *duma, veche, prikaz, derzhava, tisyatskiy,* and *stareyshina.*

P. I. Pestel' directly referred to the experience of the United States as an important reason for his conversion to republican views. Testifying before the Committee of Inquiry, he said:

> My conversion from a monarchical-constitutional to a republican mode of thinking has been effected primarily by the following factors and considerations: Destutt de Tracy's work in the French language impressed me very much. He proves that any government under which one person is the head of state, especially if this office is hereditary, will inevitably end in despotism. All newspapers and political writings have so much extolled the growing prosperity of the North American United States, which they attributed to their state organisation, that this seemed to me to be a clear proof of the superiority of the republican government. [45]

Judging by the testimony of Decembrist S. M. Semenov, Pestel, had referred to the American experience in his historical report at a meeting of the Korennaya uprava [Supreme Council] of the Soyuz Blagodenstviya [Union of Welfare] held early in 1820 at the home of Fedor Glinka in St. Petersburg. "When in 1819 or 1820 Pestel arrived at the Council, the discussion concerned the advantages or disadvantages of various forms of government. Pestel sought to prove the superiority of the government of the United States of America over all others. All those present agreed with Pestel that the government of the United States of America was better than all the other forms of government known hitherto." When the vote was taken, all declared in favor of a republic. The famous phrase of N. I. Turgenev, "Le président— sans phrases," explicitly and concisely summed up the discussion: a republic is preferable; why waste time and beat about the bush? [46]

Of considerable interest are the views on the United States held by K. F.

Ryleyev, head of the Northern Society. Though in his private conversations the poet "always advocated a restricted monarchy," at the bottom of his heart he "preferred the mode of government of the North American United States, in the belief that the mode of government of this Republic is most convenient for Russia with its vast territory and the multinational composition of the peoples inhabiting it." This was precisely what Ryleyev said to many members of the society "and, among others, to Nikita Muravev, urging him to make some changes in his constitution, in line with the Constitution of the United States, leaving, however, monarchical forms." [47] When directly asked by Pestel what form of government was preferable for Russia, Ryleyev said that "the most convenient form of government for Russia appears to be the regional government of the North American Republic under an emperor whose power ought not to be much greater than that of the President of the States." Ryleyev also concluded, "In our time even an ambitious man, if he is reasonable, of course," said Ryleyev, "would sooner wish to be a Washington than a Napoleon." [48]

The facts given above show that the advanced section of the Russian society and, notably, such personalities as A. N. Radishchev, P. I. Pestel', N. M. Murav'yev, and, later, also A. I. Herzen, N. G. Chernyshevskiy, and others closely followed the revolutionary movement in Western Europe and America and in particular, gave a high appraisal of the American War of Independence, the Constitution of 1787 and the activities of Washington and other outstanding American revolutionaries. They took an interest in the current developments in America and read works by American authors (mainly in French translations) as well as books on the history of the United States. But these facts should not, of course, lead us to believe that the American Revolution was the principal cause of the growth of a revolutionary mood in Russia or that the Decembrists uncritically accepted what they had read and blindly copied the West European or American experience. This was precisely and aptly expressed by the Decembrist A. V. Podzhio:

Surely we could not, reading some Warden,[49] borrow his convictions and try to introduce in Russia a republic similar to the one he discusses. The high complexity serves as a force and bulwark for the United States. We had apprehensions of this, lest through the introduction of a federal government our state should fall into pieces, for there are nine million inhabitants there and here we have forty million. Over there there are English settlers and here we have indigenous inhabitants of Russia! ... Over there vengeance was directed against external foes, and over here we sought the enemy among ourselves. ... Of course, we borrowed from the books, read all the statutes, the jury and the like, but the thoughts of a rising, resolved, courage can only be explained by the fact that all this originated not from books but in our hearts, among all the passions raging in them! This is the fountainhead of all our designs from which the latter evolved with all-consuming flames.[50]

Podzhio's testimony is highly important to us. The Americans fought first of all against an external enemy. They fought for independence, against the tyranny of the British crown. Russia and Russian society were confronted with different tasks. They had to fight not for national independence but for the abolition of serfdom, for a radical reorganization of the existing system and for the overthrow of the tsarist autocracy.

Notes

[1] Karl Marx and Friedrich Engels, *Sochineniya* [Works], 2d, Russian ed., 39 vols. in 42 (Moscow: Gos. izd-vo polit. lit-ry, 1955–66), 23:9 and 16:17.

[2] John Ledyard to W. S. Smith, August 20, 1787, John Ledyard, *Journey Through Russia and Siberia, 1787–1788: The Journal and Selected Letters*, ed. S. D. Watrous (Madison: University of Wisconsin Press, 1966), pp. 129–30.

[3] "The Irtysh Turning Into an Ipokrena," February 1790, pp. 156–57.

[4] Marx and Engels, *Sochineniya*, 39:128.

[5] "Secret report of the College of Foreign Affairs to Catherine II, July 31 (August 11), 1779," *Arkhiv Kniazia Vorontsova* [Archive of Prince Vorontsov] (Moscow, 1888), 34:388–405. The original is in the Archive of Russia's Foreign Policy, fond Secret Opinions, 1725–1798, file 597, sheets 100–114.

[6] See M. M. Safonov, "Konstitutsionnyy proyekt N. I. Panina–D. I. Fonvizina" [Constitutional project of N. I. Panin–D. I. Fonvizin], *Vspomogatel'nyye istoricheskiye distsipliny* [Ancillary historical disciplines] 6 (Leningrad, 1974): 261–80.

[7] For more details see Richard B. Morris, *The Peacemakers: The Great Powers and American Independence* (New York: Harper & Row, 1965), pp. 169–70; D. M. Griffiths, "Nikita Panin, Russian Diplomacy, and American Revolution," *Slavic Review* 28, no. 1 (March 1969): 13–15.

[8] See note on peace mediation approved by Catherine II on January 22 (February 2), 1781, Archives of Russia's Foreign Policy, fond Russia's Relations with Austria, file 632, sheets 24–33. The text of the note is being published in *Amerikanskiy yezhegodnik* [American annual] (Moscow, 1975).

[9] See "Letters of Empress Catherine II to Baron Melchior Grimm," *Sbornik imperatorskogo russkogo istoricheskogo obshchestva* [Collection of the Imperial Russian Historical Society], 23 (St. Petersburg, 1878); "Letters of Baron Melchior Grimm to Empress Catherine II," ibid., 33 (St. Petersburg, 1881).

[10] *Zapiski knyagini Dashkovoi* [Notes of Princess Dashkova], ed. N. D. Chechulin (St. Petersburg, 1907), p. 137.

[11] *Un Diplomate français à la cour de Catherine II, 1775–1780; Journal intime du chevalier de Corberon . . .* , 2 vols. (Paris: Plon-Nourrit et cie., 1901), 2:49.

[12] See N. N. Bolkhovitinov, *Stanovleniye russko-amerikanskikh otnosheniy, 1775–1815* [The beginnings of Russian-American relations, 1775–1815] (Moscow: Nauka, 1966), pp. 91–129;

M. N. Nikolskaya, "Russkaya pechat' o voine Severnoi Ameriki za nezavisimost' v XVIII veke" [The Russian press on the war of North America for independence in the 18th century] (Cand. Sc. thesis, Moscow, 1968).

13 N. M. Karamzin, "O knizhnoi torgovle i lyubvi k chteniyu v Rossii [On the book trade and love of reading in Russia], *N. I. Novikov i ego sovremenniki* [N. I. Novikov and his contemporaries] (Moscow, 1961), p. 415.

14 "Kratkoye opisaniye zhizni i kharaktera gen. Vashingtona" [Brief description of the life and character of General Washington], *Pribavleniye k Moskovskim Vedomostyam*, 1784, pp. 362, 369 (nos. 46 and 47).

15 Among them we can mention the following: "On the Influence Exercised by the Independence of the North American United Regions on the Political State of Europe," *Pribavleniye k Moskovskim Vedomostyam*, 1784, pp. 306, 313, 321, 329, 337; "Reflections on Undertakings Related to Trade With North America," ibid., 1783, pp. 302, 305, 309, 311; "The Mode of Government and Civil Statutes in America," ibid., 1783, p. 516; "General Description of American Morals," ibid., 1784, pp. 489, 497, 505, 513, 521; "News of Pennsylvania," ibid., 1784, no. 18, p. 137; "Europeans' Trade in America," ibid., 1783, p. 265 and elsewhere.

16 *St. Peterburgskiye vedomosti* 50, October 26 (November 6), 1781.

17 D. M. Ladygin, *Izvestiye v Amerike o seleniyakh angliyskikh, v tom chisle nyne pod nazvaniyem Soyedinennykh Provintsiy, vybrano perechnem iz noveyshikh o tom prostranno sochinitelei* [A report on the English settlements in America, including those now designated as the United Provinces, compiled on the basis of a number of books by modern authors] (St. Petersburg, 1783), pp. 58–59.

18 [Weekly reports of the Free Economic Society for 1788], vol. 2, pp. 164–65.

19 M. Karl Philip Michael Snell, *Von den Handlungsvortheilen, welche aus der Unabhängigkeit der Vereinigten Staaten von Nord-Amerika für das russische Reich entspringen* (Riga: Johan Friedrich Hartknoch, 1783), p. 5.

20 Ibid., pp. 5–6.

21 C. Bellini to F. V. Karzhavin (in Italian), March 1, 1788, Manuscripts Department, Institute of Russian Literature, fond 93, no. 2, file 100, sheet 87.

22 F. V. Karzhavin, *Frantsuzskiye, rossiyskiye i nemetskiye razgovory v pol'zu nachinatelei* . . . [French, Russian and German conversations for the benefit of beginners] (St. Petersburg, 1803), p. 64.

23 [Fedor V. Karzhavin], *Novoyavlennyy vedun, povedayushchiy gadaniya dukhov* . . . [A new fangled wizard conveying divinations of the spirits] (St. Petersburg: I. K. Shnor, 1795), p. iv.

24 Ibid., p. 71.

25 [F. V. Karzhavin], *Kratkoye izvestiye o dostopamyatnykh priklyucheniyakh kapitana d'Civila* . . . [A brief report on the memorable adventures of Captain d'Civil . . .], trans. F[edor] K[arzhavin] (Moscow, 1791), pp. 26–27. Recently, V. I. Rabinovich devoted a special work to Karzhavin's American journey. The author was carried away by his imagination a bit and presented his hero almost as another Radishchev or, at any rate, as his associate and friend, an American correspondent of N. I. Novikov's, and an active participant in the American War of Independence. See Valeriy I. Rabinovich, *S gishpantsami v Novyy York i Gavanu* [With the Spaniards to New York and Havana] (Moscow: Mysl', 1967), pp. 18–25, 68–69, and elsewhere.

²⁶ Translated by Elena Levin.

²⁷ V. P. Semennikov, *Radishchev: Ocherki i issledovaniya* [Radishchev: essays and investigations] (Moscow-Petrograd, 1923), p. 7. Semennikov's view has won wide recognition among specialists and the ode "Vol'nost' " is usually dated 1781–83. A. N. Radishchev, *Complete Works*, 3 vols. (Moscow-Leningrad, 1938–52), 1:444n.; *Vol'naya russkaya poeziya vtoroy poloviny XVIII–pervoy poloviny XIX veka* [Free Russian poetry of the second half of the 18th century and the first half of the 19th century] (Leningrad, 1970), p. 120. Not so long ago G. Shtorm, a writer, advanced a hypothesis to the effect that the four stanzas of the ode (including the 46th verse relating to America) were written by Radishchev much later, toward the end of his life, most probably in 1799 (see G. Shtorm, "Potayennyy Radishchev" [Hidden Radishchev], *Novyy Mir*, no. 11 (1964): 144–48, 156). In the view of D. S. Babkin, the ode was created in three stages (before the manuscript of "The Journey" was submitted for censorship, during its publication, and, lastly, after the publication of the book and Radishchev's return from exile, when he wrote, in particular, the 46th stanza). See Dmitriy S. Babkin, *A. N. Radishchev* (Moscow-Leningrad, 1966), pp. 100–102.

²⁸ "Preliminary peace resolutions" between the United States and Great Britain were published by *St. Peterburgskiye vedomosti* on February 17 (28), 1783, and on September 22 (October 3), 1783, the same newspaper carried a report on the signing of the Definitive Peace Treaty in Paris.

²⁹ From a section entitled "A Brief Account of the Origin of Censorship" in the chapter "Torzhok." Radishchev, *Complete Works*, 1:346–47. See also Max M. Laserson, *The American Impact on Russia: Diplomatic and Ideological, 1784–1917* (New York: Macmillan, 1950), pp. 66–67. As A. I. Startsev showed convincingly in his doctoral thesis, Radishchev became acquainted with the American constitutional materials through the French publication *Recueil des loix constitutive des colonies angloises confédérées sous la denomination d'Etats-Unis de l'Amérique Septentrionale—auquel on a joint les Actes d'Indépendance, de Confédération et autre Actes du Congrès général, traduit de l'anglois. Dedié à M. le Docteur Franklin* (À Philadelphie et se vend à Paris, 1778). See A. I. Startsev-Kunin, "Amerikanskaya revolyutsiya, Radishchev i russkoye obshchestvo XVIII veka" [The American Revolution, Radishchev and Russian society of the 18th century] (doctoral thesis, Moscow, 1946), pp. 226, 299–303; also see Leonard N. Beck, "Pennsylvania and Early Russian Radicals," *Pennsylvania Magazine of History and Biography* 75 (April 1951): 194–95.

³⁰ Radishchev, *Complete Works*, 1:334.

³¹ Ibid., 316–17.

³² A. V. Khrapovitskiy, *Pamyatniye zapiski* [Memoranda] (St. Petersburg, 1874), p. 340.

³³ "Constitution of the North-American Regions," *Dukh zhurnalov*, part 38 (1820), book 2, pp. 73–88; book 3, pp. 97–116; book 4, pp. 157–64.

³⁴ My detailed study of the question on the basis of analysis of the contents of the journal and documents of the archives of tsarist censorship has been published in *Amerikanskiy yezhegodnik*. See N. N. Bolkhovitinov, "Amerikanskaya tema na stranitsakh *Dukha zhurnalov*, 1815–1820" [The American theme as reflected in *Dukh zhurnalov*, 1815–1820], *Amerikanskiy yezhegodnik, 1972* (Moscow, 1972), pp. 266–302.

³⁵ For details see David Hecht, *Russian Radicals Look to America, 1825–1894*, (Cambridge: Harvard University Press, 1947); Laserson, *The American Impact;* D. Boden, *Das Amerikabild*

im russischen Schrifttum bis zum Ende des 19. Jahrhunderts (Hamburg; Crarn, De Gruyter, 1968).

[36] P. G. Kakhovskiy to General Levashov, February 24 (March 8), 1824, cited in A. K. Borozdin, *Iz pisem i pokazaniy dekabristov* [From the letters and evidence given by the Decembrists] (St. Petersburg; Izdaniye M. V. Pirozhkova, 1906), p. 12; P. Y. Shchegalev, "Petr Grigoryevich Kakhovskiy, *Byloye*, no. 1 (January 1906), p. 148.

[37] V. D. Vol'khovskiy to V. G. Kyukhel'beker, March 7 (19), 1823, *Literaturnoye nasledstvo* [Literary legacy], 59:483.

[38] Moscow University, Department of the History of Russian Philosophy, *Izbrannye sotsial'no-politicheskiye i filosofskiye proizvedeniya dekabristov* [Selected sociopolitical and philosophical works of the Decembrists], ed. I. Ya. Shchipanov, (Moscow, Gos. izd-vo polit. lit-ry, 1951), 2:374. V. G. Bazanov, *Vladimir Fedoseyevich Rayevskiy* (Leningrad-Moscow, 1949), pp. 99, 113, and elsewhere.

[39] *Vosstaniye dekabristov* [The uprising of the Decembrists], 13 vols. (Moscow: Gos. izd-vo, 1925–75), 9:254.

[40] John Adams, *A Defence of the Constitutions of Government of the United States of America* . . ., 3 vols. (London; J. Stockdale, 1794); Thomas Jefferson, *Manuel du droit parlementaire; ou précis des régles suivies dans le Parlement d'Angleterre et dans le Congrés des États-Unis* . . . (Paris: H. Nicolle, 1814).

[41] David Ramsay, *The History of the American Revolution*, 2 vols., (London, J. Johnson, 1791). (The first edition appeared in Philadelphia in 1789.); H. M. Brackenridge, *Histoire de la guerre entre les États-Unis d'Amerique et l'Angleterre (1812–1815)*, 2 vols. (Paris, 1820).

[42] Cited in S. S. Volk, Istoricheskiye vzglyady dekabristov [Historical views of the Decembrists] (Moscow-Leningrad, 1958), p. 250.

[43] Cf., respectively, Henry Steele Commager, ed., *Documents of American History*, 7th ed. (New York, Appleton-Century-Crofts, 1963), 1:138–45; N. M. Druzhinin, *Dekabrist Nikita Muravev* [The Decembrist Nikita Muravev] (Moscow, 1933), pp. 306–63.

[44] Druzhinin, *Dekabrist Nikita Muravev*, p. 179.

[45] *Vosstaniye dekabristov*, 4:91b; Destutt de Tracy, *Commentaire sur l'Esprit des lois de Montesquieu* (Paris, 1819); E. M. Dvoichenko-Markov, "Jefferson and the Russian Decembrists," *American Slavic and East European Review* (October 1950): 162–67.

[46] *Vosstaniye dekabristov*, 4:101–2; S. S. Landa, "Formirovaniye revolyutsionnoy eidologii dekabristov, 1816–1825" [Formation of the revolutionary ideology of the Decembrists, 1816–1825]. (doctoral thesis, Leningrad, 1971), p. 286 (Central State Historical Archives, fond 48, storage number 67, sheet 40).

[47] *Vosstaniye dekabristov*, 1:175, 211, and elsewhere.

[48] Ibid., p. 178.

[49] Reference is to: D. B. Warden, *Description Statistique, Historique et politique des Etats Unis de l'Amérique Septentrionale* . . ., 5 vols. (Paris: Rey et Gravier, 1820), vol. 5. This work was known to many members of the society and was listed in the catalog of F. P. Shakhovskoy's library; N. I. Turgenev and many others were acquainted with it.

[50] *Vosstaniye dekabristov*, 9:43.

Nikolai N. Bolkhovitinov is a senior research associate at the Institute of General History of the Academy of Sciences USSR and a member of the editorial boards of the journal New and Contemporary History *and the* American Annual. *From 1967 to 1974 he served as lecturer and consultant on American history at Moscow University. In 1974–75 he also taught at Simferopol University in the Crimea.*

Mr. Bolkhovitinov, who holds a doctor of historical sciences degree, has published a number of studies relating to the United States, including The Monroe Doctrine *(1959),* The Beginnings of Russian-American Relations, 1775–1815 *(1966), and* Russian-American Relations, 1815–1832 *(1975). For the 200th anniversary of the United States, a new book by Mr. Bolkhovitinov,* Russia and the United States War of Independence, *is to be issued by the Mysl' Publishing House in Moscow.*

Recently I have been collaborating with some scholars at the Colegio de Mexico on an anthology comparing some of the principal issues and objectives of the Mexican War for Independence, 1810–24, and our own American Revolution, and both the Mexican editors and I myself have been challenged by the complexities of the problem. The American anticolonial war for independence was, of course, an example to the entire Western Hemisphere, and although the independence movement in Latin America was triggered by the Napoleonic wars and much of the ideology was influenced by French Enlightenment thought, the parallels to the American precedents in the area of constitutionalism, to federalism, and to reform are simply too numerous to be considered entirely coincidental. I am not privy to the views of the next speaker, a long-time specialist in Latin American affairs who is currently completing a study of Spanish liberalism which will be published under the title The Cádiz Experiment in Central America, 1808–1826, *but I know that there is much that he has to impart which all of us will find fresh and suggestive. It is my pleasure to introduce Professor Mario Rodríguez of the University of Southern California, who will address us on the topic of the impact of the American Revolution on the Spanish- and Portuguese-speaking world.*

The Impact of the
American Revolution on the
Spanish- and Portuguese-Speaking World

MARIO RODRÍGUEZ

Colonies are like fruit that stay on the tree until it is ripe: once they are self-sufficient, they will go the way of Carthage, *which some day will happen to America.*[1]

A. R. J. Turgot, Sorbonne, 1750

A DISTINGUISHED MAN OF LETTERS, Valentín de Foronda represented Spain in Philadelphia from 1801 to 1809. In the halls of the American Philosophical Society, this native of the Basque country informed his colleagues of cultural developments in Spain and encouraged the exchange of publications. As an expert in economics, Foronda marveled at the burgeoning prosperity and population growth of the young American republic—information which he compiled for his countrymen. After eight years' residence in the new nation, he knew the United States better than any Spaniard of his day. When he returned to Spain, therefore, Foronda constituted an indispensable resource for the Cádiz government that was forging a blueprint and a constitution for a modern Spanish nation. He spoke with authority about the open and liberal society that he had known in the United States.[2]

As a fervent advocate of laissez-faire economics, Foronda questioned the premises of Spain's colonial system. To stimulate a discussion on this theme among Spanish economists, he published a pamphlet in 1803 entitled *A Letter Concerning What a Prince Should Do Who Has Colonies at a Great Distance.*[3]

In this allegory, the Basque author analyzes a dream for his friend the prince. "I imagined," he begins, "that you were the master of an immense territory . . . resembling our Americas in every respect." In Europe your principality "needed to round it out a little kingdom that was its neighbor, and a fortress that belonged to a commercial nation." The allusions were to Portugal and English Gibraltar—two coveted objectives of Spanish national policy. These possessions could belong to the prince, Foronda continued, if he were amenable to some trades: first, the exchange of his mainland colonies overseas for the European territory of Portugal, and second, the transfer of some Caribbean islands for Gibraltar. The remainder of his colonial holdings could be sold to "commercial companies and to those princes who crave to own lands thousands of leagues from home, when they have more than enough in their own [country]."

In this new context the prince's nation could gain many advantages, especially with the adoption of free trade. He would now have a strong peninsular country with natural defenses and excellent resources. Moreover, war—that "monstrous devourer of the public tranquility"—would be a thing of the past, thus sparing the productive lives of many farmers and laborers who formerly served in the armed forces. The extensive imperial bureaucracy would be superfluous, and the savings from the liquidation of the colonies and the navy would yield the needed capital for the nation's infrastructure and educational establishment. Now that the prince no longer entertained "warlike ideas," he could also eliminate expensive ambassadorial posts, thus extricating his country from Europe's selfish diplomacy.

Colonialism, in short, was an untenable proposition. To prove his point, Foronda cited the example of the United States—a common device among anticolonialist writers:

Is there a country on the globe where the inhabitants live with more comforts and abundance than in the United States of North America? No. Do they have colonies at great distances in order to have an outlet for their goods? No. And yet they exported ninety-three million dollars worth of goods in the year 1801.

The author listed the exports involved, all of them nonmetallic, and stressed the fact that he had not accounted for all the sources of wealth in the United States. "It is not necessary," he concluded, "to possess colonies or mines for a nation to be rich." [4]

The Foronda letter sets the tone for this presentation. We will analyze first the official reaction of Spain and Portugal to the implications of the American Revolution, then the vogue of anticolonialism in the Hispanic world, a movement stimulated by the independence of the English colonies, and finally the revolutionary example of the United States in the other Americas.

England's victory in the Seven Years' War made a shambles of the balance-of-power system in the world, and the humiliating defeats at Havana and Manila continued to rankle in the minds of Spanish leaders. Charles III of Spain, who ruled from 1759 to 1788, felt so bitter about the British that Turgot despaired of complications for France at the time of the American Revolution.[5] A staunch economic nationalist, King Charles resented the inroads that Englishmen had made in the colonial trade through the slave contract in the first half of the 18th century. It galled him, moreover, that his nation depended so heavily upon foreign manufactures. To offset this dependence, he urged a talented group of Spanish ministers to develop a strong national economy. The accomplishments were impressive. Spaniards discovered a knack for economic matters, and the study of "political economy" virtually obsessed some of the best minds in Spain. By the 1780's Spaniards were supplying more than half of the manufactures in the colonial traffic, a threefold increase over previous inputs.[6]

Spanish leaders sensed that the American Revolution marked the successful beginning of anticolonialism in the New World. They too had faced ugly demonstrations overseas in the post-1763 period, challenging the imposition of defense taxes. The tobacco monopoly of 1767 was especially objectionable to the Spanish Creoles.[7] José de Abalos, a Venezuelan official, wrote to Charles III in 1781 noting the "vehement desire for independence" among Spanish Americans, who might resort to sedition as had recently been the case in Peru and New Granada. According to Abalos, the colonial victories in North America made the situation even more critical.[8] This awareness of the American Revolution's meaning for the Spanish colonies helps to explain the almost pathetic policy of nonrecognition and the containment of the American cause by Spain, so trenchantly described in *The Peacemakers* by Professor Richard B. Morris.[9]

The Portuguese government likewise resented the British, despite a long-standing friendship with England. As head minister of José I from 1755 to 1777, the marquis de Pombal was an inveterate anglophobe who believed that Brazil's gold riches of the first half of the 18th century had been usurped by the British thanks to the Methuen Treaty of 1703. To reverse this pattern, Pombal contrived a program of "nationalization" that favored the Portuguese and Brazilians at the expense of foreigners. These nationalistic measures, moreover, worked out better than expected. The decline of gold production at midcentury further reduced the English advantage in the Luso-Brazilian economy, arousing bitter feelings among the British interests affected. Europe's oldest alliance, in short, was under strain at the time of the American Revolution.[10]

Alarmed at the results of the Seven Years' War, Pombal was afraid that an unchecked British power in the New World might lead eventually to the seizure of Brazil. For a time it appeared that this apprehension would unite the Iberian powers against the common foe—a prospect that further aggravated relations between the British and the Portuguese governments. When Pombal heard of the trouble in North America, his anxiety about English intentions evaporated.[11]

Instead, Portugal embarked upon an aggressive campaign in 1775 to win British support for Pombal's expansionist designs in South America. In July 1776, Pombal took a stand against the American Revolution by closing all ports to the English rebels, a move that exposed his countrymen to the attacks of American privateers.[12] By August of that year, the Portuguese minister exhorted the English leadership to block the naval activities of the French and Spanish Bourbons at Brest and at Cádiz in order to deprive Americans of "the resources they at present rely upon." [13] England rejected his advice since it would have brought general war to Europe.

Pombal's devious relations with Spain explain the maneuvers mentioned above. While on the one hand he was assuring Spaniards that he wanted a friendly settlement of the Rio Grande do Sul confrontation, on the other he had ordered an attack upon the Spanish challengers. Spain countered this duplicity by outfitting the largest armada that had ever been sent to the New World, 116 ships and over 19,000 men. It left Cádiz on November 15, 1776, causing a stir in the diplomacy of the American Revolution. The armada proceeded to southern Brazil, where it thoroughly overwhelmed the enemy.[14] This striking success helps to account for Spain's eagerness to join with France in an attempt to invade England during the summer of 1779, a daring stroke that might have ended the war. That armada, however, was a dismal and costly failure.

Since Spain's role in the American Revolution is well known, let us concentrate instead on the momentous impact of that conflict upon the Spanish world.[15] To begin with, it brought Spanish officials and subjects into direct contact with English Americans on a larger scale than ever before, and these relationships had major ideological and economic consequences. Governor Bernardo de Gálvez of Louisiana struck up a close friendship with Oliver Pollack, who wanted to honor the Spaniard by placing his portrait in the American Congress. The Cuban General Juan Manuel de Cagigal was a great admirer of Washington's military genius.[16] The merchant Juan de Miralles cooperated enthusiastically with American leaders and helped to expedite

Spanish aid to the revolutionaries. Moreover, Miralles was vital in propagating the hemispheric image of our first President.[17] The Venezuelan Francisco de Miranda fought in the battle of Pensacola and, many years later, claimed that it was there that he first conceived of the program to liberate Spanish America.[18]

The financial drain of the American Revolution weakened Spain's position as a world power in the long run. The outfitting of various armadas (to Brazil, to England, and to Gibraltar) was expensive; so were the campaigns in the Floridas and in the Caribbean. If we add to this the cost of pacifying the rebellions in Peru and New Granada in the early 1780's, we can appreciate the financial predicament of the Spanish nation. The trend toward bankruptcy accelerated after the French Revolution of 1789, undermining Spain's rating as a European power and isolating her from her former colonies.

In a lengthy memorandum of 1776 to the Bourbon governments, Turgot emphasized that the rebellion of the English colonies marked a dramatic change in the relationship between Europe and the Americas. Anticolonialism was now a fact of life, and Spain, in particular, would do well to reckon with this reality.[19] There is some evidence to suggest that both Iberian powers tried to accommodate themselves to the new situation vis-à-vis their colonies.

As part of the nationalization program, Pombal adopted a strategy of tightening his control overseas by inviting Brazil's moneyed interests to participate in the government of their respective regions. Thus, he identified the colonial plutocracy with the interests of the mother country—a tactic that worked well so long as both interests were compatible.[20] The encouragement of regional interests, however, involved the risk of eventual separation if conditions changed. This regional, or federalistic, approach was also evident in the reforms of Charles III of Spain. It is not clear whether Spaniards were emulating their neighbor's example or whether the change resulted from the fashion of laissez-faire thought in Europe. At any rate, as noted by the Venezuelan official in 1781, the American Revolution contributed a sense of urgency to the reform movement in the Hispanic world.

The Spanish government announced a program of "free trade" in 1778 which liberalized the base of the colonial economy by opening up more ports. It was not true free trade, however, since all traffic between the Spanish colonies and Europe had to proceed via ports in Spain. The use of the term *free trade*, so popular among anticolonialists, may have resulted from the vogue of laissez-faire economics at the time, or it may have been intended to placate Spanish Americans so that they would not follow the revolutionary pattern of North Americans. It is also notable that "free trade" reform was accompanied by the authorization to establish new merchant guilds (*con-*

sulados) in Havana, Buenos Aires, Santiago de Chile, and Bogotá.[21] Other regions clamored for their own corporations; and in the early 1790's, a second group of consulados was authorized, suggesting that Spain had adopted the same regional tactic that we have described for Pombal's Brazil.[22] The new consulados, moreover, differed in their orientation from the older ones at Lima and Mexico City. Let us take the Guatemalan corporation as an example. It was open to both white merchants and landowners with fortunes over 20,000 pesos. The representation was regional (all of Central America) and not just limited to Guatemala City, the capital. Moreover, the Guatemalan consulado was progressive in outlook and dedicated to the economic development of the entire region. In 1811, it even proposed agrarian reform in the modern sense.[23]

Professor John Lynch has referred to the reforms of the 1770's as the "second conquest" of Spanish America, one in which the authorities in Madrid were determined to fasten their control over Spanish Creoles. Certainly this was the intent, but the use of the regional tactic was counterproductive in that it prepared the moneyed interests of America for eventual independence.[24] Many founding fathers of the Spanish American nations played an active role in these regional consulados and economic societies, thoroughly infused with the enlightened thought of the times.[25] To what extent the success of federalism in the United States encouraged the adoption of the regional strategy is a question that requires further study. We have already noted Foronda's admiration for the young republic's economic progress.

There was another reform proclaimed in 1787 which advocated the equality and union of the Spanish world. It apparently was Charles III's wish that his overseas subjects should enlist in local militias and agree to pay substantial taxes for the upkeep of the Spanish navy. There seems to have been an effort at this time to open up governmental positions to colonials in order to minimize the hostility between American Spaniards (*españoles americanos*) and European Spaniards (*españoles europeos*).[26] We need to study the execution of this reform, for it implies a conscious awareness of the anticolonialist potential in the Spanish Empire. In Central America, for example, Creoles and Spaniards shared the available municipal posts in Guatemala City.[27]

Spain and Portugal, moreover, favored a gradualist solution to the problem of anticolonialism, that is, they considered setting up federative monarchies overseas. Pombal, for example, urged his English ally to accept such a solution in 1775 by allowing a special parliament for North America.[28] It will be recalled that the count of Floridablanca likewise recommended a similar settlement before Spain entered the war against England, and he continued to favor this solution rather than accept the fact of American independence, so distasteful to him.[29] The Iberians, of course, did not invent the notion of feudal monarchies, which had a long historical tradition in Europe; moreover, other European statesmen were advocating this approach without much success as far as the American Revolution was concerned. It should be stressed, however, that the establishment of a federative monarchy in the colonial area, which might lead to a commonwealth arrangement, was a workable solution to anticolonialism on the part of the European powers.

At the turn of the century, some progressive figures in the Portuguese government looked with favor upon a scheme to transfer the royal court to Rio de Janeiro, recognizing that Brazil after all was the effective center of the Portuguese-speaking world from many points of view. As might be expected, the project flattered the Brazilians and ensured their loyalty to the government. Scheduled for 1803, the move was delayed by Portuguese nationalists. Yet it occurred in late 1807, just before the French took Lisbon.[30] The so-called "Brazilian Inversion" was a source of pride to Portuguese Americans—the ex-colony was now the metropolis and the ex-metropolis the colony. In 1815 Brazil gained the rank of kingdom, and the prospects for a federative monarchy were promising as the Napoleonic wars came to an end. During the 1821–22 hassle with the Lisbon authorities, Brazilian Americans favored a dual monarchy, but the mother country rejected the notion outright. Once Brazilian independence was a fact, the positions were reversed. Now Portuguese commissioners offered the federative solution and the Brazilian elite, like their English counterparts many years earlier, refused the offer, determined to guide their own destiny.[31]

The solution of a federative monarchy had a special attraction for the Spanish-speaking world. The Venezuelan official José de Abalos had recommended such a program in order to thwart anticolonialism and the example of the English colonies.[32] The most renowned advocate of the solution, however, was the count of Aranda, who made the Peace of 1783 possible by defying his instructions from Madrid. Although the authenticity of his 1783 letter to Charles III has been questioned, there is no debate about his 1786 proposals for imperial reorganization.[33] In the earlier project, Aranda allegedly recommended the division of the New World possessions among three Spanish princes, all linked by blood to the emperor in Madrid. With a common defense system and a reciprocal trade program, the Spanish world could thus protect itself against that ungrateful "pygmy," the United States, who as the "colossus" of the future would inevitably press upon the lands of Spanish America. Three years later, the count suggested the exchange of Spanish Peru, and even Chile if required, for European Portugal. Elsewhere, in the Plata a Spanish prince would reign and from Quito north the authorities in Madrid would maintain their control. The count of Floridablanca, Aranda's rival, refused to have anything to do with such projects.[34]

During the ensuing reign (1788–1808), Charles IV seriously considered the establishment of feudal monarchies overseas. Manuel Godoy, his favorite, urged the creation of a federative monarchy in Spanish Louisiana, an enlightened constitutional government that might attract American royalists and thus counter the influence of the United States government. There was another plan to divide Spanish America among Charles IV's two younger sons, his nephew Pedro, and Manuel Godoy himself, the "Prince of Peace." They were to act as viceroys for Spain, a project that had special appeal to the Spanish king. Unstable conditions in Europe, however, worked against the implementation of this scheme.[35]

As Napoleon's forces invaded the Iberian Peninsula in 1807–8, the new situation found loyal Spaniards underground and in the resistance movement. Napoleon captured the Spanish monarchs and held them prisoners in southern France while he placed his brother on the throne as Joseph I of Spain. The Napoleonic dynasty immediately sent out documentation to Spanish America announcing the change in government and welcoming officials overseas to continue in office, a proposal that sparked a fierce struggle for power between the Spanish hierarchy in America and the local Creoles. Meanwhile, in Spain, the provisional governments fought valiantly to oust the French invaders, supported by large financial contributions from America. Little by little, however, the provisional regime of Spain retreated southward to the port of Cádiz in late January, 1810. Refusing to be pushed into the sea, Spaniards withstood the siege of Cádiz for the next few years and thus gave loyal Spain a chance to embark upon a program of liberal reform that seemed to offer a solution to the colonial question.

During the second constitutional period in Madrid from 1820 to 1823, talk about establishing monarchies overseas was common. The Mexican delegation, for example, proposed the creation of three kingdoms in America, closely linked with the government of Ferdinand VII in Spain. The pride of the European, however, would not accept the arrangement. Yet, the dream of creating monarchies in the New World persisted throughout the 19th century as the Pan Hispanic movement strove to reconcile the differences between Spain and her former colonies. It failed to achieve the vaunted commonwealth relationship.[36]

The movements of anticolonialism and laissez-faire tended to complement each other. The acceptance of the new economic orientation in the Hispanic world, moreover, fostered an attack upon the mercantilist assumptions of the colonial system. Not all advocates of laissez-faire accepted the rejection of colonialism, to be sure, but the freedom to discuss the laissez-faire authors made it possible for anticolonialism to spread widely throughout the Spanish- and Portuguese-speaking world. The colonial areas were especially vulnerable and receptive to the new ideas. Since the American Revolution and its product the United States of America were identified with the new system of freedom, anticolonialist writers utilized the examples to the utmost, just as Foronda had done in his 1803 publication.

The impact of the Enlightenment upon the Hispanic world is well known to the students of that area, thanks to the significant contributions of many scholars since World War II.[37] It is not surprising, therefore, to learn that the *Wealth of Nations* by Adam Smith, which appeared in 1776, soon came to the attention of Spanish and Portuguese readers in the original English or, a few years later, in the French translation. Gaspar de Jovellanos, for example, who had read the English, French, and Spanish versions, once remarked with admiration, "How well he proves the advantage of free trade with the colonies."[38] The four-volume Spanish translation of 1794 by José Alonso Ortiz underscored the anticolonialist issue because the translator, in his commentary, argued the opposing point of view on the colonial question. Another prominent critic of Smith's anticolonialism was Ramón Lázaro de Dou y de Bassols, a Catalan industrialist.[39] Defending Smith's position, on the other hand, were such worthies as Valentín Foronda and Alvaro Flórez Estrada. The Spanish public, of course, benefited from the debate.[40] Smith's ideas were also popularized by the French economist Jean Baptiste Say and by Jeremy Bentham, an Englishman who left a deep imprint upon the Spanish world with his ideas on utilitarianism.[41]

Adam Smith's recognition in the Spanish world was brought out in 1807 in connection with university curriculum reforms. The government gave the institutions of higher learning a choice between two authors for the subject of political economy—J. B. Say or Adam Smith.[42] In either case, Spanish college students learned about laissez-faire and anticolonialism in the classroom.

The influence of the French Physiocrats in the Spanish- and Portuguese-speaking world is also well established. Since agriculture was the main economic activity in these areas, it is understandable that the ideas of François de Quesnay and his colleagues should be so popular. The point is documented by the appearance of the *Informe de Ley Agraria* in 1795, a thorough study of Spain's agrarian problem. The author was Gaspar de Jovellanos, whom we have already mentioned as an admirer of Adam Smith. The Informe was not exclusively his work, although Jovellanos did more than his share of the research. It was above all the product of the Economic Society of Madrid who was asked to investigate the theme in 1780 by the Council of Castile. For over a decade the best minds of Spain labored conscientiously in the review and evaluation of the world's literature on agriculture from the time of the Romans forward. Smith was cited in the Informe, and agricultural production figures for the United States demonstrated the operations of a free society. The conclusions of this famous report were significant—and we must remember that the Spanish government paid for its publication.

The Informe of 1795 minced no words in attacking the paternalism and centralization of the Bourbon government in Spain. On the other hand, it supported laissez-faire without equivocation and suggested a form of economic federalism that would permit the people of a region to have a say in its development. It opposed useless wars that involved nothing more than national pride or the greed of mercantile interests, and it stressed the fact that agriculture should have priority in the Spanish economy.[43] From the standpoint of Spanish America, it is probable that the Informe may have influenced the regionalist tactic mentioned in the previous section.

Moreover, the laissez-faire commitment in the Informe persisted through the constitutional periods at Cádiz and at Madrid in the first quarter of the 19th century. The same trend is evident in the Portuguese-speaking world; and it is notable that the first decree issued in Brazil by the Portuguese government in 1808 proclaimed "free trade." [44]

The popularity of laissez-faire thought in the Spanish world, as well as its implications for anticolonialism, was reflected in a decree of January 22, 1809, declaring that the overseas territories of Spain were integral parts of the nation and not colonies.[45] In effect, Spaniards had outlawed colonialism.

From 1810 to 1814 the American delegation at the Parliament or *Cortes* of Cádiz unanimously advocated laissez-faire economics and the eradication of all vestiges of the old colonial system. Americans and their Asian colleagues presented 11 demands to the Cortes of Spain on December 16, 1810, insisting upon effective equality with Peninsulars and many other reforms.[46] These demands were debated openly and heatedly in the parliamentary sessions of January–February 1811, and the published minutes of those meetings circulated widely throughout the Spanish world. All the anticolonialist arguments of European authors came out in these debates, and whenever the ex-colonials encountered resistance, which was often, they reminded their peninsular colleagues of the mistakes that England had made with regard to her North American colonies.

Throughout the spirited discussions, Americans evoked the notorious "Black Legend" characterization of Spain's tyranny and despotism during the colonial centuries, almost as if they had memorized Abbé Raynal's *Histoire Philosophique et Politique des Establissements et du Commerce, des Europeens dans les Deux Indes*. Americans, of course, did not need Raynal as a source for the Black Legend. The point is that American deputies at Cádiz employed the stereotype as an anticolonialist weapon. Its effect was to polarize opinion at Cádiz between European and American to the point that even sympathetic Spanish liberals were put on the defensive and ended up by elaborating a "White Legend" stereotype of Spain's beneficent rule overseas.[47] Moreover, the arrogance of certain Spaniards and the innuendoes of inferiority, so distasteful to Americans everywhere since the 18th century, widened the gap between Europeans and the New World delegation at Cádiz.[48] Americans, on the other hand, believed strongly in their own superiority; and the success of their English counterparts in North America supported this conviction, all of which built up a fierce pride in the New World and its destiny—a "mystique" which Professor Whitaker has called the "Western Hemisphere Idea." Others referred to it as the "American System." [49]

The unwillingness of the European mother countries to grant effective and equal political representation, the refusal of Spaniards to yield on "free trade" at both Cádiz and Madrid, and the annoying airs of superiority by Europeans left the Spanish and Portuguese Americans no alternative but independence.[50]

There were other Frenchmen besides the Physiocrats who influenced anticolonialism in the Hispanic world. The abbé Raynal's history, first published in 1770 and expanded in 1781 to include his impressions of the American Revolution, had a wide circulation despite the prohibitions of the Spanish Inquisition. It appears that Raynal's favorable coverage of Portuguese America made it more popular in Brazil than in Spanish America.[51] Spaniards, on the other hand, resented the Black Legend exaggerations of the French author. Nevertheless, an expurgated version by the marquis de Almodóvar, still bearing the anticolonialist message, was permitted to circulate by the Spanish government.[52]

More important than Raynal among Spanish readers was the abbé de Pradt, who claims to have been inspired by his countryman Raynal.[53] His book *Les Trois Ages des Colonies* appeared in 1802. The expanded version of 1817, however, was far more useful because of its comments on the Spanish American Revolution. The Spanish reading public—more than the Portuguese, it seems—clamored for translations of his many works, and some nine volumes circulated throughout Spain and Spanish America. More of his works were translated into Spanish than into any other language.[54]

Although the abbé employed all the arguments of the anticolonialists and cited the increased trade between the United States and England since the American Revolution as proof of the inadequacy of colonialism, he was nonetheless an imperialist at heart. Raynal had exclaimed: "Unhappy Europeans! Why have you Colonies?" Pradt said: "Happy Europeans! Is it possible to congratulate you too highly for possessing Colonies?" In effect, Pradt was an advocate of the new colonialism, that "Invisible Empire" of Europe over America. And in this relationship he envisioned the leadership of France at the expense of England. The means of exploitation would be the establishment of federative monarchies in the New World, closely connected with European dynasties. Recognizing the attraction of the "republicanism" of the United States in the Hispanic Americas, Pradt proposed to counter this influence by encouraging liberal constitutional monarchies. If we keep in mind the appeal of the Cádiz movement in Spanish America, we can thus appreciate the abbé's popularity. Moreover, his insistence upon the inevitability of Spanish American independence and his use of the successful example of the United States were both instrumental in molding a psychology of independence in Hispanic America.[55]

The Spanish- and Portuguese-speaking world learned of the American Revolution through direct contacts and by publications. Francisco de Miranda, for example, went on an extended tour of the young republic in 1783 and 1784, noting his impressions in a diary.[56] Because of Spain's involvement in the war, books describing the military conflict appeared almost immediately. A more complete study was published in 1793.[57]

Many Spanish and Portuguese reader who knew English and French had a greater range of publications to choose from in learning about the American Revolution and the United States. Their libraries included these works. Out on the frontier of Louisiana, for example, Governor Manuel Gayoso de Lemos had David Ramsay's two-volume history of the conflict, Thomas Jefferson's *Notes on Virginia*, and some pamphlets of 1775 and 1780 on American grievances. He also had a copy of Almodóvar's version of Raynal's *Histoire*.[58] Brazilian libraries likewise contained literature of the American Revolution and the legal documents associated with it.[59]

An influential account of the American Revolution was written by a native of Quito, Ecuador—Antonio de Alcedo y Bexarano—and published under the title *Diccionario geográfico-histórico de las Indias Occidentales o América*

(5 vols., Madrid, 1786–89). Based upon numerous references, in a wide variety of languages, relating to the history of the Western Hemisphere, Alcedo's work included an objective account of the British colonies in North America, how they were formed, the nature of the area and its people, and the causes for rebellion. Moreover, Alcedo reproduced in its entirety a revolutionary handbill circulated in Boston and elsewhere in the colonies in 1774. The final line must have impressed Spanish readers in the New World: "Awaken then, Americans, never before has the region that you inhabit seen itself covered by such dark clouds. You are called rebels because you do not want to pay tribute; justify your pretensions with your valor, or seal the loss with all your blood."[60]

Despite the reluctance of their nation to recognize the English Americans, Spaniards were nonetheless curious about the young country and its people. Professor Morris has noted Floridablanca's curiosity and how much time John Jay spent in satisfying his questions about the United States.[61] Another prominent Spanish official, Pedro Rodríguez de Campomanes, a great economist and advisor to Charles III, was interested in establishing an intellectual connection with the American Philosophical Society. He became an honorary member of the Philadelphia organization and, through his chairmanship of the Spanish Academia de Historia, encouraged a profitable exchange of books and minutes between the two organizations. In 1784 the academy invited Benjamin Franklin into its ranks for his recognition of Spanish letters. And there were many other Spanish and Portuguese scientists, diplomats, and literary figures who became members of American intellectual associations, an experience in cultural exchange that has been recorded in Professor Harry Bernstein's *Origins of Inter-American Interest*.[62]

The American Revolution stimulated and expanded the economic contacts between the United States and the Hispanic area. The trade between Spain and the young republic was substantial, and whenever Spain could not service her colonies during the French revolutionary and Napoleonic periods, neutral shipping, like that of the United States, was permitted temporarily to frequent Spanish American ports. To be sure, Spain's policy was inconsistent, but whether legal or illegal, the traffic with North Americans increased notably in the nearby Caribbean area and even expanded into the ports of South America. American consuls and merchants made their presence felt everywhere; they were living examples of the American Revolution and proudly displayed copies of the key documents in their nation's history. Moreover, their optimism and faith in their young country inspired the other Americans to emulate their example.[63]

The first serious conspiracy in the Hispanic Americas to follow the pattern of the English colonies unwound itself in the interior of Brazil at Minas Gerais in 1789, the so-called "Inconfidencia" or Tiradentes' Conspiracy. Although it aborted, the men involved in the planning were thoroughly familiar with the literature of the American Revolution and the anticolonialists, and as early as 1786 one of them had communicated with Thomas Jefferson about their expectations of duplicating the American example. As men of property, for the most part, they felt the effects of the depression in the gold fields and imagined that their grievances toward the mother country paralleled those of the English Americans a few years earlier.[64]

In 1798 another insurgency broke out in Bahia, but this one followed the French and Haitian pattern of social revolution. As a result, it frightened the white elite of Brazil because the rebel leaders were black. Moreover, the Brazilian whites were moving toward an accommodation with the enlightened officials of the Portuguese government. In their view republicanism had been discredited by its identification with the excesses of the French and Haitian revolutions. Above all, the Brazilian elite wished to avoid social chaos.[65]

Terrified at the outbreak of the French Revolution, even more so than he had been of the American Revolution, the count of Floridablanca desperately tried to turn back the clock on enlightened thought in his country. In 1790 the Inquisition banned a host of allegedly subversive books, and in the following year Floridablanca closed the economic societies in Spain and suspended all periodicals that spread ideas of the Enlightenment.[66] A royal order prohibited the circulation of medals overseas commemorating the American Revolution with the provocative words *Libertad Americana*.[67] The effect of this persecution, as well as the new wave of persecution in 1801, was to force the independence movement in Spanish America underground. It also disenchanted many Spanish subjects overseas by reminding them of their subservience to a distant and arbitrary mother country in Europe.[68] It is important to recognize, however, that these episodes of censorship in the Hispanic world were not always enforceable or long lasting.

A Peruvian Jesuit wrote a letter in 1791 which underscored the results of such persecution. Published in 1799 by Francisco de Miranda and widely circulated throughout the Spanish world, the letter was addressed to all Spanish Americans. Father Juan Pablo Viscardo y Guzmán pointed out in his message that increased taxation had been a basic grievance in the uprisings of Peru and New Granada during the early 1780's. He pleaded with his readers, moreover, to reject the promises made by Spain in the decree of July 8, 1787, announcing the "system of union and equality." It was merely a scheme to force Americans to pay from one-half to one-third of Spain's naval expenses. The Spanish government had always violated the rights of Americans, and it was time for Spanish America to emancipate herself. A big continent should not have to depend upon a weak nation like Spain. Then came his famous quotation on the American Revolution: "The valor with which the English colonies of America have fought for their liberty, which they gloriously enjoy, covers our indolence with shame; we have yielded to them the palm with which they have been the first to crown the New World by their sovereign independence." [69]

Others followed Father Viscardo into the revolutionary camp. In 1794, Antonio Nariño of Colombia was brought before the Spanish authorities for his revolutionary publications and translations, including *The Rights of Man* by Thomas Paine. A printer like his hero Benjamin Franklin, whose portrait he owned, Nariño defended his admiration for the United States with these words: "Oh Fatherland of the Franklins, of the Washingtons, of the Hancocks, and of the Adamses, who is not glad that they lived both for themselves and for us." Although Nariño was imprisoned for his audacity, with the independence of his country he reappeared as an editor of *La Bagatela*, inspiring his readers with the message of the American Revolution.[70]

Francisco de Miranda's odyssey in behalf of the liberation of Spanish America is too well known to repeat here. It ended in failure in 1806, but the preliminary document signed in Paris on December 27, 1797, provides some meaningful insights. It reveals, for example, that there were cells of collaborationists throughout the New World and Spain—two of the men who signed the document had been sent to Paris by the underground junta in Madrid. The first article of the document, moreover, highlighted the argument and the approach employed by potential revolutionaries in Spanish America since the outbreak of the American Revolution: it was to remind the English that they had lost their colonies in North America because of Spain's intervention in the revolution. It was now England's turn to reciprocate! The prospective alliance between England and Spanish America offered commercial attractions to the British. The allies agreed to sponsor the construction of passageways across both Panama and Nicaragua, and there were plans for a hemispheric gathering of the Spanish-speaking sections. The United States could join the alliance if it provided a corps of 5,000 infantrymen and 2,000 cavalrymen for the emancipation movement. Such a force would also be made available for the defense of the new Spanish American nation in the event of a future attack.[71] The United States, however, held back on the project, feeling that England stood to gain most from the arrangement.[72]

As Spanish Americans committed themselves to independence, they chose the American Revolution as their guiding star. In addition to their own heroes and symbols that emerged from the emancipation of Hispanic America, they also utilized those of English America. They took pride in the military genius and political shrewdness of George Washington, the scientific prowess and practicality of Benjamin Franklin, and the political insights of Thomas Paine and Thomas Jefferson, only to mention the more recognizable figures in the Spanish- and Portuguese-speaking world. All the famous documents of the American Revolutionary period were translated and commented upon by publicists in the New World, and Spanish Americans borrowed liberally from them in drawing up their own governmental systems. The success of federalism in the United States particularly impressed them, the more so because it buttressed their own historical inclinations and the Bourbon and Pombalian reforms of the late 18th century. The Cádiz Constitution of 1812 also pointed them toward the benefits of federalism.

It is interesting to note that even Napoleon's spies in the New World resorted to the example of the United States in order to advance their master's designs upon the Western Hemisphere. When Napoleon realized that the Americans were not welcoming his brother's regime in Spain but, on the contrary, were financing the resistance movement on the peninsula against the French, he reversed his former strategy to one in favor of American independence, hoping thus to tie the grateful new countries to his influence at the expense of England and the United States. He instructed his spies to guide the Creoles as follows:

> You will demonstrate to them the difference that exists between the United States and the Spanish Americas; the happiness that those Americans enjoy, their progress in commerce, agriculture, and navigation, and the pleasure that they derive from being free of the European yoke, just with their own patriotic and elected government; and you will assure them that with the freedom of Spain's Americas, they will be the legislators of the universe.[73]

The appeal of the United States model was particularly strong in northern South America from 1810 to 1812. The Venezuelan Juan G. Roscio once again translated Paine's *Rights of Man* in 1810, and his countryman Manuel García de Sena circulated translations of other writings by Thomas Paine, in addition to the Articles of Confederation, the Constitution of the United States, and the state constitutions of Connecticut, Massachusetts, New Jersey, Pennsylvania, and Virginia. Extracts of these publications appeared frequently in Venezuelan periodicals that were available from 1812 to 1824.[74] The fiery Colombian Miguel de Pombo made the same writings available to the founding fathers of his country who drew up the Charter of 1811. He told his countrymen that the Constitution of the United States "has promoted the happiness of our brothers of the North and will promote our happiness also, if we imitate their virtues and adopt their principles." [75] On another occasion, Pombo told an audience in Bogotá that "the American voice is raised and it has sworn to avenge the blood of its Franklins and Washingtons." [76]

The future nations of southern South America likewise acknowledged their debt to the United States. The following verse appeared in the *Gazeta de Buenos Aires* on October 25, 1810:

> If there was a Washington in the North land,
> We have many Washingtons in the South;
> If arts and commerce have prospered there.—
> Courage, fellow countrymen:
> Let us follow their example. [77]

In another issue of the same periodical, the famous Argentine Mariano Moreno quoted from Jefferson's *Notes on Virginia* on the theme of federalism. [78] General Manuel Belgrano took pride in his translation of Washington's Farewell Address; even José Gaspar de Francia, the dictator of Paraguay, spoke warmly of the United States. [79] So did José Artigas of Uruguay. [80]

The North Carolinian Joel Poinsett was a key influence in both Argentina and Chile from 1810 to 1814, as he was 10 years later in Mexico as well. In Chile, he collaborated with José Miguel Carrera, one of the liberal leaders. He was also a good friend of the liberal priest Camilo Enríquez, editor of various periodicals of the time, who overflowed with enthusiasm and admiration for the United States, the "Sun of America" and the "beacon which we should follow." [81]

It is impossible to exhaust here today the vein of admiration for the American Revolution that existed in the Hispanic world. Suffice it to say that the successful movement in North America served as inspiration for the emancipation of the Americas to the south. It was perhaps an inevitable development, for anticolonialism was a movement whose time had come. As believers in the Enlightenment, the white American elites in Spanish and Portuguese America felt an affinity for their English-speaking brothers to the north, whose grievances toward the European mother country and the oppressive colonial system they could understand. Moreover, they resented the degrading relationship vis-à-vis their European counterparts, implying that Americans were in some way inferior. This made no sense to Americans of the New World, and if they could not achieve equality with the European whites, they then preferred to go it alone. Besides, with all the bountiful resources of America, of what value was a Europe that was continually at war?

We are now beginning to appreciate the fact that the elites of Brazil and Spanish America actually preferred constitutional monarchy for their areas, since it would provide historical continuity and preserve order in racially and culturally divided societies. Moreover, the American Revolution appealed to these elites precisely because it produced an exemplary republic in almost the classical sense. This was not true of the French Revolution and the Haitian debacle of the 1790's, which discredited republicanism in their midst. Francisco de Miranda understood this point. He told a friend of his in 1799 that they had two examples before them: the American Revolution and the French Revolution. His advice was: "let us imitate discreetly the former; let us avoid with utmost care the fatal effects of the latter." [82]

The American Revolution had a dramatic impact upon the Spanish- and Portuguese-speaking world, much more than is usually realized. Yet it is not surprising that it did if we consider that these were the areas where anticolonialism was bound to reassert itself. Moreover, the resort of the Iberian mother countries to what could be called federalistic reforms, as well as the consideration given to proposals in behalf of federative or feudal monarchies overseas, heightened the realization everywhere that the old colonial relationship was changing, along the lines that Turgot had predicted in 1750. Also, the encouragement of laissez-faire economics in both countries led to the insistence upon free trade and the corresponding rejection of mercantilist assumptions. The events at Cádiz demonstrated the logical conclusion of the trend that had been unleashed in the Hispanic world. And the model of the United States as the open society of the future, as well as the stimulus that it gave to the movement of anticolonialism in the New World, combined to promote the spread of the "Greater American Revolution" from 1775 to 1825, a notion which the late Herbert Eugene Bolton used to stress among his students at Berkeley.

Notes

[1] Anne Robert Jacques Turgot, Second discours, Sorbonne, December 11, 1750, *Oeuvres de Turgot*, ed. Eugène Daire and Hippolyte Dussard, 2 vols. (Paris: Guillaumin Libraire, 1844), 2:602.

[2] J. R. Spell, "An Illustrious Spaniard in Philadelphia, Valentín de Foronda," *Hispanic Review* 4, no. 2 (April 1936), 136–40; José de Onís, "Valentín de Foronda's Memoir on the United States of North America, 1804," *The Americas* 4, no. 3 (January 1948): 351–87.

[3] Robert S. Smith, "A Proposal for the Barter and Sale of Spanish America in 1800," *Hispanic American Historical Review* (hereafter *HAHR*) 41, no. 2 (May 1961), 275–86. The letter is dated March 1, 1800, but the publication date was 1803 (Philadelphia). The Spanish title is: *Carta sobre lo que debe hacer un príncipe que tenga colonias a gran distancia.*

⁴ Ibid., pp. 285–86.

⁵ "Mémoire sur la manière dont la France et l'Espagne devaient envisager les suites de la querelle entre la Grande-Bretagne et ses colonies," April 6, 1776, *Oeuvres de Turgot*, 2:551–85; for specific allusions to Charles III, see pp. 566, 569, and 582.

⁶ Richard Herr, *The Eighteenth-Century Revolution in Spain* (Princeton: Princeton University Press, 1958), p. 147, as well as the entire chapter 5, "Industrial Renaissance and Stagnation," pp. 120–53. See also Ramón Ezquerra, "La crítica española de la situación de América en el siglo XVIII," *Revista de Indias* 22 (January–June 1962), 159–286, which discusses the reformers of this period.

⁷ Consulta, Consejo de Estado, Cádiz, March 17, 1813, Archivo Histórico Nacional (Madrid), Sección Estado, Libro 50, 104 folios, reviewing the tobacco question up to that date.

⁸ Carlos E. Muñoz Oraá, "Pronóstico de la independencia de América, y un proyecto de monarquías en 1781," *Revista de Historia de América* (México), no. 50 (December 1960), 439–73 (document on pp. 460–69).

⁹ Richard B. Morris, *The Peacemakers; the Great Powers and American Independence* (New York: Harper Torchbook edition, 1970), pp. 14–66, 95–121, 150–51, 218–47, 278–79, 305–10, 320–27, 341–44, 388–425, 457.

¹⁰ Kenneth R. Maxwell, *Conflicts and Conspiracies: Brazil & Portugal 1750–1808* (Cambridge: Cambridge University Press, 1973), pp. 19, 22, 32–38, 42, 49–59, 71–72, and his article "Pombal and the Nationalization of the Luso-Brazilian Economy," *HAHR* 48, no. 4 (May 1968): 608–31. Also consult the study by S. Sideri, *Trade and Power: Informal Colonialism in Anglo-Portuguese Relations* (Rotterdam: Rotterdam University Press, 1970).

¹¹ Maxwell, *Conflicts*, pp. 33–38, especially footnote 2, p. 35.

¹² Dauril Alden, "The Undeclared War of 1773–1777: Climax of Luso-Spanish Platine Rivalry," *HAHR* 41, no. 1 (February 1961): 55–74; Raul D'Eça, "Colonial Brazil as an Element in the Early Diplomatic Negotiations Between the United States and Portugal, 1776–1808," in A. C. Wilgus, ed., *Colonial Hispanic America* (Washington: George Washington University Press, 1936), pp. 551–57, especially pp. 551 and 553.

¹³ Richard W. Van Alstyne, *Empire and Independence; the International History of the American Revolution* (New York: John Wiley & Sons, 1965), pp. 93–94, quoting at length a letter from Walpole to Weymouth, no. 39, August 17, 1776, SP 89/82, PRO.

¹⁴ Alden, "Undeclared War," pp. 67–69, 71–73.

¹⁵ In addition to the works already cited by Morris and Van Alstyne, see Samuel Flagg Bemis, *The Diplomacy of the American Revolution* (Bloomington: Indiana University Press, 1957); Manuel Conrotte, *La Intervención de España en la Independencia de los Estados Unidos de la América del Norte* (Madrid: Librería general de Victoriano Suárez, 1920); and Juan F. Yela Utrilla, *España ante la guerra de la independencia de los Estados Unidos*, 2 vols. (Lérida: Gráficos Academia Mariana, 1925).

¹⁶ John W. Caughey, *Bernardo de Gálvez in Louisiana, 1776–1783* (Berkeley: University of California Press, 1934), p. 101; James A. Robertson, "Spanish Correspondence Concerning the American Revolution," *HAHR* 1, no. 3 (August 1918): 299–316; José de Onís, *The United States as Seen by Spanish American Writers, 1776–1890* (New York: Hispanic Institute in the United States, 1952), pp. 32, 38, quoting a letter from Cagigal to Washington dated May 25, 1783.

[17] Helen Matzke McCadden, "Juan de Miralles and the American Revolution," *The Americas* 29, no. 3 (January 1973): 359–75; see also Herminio Portell Vilá, *Juan de Miralles, un habanero amigo de Jorge Washington* (Havana: Sociedad Colombista Panamericana, 1947).

[18] William S. Robertson, *Hispanic American Relations With the United States* (New York and London: Oxford University Press, 1923), p. 61, referring to an article by Miranda entitled "Emancipation of Spanish America" which appeared in the *Edinburgh Review* (1809.)

[19] "Mémoire," April 6, 1776, *Oeuvres de Turgot*, 2, 559, 563, 565–66 (on Spain).

[20] Maxwell, *Conflicts*, pp. 44–46.

[21] Robert S. Smith, "*The Wealth of Nations* in Spain and Hispanic America, 1780–1830," *Journal of Political Economy* 65, no. 2 (April 1957): 121; Harry Bernstein, *Origins of Inter-American Interest, 1700–1812* (Philadelphia: University of Pennsylvania Press, 1945), p. 10. In Juan Sempere y Guarinos, *Ensayo de una biblioteca española de los mejores escritores del reynado de Carlos III*, 6 vols. (Madrid: Real, 1785–89), 2:91–93, much credit for the free-trade decision is given to Pedro Rodríguez de Campomanes, a strong advocate of freeing trade within the peninsula and overseas as well as the elimination of the single customhouse at Cádiz. Elsewhere (1:138–40), it was also suggested that Spaniards were reacting to Raynal's *Histoire*. Hoping that the free-trade measure would stimulate national industry, the count of Floridablanca encouraged the economic societies of Spain to capitalize upon the opportunity (1:143).

[22] Irving A. Leonard and Robert S. Smith, "A Proposed Library for the Merchant Guild of Veracruz," *HAHR* 24, no. 1 (February 1944): 84, referring to the case of the Vera Cruz merchants who petitioned for the establishment of a consulado in 1781, realizing it on April 25, 1795.

[23] The initial petition appears in "Reglas porque se ha de gobernar el nuevo Consulado que se debe establecer en la Nueba Ciudad de Goathemala . . .," Guatemala City, October 24, 1787, Archivo General de Centroamérica, Al. 5, legajo 2266, expediente 16437; and "Apuntamientos sobre la agricultura y el comercio del Reyno de Guatemala," March 29, 1811, in *Economía guatemalteca en los siglos XVIII y XIX*, 3d ed. (Guatemala City: Universidad de San Carlos de Guatemala, 1970), pp. 21–70, a remarkable document that illustrates many of my generalizations about laissez-faire economics in the next section.

[24] John Lynch, *The Spanish-American Revolutions, 1808–1826* (New York: W. W. Norton & Co., 1973), pp. 4–10. Among the reforming ministers of Charles III who urged more involvement of the Americans in order to ensure their loyalty was Pedro Rodríguez de Campomanes, a Spanish economist who was influenced by Adam Smith and the French Physiocrats. See Ezquerra, "Crítica española," pp. 217–23.

[25] R. S. Smith, "*Wealth of Nations* in Spain," pp. 121–25.

[26] Francisco Iturri to Colonel Antonio de Alcedo, March 11, 1789, *The Americas* 8, no. 1 (July 1951): 88, quoting the decree of July 8, 1787, as follows: "mientras se examina lo q.e más convenga a la felicidad de mis vasallos de éstos, y aquellos dominios, y al sistema de unión, e igualdad de unos y otros, qe deseo eficazmente se establesca." While this Jesuit father favored the decree, another one warned that it was insincere and calculated to enslave the Americas. See Juan Pablo Viscardo y Guzmán, *Lettre aux Espagnols-Américans* (Philadelphia, 1799), reproduced in the appendix of Carlos A. Villanueva's *Historia y Diplomacia, Napoleón y la independencia de América* (Paris, Garnier Hermanos, 1911), pp. 295–321 (see especially p. 316). For the Spanish translation, *Carta dirigida a los españoles americanos. Hermanos y compatriotas* (London, 1801), see the appendix of Manuel Giménez Fernández'

Las doctrinas populistas en la independencia de Hispano-América (Seville: Escuela de Estudios Hispano-Americanos de Sevilla, 1947), pp. 645–66.

²⁷ The cooperation of Americans and Spaniards in the city government of Guatemala City was exemplary. By 1810 both groups favored economic development of Central America. They differed, however, on the issue of free trade. The Americans advocated a free program in the *Instrucciones para la constitución fundamental de la monarquia española y su gobierno de que ha de tratarse en las próximas cortes generales* (Guatemala City: Editorial del Ministerio de Educación Pública, 1953), which formed the instructions of October 16, 1810 to the Guatemalan deputy at Cádiz; the protectionist views of four Spaniards, on the other hand, appear in the "Apuntes Instructivos pa. 'el Diputado de Cortes de Guatemala," Guatemala City, December 20, 1810, in *Revista de la Facultad de Ciencias Jurídicas y Sociales de Guatemala*, series 3.a, vol. 2, no. 1 (March–April 1939), 136–59.

²⁸ Dauril Alden, "The Marquis de Pombal and the American Revolution," *The Americas* 17, no. 4 (April 1961): 369–82, with the document dated November 28, 1775.

²⁹ Morris, *Peacemakers*, pp. 150–51.

³⁰ Kenneth R. Maxwell, "The Generation of the 1790s and the Idea of Luso-Brazilian Empire," in Dauril Alden, ed., *Colonial Roots of Modern Brazil* (Berkeley: University of California Press, 1973), pp. 107–44, focuses on this theme, which is also treated in his book *Conflicts* (see note 10).

³¹ Alan K. Manchester, "The Rise of the Brazilian Aristocracy," *HAHR* 11, no. 2 (May 1931): 164–68; Clarence H. Haring, *Empire in Brazil; a New World Experiment with Monarchy* (Cambridge: Harvard University Press, 1958), pp. 12–13, 27–28.
A comprehensive and timely volume has come out since the completion of this manuscript: A. J. R. Russell-Wood, ed., *From Colony to Nation: Essays on the Independence of Brazil* (Baltimore and London: Johns Hopkins University Press, 1975). Professor Russell-Wood introduces the series of essays with a masterly review of the colonial period, "Preconditions and Precipitants of the Independence Movement in Portuguese America," pp. 3–40. The section on political aspects includes studies by Emília Viotti da Costa ("The Political Emancipation of Brazil," pp. 43–88), Maria Odila Silva Dias ("The Establishment of the Royal Court in Brazil," pp. 89–108), and Stanley E. Hilton ("The United States and Brazilian Independence," pp. 109–29), underscoring the competition of monarchy versus republic in the relations of the two countries. The second part, on social aspects, contains significant studies by Stuart B. Schwartz ("Elite Politics and the Growth of a Peasantry in the Late Colonial Period," pp. 133–54) and Richard M. Morse ("Brazil's Urban Development: Colony and Empire," pp. 155–81). The final section, on cultural aspects, includes articles by Manoel Da Silveira Cardozo ("The Modernization of Portugal and the Independence of Brazil," pp. 185–210) and E. Bradford Burns ("The Intellectuals as Agents of Change and the Independence of Brazil, 1724–1822," pp. 211–46).

³² See note 8.

³³ For a good review of the historiography on this point, see Arthur P. Whitaker, "The Pseudo-Aranda Memoir of 1783," *HAHR* 17, no. 3 (August 1937): 287–313, which argues against its authenticity, and Almon R. Wright, "The Aranda Memorial: Genuine or Forged?," *HAHR* 18, no. 4 (November 1938): 445–60, which raises some doubts about the Whitaker position.

³⁴ "Dictamen reservado que el conde de Aranda dió al Rey sobre la independencia de las

colonias inglesas, después de haber hecho el tratado de paz ajustado en Paris el año de 1783,"
in Pedro de Urquinaona y Pardo, *Resumen de las causas principales que prepararon y dieron
impulso a la emancipación de la América española* (Madrid: L. F. de Angulo, 1835), pp. 62–68.
See also Mark Van Aken, *Pan Hispanism: Its Origin and Development to 1866* (Berkeley:
University of California Press, 1959), pp. 1–3; Ezquerra, "Crítica española," pp. 213, 215–16.

[35] Ibid., pp. 248–52.

[36] Van Aken, *Pan Hispanism*, pp. 3–16.

[37] In addition to the work by Professor Herr, already cited, see Arthur P. Whitaker, ed.,
Latin America and the Enlightenment, 2d ed. (Ithaca: Cornell University Press, 1961); John
Tate Lanning, *The Eighteenth-Century Enlightenment in the University of San Carlos de Guate-
mala* (Ithaca: Cornell University Press, 1956); R. S. Smith, *"Wealth of Nations* in Spain,"
pp. 104–25; Irving A. Leonard and R. S. Smith, "A Proposed Library," pp. 84–102. For the
Portuguese-speaking world, see the two articles by E. Bradford Burns, "The Role of Azeredo
Coutinho in the Enlightenment of Brazil," *HAHR* 44, no. 2 (May 1964): 145–60, and "The
Enlightenment in Two Colonial Brazilian Libraries," *Journal of the History of Ideas* 25, no. 3
(July–September 1964), 430–38.

[38] R. S. Smith, *"Wealth of Nations* in Spain," p. 107. The popularity overseas of Adam
Smith, as well as of the French Physiocrats, is illustrated in the *Gazeta de Guatemala*, which
frequently quoted them; see, for example, the issues of July 7, 1800 (Physiocrats), and June
30, 1800, in which the editor referred to Adam Smith as a man with "pelo en pecho" (hair
on his chest)!

[39] R. S. Smith, *"Wealth of Nations* in Spain," pp. 109, 113–19.

[40] Ibid., p. 106; see also Valentín de Foronda, *Cartas sobre los asuntos más exquisitos de la
economía política, y sobre las leyes criminales*, 2 vols. (Madrid: M. González, 1789–94), and
Alvaro Flórez Estrada, *Examen imparcial de las disensiones de la América con la España* ...
(Cádiz: D. M. Ximénez Careño, 1812), a bitter attack upon the colonial trade system of
Spain.

[41] W. Stark, *Jeremy Bentham's Economic Writings*, 3 vols. (reprint ed., New York: Burt
Franklin, 1952–54), 1:48–51, referring to Bentham's popularity in Spain from 1820 to 1821.
Impressed with the writings of Josiah Tucker and others, Bentham also attacked the financial
burden of having a navy and of fighting colonial wars (1:211–18). During the French Revolution he wrote a pamphlet entitled "Emancipate your Colonies," which received much publicity in France; there is also an unpublished manuscript which he wrote for his Spanish friends
entitled "Rid yourselves of ultramarina" (1:37–38).

[42] Acta, July 20, 1820, Diario de las Cortes (Madrid), 1:210, alluding to the royal cédula
of July 12, 1807.

[43] Gaspar de Jovellanos, "Informe de la Sociedad económica de Madrid al Real y Supremo
Consejo de Castilla en el expediente de Ley Agraria," 1795, in Venceslao de Linares y Pa-
checo, ed., *Obras de Jovellanos*, 8 vols. (Barcelona: Imprenta Don Francisco de Oliva, 1839–
40), 7:29–185. See also "Noticia histórica del Excmo. Señor Don Gaspar Melchor de Jovellanos," by the editor of his *Obras*, 8:205–28, containing a brief biography of Jovellanos and a
digest of the Informe

[44] Maxwell, *Conflicts*, pp. 136, 224–30; E. Bradford Burns, *A History of Brazil* (New York:
Columbia University Press, 1970), pp. 101–2. José da Silva Lisboa, a follower of Adam Smith,

had been among those who advised the 1808 move. Da Costa's article (see note 31) elaborates upon the political implications of laissez-faire thought in Portuguese America, regarding it as a consequence of the rise of "industrial capitalism."

[45] Decree, Junta Central, Sevilla, January 22, 1809, Archivo Histórico Nacional (Madrid), Sección Estado, legajo 54, expediente D, documento 71.

[46] "Proposiciones que hacen al Congreso Nacional los diputados de América y Asia," Isla de León, December 16, 1810, in José Alvarez de Toledo y Dubois, *Manifiesto o satisfacción pundonorosa a todos los buenos españoles europeos, y a todos los pueblos de la América, por un diputado de las Cortes reunidas en Cádiz* (Philadelphia, 1811), a copy of which can be found in the Rare Book Room of the Library of Congress. For an English version, see William Walton, *An Exposé on the Dissentions of Spanish America* (London: Booth & Co., 1814), pp. 282–89, by an Englishman who favored free trade with Spanish America.

[47] See, for example, Agustín Argüelles, *Examen histórico de la reforma constitucional que hicieron las Cortes Generales y Extraordinarias*, 2 vols. (London: C. Wood e Hijo, 1835), 1:310–74, and 2:24–58: also, Diario de las Cortes (Cádiz), minutes of January 9 and 18, 1811, and February 13, 1811; also Semanario Patriótico (Cádiz), March 5, 1812, reflecting a typical Spaniard's view of the loose character and morality of Americans.

[48] James F. King, "The Colored Castes and the American Representation in the Cortes of Cádiz," *HAHR* 33, no. 1 (February 1953), 33–64, and his excellent analysis of the struggle over political representation in the Spanish Parliament; Antonello Gerbi, *The Dispute of the New World; the History of a Polemic, 1750–1900*, rev. and enl., trans. Jeremy Moyle (Pittsburgh: University of Pittsburgh Press, 1973), treats the reaction of the Americans to notions about the inferiority of peoples in the New World.

[49] Arthur P. Whitaker, *The Western Hemisphere Idea: Its Rise and Decline* (Ithaca: Cornell University Press, 1954); and Mario Rodríguez, *A Palmerstonian Diplomat in Central America, Frederick Chatfield, Esquire* (Tucson: University of Arizona Press, 1964), pp. 56–57, describing the opposition of the British agent to the ideological bond between the Central American liberals and the North American Ephraim George Squier.

[50] The disillusionment of Spanish Americans in both constitutional periods is captured in a pamphlet by Fernando A. Dávila entitled *Exposición del Padre Fernando Antonio Dávila, diputado por la provincia de Chiapa en apoyo de la que presentó a las Cortes la Diputación Americana en la sesión del día 25 de junio, del corriente año* (Madrid, 1821), pp. 1–28.

[51] Maxwell, *Conflicts*, pp. 82, 132, 138–39.

[52] Ezquerra, "Crítica española," p. 274; Hans Wolpe, *Raynal et sa Machine de Guerre' L'Histoire des Deux Indes et ses Perfectionnements* (Stanford: Stanford University Press, 1957)' pp. 8–9, 68–69, 112–13, 115–17; Onís, *Spanish American Writers*, p. 42. See also G. T. F. Raynal, *L'Anticolonialisme au XVIIIᵉ Siècle . . .*, ed. Gabriel Esquer (Paris: Presses Universitaires de France, 1951), with comments and an analysis of the sections in Raynal's work dealing with anticolonialism.

[53] For an excellent evaluation of the man and his work, see Laura Bornholdt, "The Abbé de Pradt and the Monroe Doctrine," *HAHR* 24, no. 2 (May 1944), 201–21; Abbé de Pradt, *The Colonies and the Present American Revolutions* (London: Baldwin, Cradock, and Joy, 1817), pp. iii–vi; Manuel Aguirre Elorriaga, *El Abate de Pradt en la emancipación hispanoamericana (1800–1830)* (Rome: Typis Pontificiae Universitatis Gregorianae, 1941), a detailed study of the abbé's influence upon specific countries of Latin America.

[54] Bornholdt, "Abbé de Pradt," pp. 201, 207.

[55] Pradt, *The Colonies*, p. 108 and elsewhere.

[56] Onís, *Spanish American Writers*, pp. 51–57, provides a summary of Miranda's major impressions; see also William S. Robertson, ed., *The Diary of Francisco de Miranda, Tour of the United States, 1783–1784* (New York: Hispanic Society of America, 1928), with an introduction and notes by the editor; and *Archivo del General Miranda*, 24 vols. (Caracas: Editorial Sur-América, 1929–50), 1:192–338, which is preceded by Miranda's "Diario de Panzacola," (pp. 141–91).

[57] Onís, *Spanish American Writers*, pp. 21–22, 39–40, citing the works of Francisco Alvarez (Madrid, 1778), Juan Bautista Muñoz (1779), and Josef de Covarrubia (1783); the last work was dedicated to the Count of Floridablanca. Odet Julien Leboucher was the author of the 1793 volume *Historia de la última guerra* (Alcalá, Spain).

[58] Irving A. Leonard, "A Frontier Library, 1799," *HAHR* 23, no. 1 (February 1943), 21–51, which comments upon and reproduces the lists of books belonging to Manuel Gayoso de Lemos. See items on pp. 37, 41, 43, 46, and 50. Perhaps the most impressive evidence of Spain's familiarity with the literature of the American Revolution and the United States in all languages was the manuscript by Antonio de Alcedo y Bexarano, "Biblioteca Americana, Catálogo de la América en diferentes idiomas y noticia de su vida y patria, años en que vivieron, y obras que escribieron," finished in Coruña, Spain, in 1807. It was originally supposed to have been the bibliography for his *Diccionario*, which is mentioned in the text of this essay. The original manuscript is in the New York Public Library. Fortunately, in honor of the Ecuadorian author, the Municipality of Quito has published the *Biblioteca* in 2 volumes (Publicaciones del Museo Municipal de Arte e Historia, vol. 32, books 1 and 2, Quito, 1964–65). It includes works covering the entire colonial period for all of the Americas. On English America, the names and works of Ramsey and Hodge are typical of those listed for the American Revolution. There are, in addition, specific references for the various states. See José de Onís, "Alcedo's Biblioteca Americana," *HAHR* 31, no. 3 (August 1951): 530–41.

[59] See E. Bradford Burn's more recent survey (note 31), as well as the articles cited in note 37.

[60] Antonio de Alcedo y Bexarano, *Diccionario geográfico-histórico de las Indias Occidentales o América*, 5 vols. (Madrid: B. Cano 1786–89), 2:104–5; also consult Onís, *Spanish American Writers*, pp. 40–41; and Charles Lyon Chandler, *Inter-American Acquaintances*, 2d ed. (Sewanee, Tenn.: University Press of Sewanee, 1917), pp. 11–12.

[61] Morris, *Peacemakers*, p. 50.

[62] Bernstein, *Origins*, pp. 55–62.

[63] Roy F. Nichols, "Trade Relations and the Establishment of the United States Consulates in Spanish America, 1779–1809," *HAHR* 13, no. 3 (August 1933): 289–313; Bernstein, *Origins*, pp. 15–51; Arthur Preston Whitaker, *The United States and the Independence of Latin America, 1800–1830* (Baltimore: Johns Hopkins Press, 1941), pp. 3–4, 38.

[64] Maxwell, *Conflicts*, pp. 61–62, 80, 82–83, 119, 125–26, 129, 132. Also see Guilherme Mota, *Atitudes de inovaçao no Brasil, 1789–1801* (Lisbon: Editorial Gleba, n.d.), pp. 25, 66–68, 124–26, arguing that because they were men of property the conspirators of Minas Gerais were attracted to the model of the American Revolution.

[65] Maxwell, *Conflicts*, pp. 219, 229.

[66] Herr, *Revolution*, pp. 258–64, describes the changing mood of the Spanish government from 1789 to 1792.

[67] Chandler, *Acquaintances*, pp. 16–17.

[68] *Gazeta de Guatemala* (Guatemala City), May 17, 1802, reproducing the royal cédula of May 19, 1801, in which Charles IV announced the appointment of censors to prohibit publications working against his authority or inciting to tyrannicide. The Economic Society of Guatemala was a victim of this persecution and did not reopen its doors for another eight years.

[69] Juan Pablo Viscardo y Guzmán, *Lettre aux Espagnols-Américains* (see note 26), pp. 314–17 and, for the quotation, 318.

[70] Chandler, *Acquaintances*, pp. 15–16, 18; see also Onís, *Spanish American Writers*, pp. 63–65. For a detailed study of the Colombian patriot, consult Thomas Blossom, *Nariño, Hero of Colombian Independence* (Tucson: University of Arizona Press, 1967).

[71] "Acta de la Convención de Paris," Paris, December 27, 1797, in Carlos A. Villanueva, *Napoleón y la independencia de América*, pp. 325–33.

[72] Ibid., pp. 87–88.

[73] Ibid., pp. 171–79, 232–45, which includes a copy of the instructions given to French spies (pp. 242–45), dated March 20, 1810, in Madrid.

[74] Robertson, *Hispanic American Relations*, pp. 70–71.

[75] Ibid., p. 77.

[76] Chandler, *Acquaintances*, p. 62.

[77] Ibid., p. 63.

[78] Robertson, *Hispanic American Relations*, p. 83.

[79] Onís, *Spanish American Writers*, pp. 36–37.

[80] Charles C. Griffin, *The United States and the Disruption of the Spanish Empire, 1810–1822* . . . (New York: Colombia University Press, 1937), p. 59.

[81] Ibid., p. 61; Chandler, *Acquaintances*, p. 81.

[82] Francisco de Miranda, *Archivo del General Miranda* 15:404.

Before accepting his present position as professor of Latin American history at the University of Southern California, Mario Rodríguez taught at Tulane University (1952–54), Yale University (1954–60), the University of Arizona (1960–66), and George Washington University (1966–72). He holds A.B., M.A., and Ph.D. degrees from the University of California at Berkeley and has been the recipient of the Morse Fellowship in History from Yale University, the Guggenheim Fellowship in History, and the James Robertson Prize of the Conference of Latin American History, American Historical Association.

Since 1959 Professor Rodríguez has been a contributing editor for the Library of Congress' Handbook of Latin American Studies. His publications include A Palmerstonian Diplomat in Central America—Frederick Chatfield, Esquire *(1964), translated into Spanish as* Chatfield, consul británico en Centro América *(1970);* Central America *(1965); and* A Guide for the Study of Culture in Central America *(1968). He is now completing a study on Spanish liberalism entitled* The Cádiz Experiment in Central America, 1808–1826.

After hearing Professor Plumb's learned exposition of the impact of the American Revolution in Great Britain, one could safely predict that the picture in Ireland would be another story. Certainly Congress felt confident of a sympathetic response when it drew up a special "Address to the People of Ireland," and most of us recall Horace Walpole's observation in June of 1776 that "All Ireland is America mad," as well as the patriot Henry Gratton's exhortation, "Look to America."

To hear more about the Irish reaction we now look to a scholar who combines scholarship and the communication arts with enviable ease and whose work on Irish revolutionary forces and Irish conflict give him indisputable credentials. For remarks on the impact of the American Revolution in Ireland, it is my privilege to call upon Professor Owen Dudley Edwards of the University of Edinburgh.

The Impact
of the American Revolution
on Ireland[1]

OWEN DUDLEY EDWARDS

SIR HERBERT BUTTERFIELD, whose immense services to the development of professional historiography in Ireland make him in the happiest sense an honorary Irishman, has observed that "there is ... in Ireland a peculiar relationship between past and present, utterly different from that peculiar relationship which the Englishman has had with his history. It involves a high consciousness of those events which one wants to celebrate and those wrongs which are to be kept in mind things which, even if they happened long ago, seem to be remembered as though they had taken place last week."[2] Therefore golden jubilees and centennials, and even bicentennials, are dangerous toys for Irish people: dangerous in that they involve elucidation of past concepts with present assumptions, dangerous even more in that they can involve hatred and bloodshed today. We are in the presence of all kinds of myths, and the preservation of myths can be a very profitable industry. I am sorry if what follows may be rather a hard look at the impact, short and long term, of the American revolution on Ireland.

Ireland, on the face of it, seemed a very natural country to be affected by the American Revolution. The English plantations in Ireland had offered various kinds of precedent for English colonial settlement in America. The colonies' constitutional relationship to the imperial Parliament offered parallels with Ireland. British legislators virtually plagiarized the Declaratory

Act of 1719, subordinating the Irish Parliament to that of Britain, when they framed the Declaratory Act of 1766. Americans looked back to Irish protests, notably that of William Molyneux in 1698, to gain additional arguments for their own case for constitutional independence under the kingship of George III.[3] The Scots painter Allan Ramsay avenged some of the insults his fellow countrymen were sustaining in America in the era of American fulminations against Lord Bute, when in 1766 he commented acidly: "At one time an American claims the rights of an Englishman; if these are not sufficient, he drops them, and claims the rights of an Irishman; and, when those do not fully answer his purpose, he expects to be put upon the footing of a Hanoverian." [4]

Ireland meant a great deal in the American world. And for a variety of reasons several of the revolutionary leaders devoted much attention to her: Washington, Franklin, Hamilton, John and Samuel Adams, James Wilson, John Dickinson, all made notable contributions here. The motives for this interest were mingled and varied. Ireland was at once a precedent and a potential convert, a diplomatic diversion and a military decoy, a target of economic pressure to exert pressure in its turn on Britain and a most favored nation embodying hope of future commercial profit. It was natural that Congress should adopt an address to the People of Ireland on 28 July 1775, in a style Professor Lyman Butterfield assigns to Samuel Adams and in which I detect a degree of Irish awareness that I credit without question to his cousin John (both were on the four-man committee).[5] John Adams's researches in Irish history were extensive and profound, yet like most of his fellow-publicists there was much he did not see, and some that he did not wish to see. He could, nonetheless, even in the midst of propaganda, question the accuracy of his picture of Ireland. But Sam Adams, of course, had a breezy confidence that the facts of any question, Ireland included, were what he wanted them to be, and while he would not have known enough on his own to give the solidity which the address to the Irish people has, the self-assurance with which it targets Ireland is his.[6] The Ireland of their day was not so much a comparable nation seeking freedom as a society whose central characteristic was sectarian conflict such that we should speak of a caste system between Protestant episcopalians, Presbyterians, and Catholics. It may very well be that an honest Irish historian should admit sectarianism to be the central theme of Irish history with the frankness, if without the racism, of Ulrich B. Phillips.[7] In 1775 only the first flickerings were emerging of a relaxation of the previous situation where the law did not, in the words of an Irish judge, presume a Roman Catholic to exist, in a country where they formed the majority. The analogy must be with present-day South Africa. However, the Presbyterians are analogous to the Cape Coloureds only in point of status: their friends tended to be the Catholics' bitterest enemies. And the American references to Irish freedom remind one uncomfortably of, say, Irish support for "the Boer fight for Freedom" at the beginning of the 20th century. In 1775 the Irish Catholics were, in American eyes, an invisible people.[8]

The only major figure who seems to have confronted sectarianism as the main issue in Ireland was in fact the repository of truth General Washington himself, though he was not to see it until 1792. Writing to his Irish supporter Sir Edward Newenham, a statesman conspicuous for his anti-Catholicism, even in Ireland, he observed:

I regret exceedingly that the disputes between the protestants and Roman Catholics should be carried to the serious alarming height mentioned in your letters. Religious controversies are always productive of more acrimony and irreconcilable hatreds than those which spring from any other cause; and I was not without hopes that the enlightened and liberal policy of the present age would have put an effectual stop to contentions of this kind.[9]

He was clearly concerned about the point, and somewhat repeated himself to Newenham on it four months later. "Of all the animosities which have existed among mankind, those which are caused by a difference of sentiments in religion appear to be the most inveterate and distressing, and ought most to be deprecated." [10] Had he realised that his Irish votary was peculiarly prone to that animosity? At all events he stands as our witness that the impact of the American Revolution in Ireland had been decidedly limited as far as a direct ideological effect in combatting sectarianism is concerned. But—dare one say it?—was George Washington absolutely truthful? Congress in 1774 had played coyly enough with the anti-Catholic issue. [11] Congress in 1775 was producing addresses of a sufficiency of invective and vagueness to cater to such prejudices in their audiences as they might.

Congress's Address to the People of Ireland left it nicely open as to whether the unrepresentative, unreformed, Protestant episcopalian Irish Parliament was what was addressed or whether the Protestant episcopalian elite was also included, or the Presbyterian elite, or the Catholic elite, or the mass of Protestants, or all the people of Ireland. Did they mean Sir Edward Newenham, Ireland's most vocal supporter of the insurgent Americans, or did they also mean the agrarian outlaws or Whiteboys, Dowling and Kavanagh, who in Carlow on September 4, 1775, were whipped "from Fenagh to the Church" in the presence of Sir Edward and other "respectable Gentlemen" who proposed to turn out for the two scheduled repeat performances?[12] Did they mean the gentleman who would be robbed at Islandbridge, on the outskirts of Dublin, that September, or did they also mean the highwayman who, having taken the gentleman's cash, handed back his watch, saying "that he never distrained when the Rent was paid," which was wise of him as the authorities were swift in picking up stolen watches? [13] Did they mean William Donoghue, an indentured servant who, while Sam Adams was writing, was running from Dublin to the wilds of his native Kerry, apparently with several stolen articles of plate and clothing, he being about 16, with "a fresh Complexion, black Hair, and a remarkable good Countenance," wearing a "green Frock, Buff Waistcoat, Leather Breeches, and a round Hat with a Silver Band," or did they only refer to his master, James McLoughlin, apothecary of Temple Bar, who hoped from the above description to ensure that "some gentleman will apprehend and lodge him in Jail, and send Notice to his Master; as it would be a real Good to bring all such Offenders to a public Punishment," the which in the then state of the criminal law would presumably have been hanging? [14] Did they mean infant trade unionism, as represented by the Journeymen Skinners of Watling Street, who "makes Bould to rite these few lines" to the commanding officer of the Barracks of Dublin "letting your Honour no that there is a debate between Masters and Men and is out of Employment this Eight Weekes by the manes of some of the Soldgers of the Barricks Working in our Placeses and as long as those Workes we are kept out So Sir if your Honour wid be pleased to keep thoes Men in thire Barrick until Matters is made up thin the may work as long as the like but if the are not kept at Hom you will be so maney Men out of Pocket by it Sir your Humble Servant, P., S and Sir wee for your Honour will pray"? Did they mean—and there was little limit to the optimism of American committees of correspondence in choosing an audience—Lord Lieutenant Harcourt who proclaimed a speedy and condign punishment for the authors of that appeal together with £100 being paid for information leading to the conviction of each of the first three persons sentenced for authorship of it? [15] Did they mean the Roman Catholic authorities, still interdicted but permitted to discharge their illegal functions without undue harassment, especially as they rose to such occasions as this: "Now we think it highly incumbent on us at this juncture to express our utmost Horror and Detestation of such audacious villainy," the author of the anonymous appeal and his accomplices having not only incurred "the Indignation of Almighty God" and the just penalty of the laws "but also" (if "unhappily" they were Roman Catholics) the "most severe Censures" of the Church, whose authorities "absolutely require" discovery of "such Miscreants" so as to receive due expulsion from the fold? [16] Even if their Ireland did not go beyond Dublin, which Dublin did they mean? The viceroy's son had written to a friend less than two years before:

This is the most dirty, the most gloomy, the most stinking, and the ugliest city I ever was in. Most of the streets are narrow; all that are paved are paved like the most neglected and unfrequented streets of London before the improvements; several are half-paved only; many not at all. Added to this, every kind of filth is thrown into the huge stream of black mud that gently flows through the town; so you may imagine what a villanous place this is. Half the inhabitants are in absolute rags, and one-third of them without shoes or stockings, and almost naked. There are no flat pavements for foot-passengers, therefore I shall never attempt walking in the streets; and you cannot stop in a carriage without being surrounded with such a crowd of importunate beggars that, compared with Dublin, the towns in Flanders are, in that respect, free from those nuisances.

All the lower people are idle, drunken, and universally thieves, but the Castle is where they shine the most in their profession; there are, perhaps, 4 or 5 false keys to every room, and to every table and chest of drawers in those rooms, for which reason the locks are very frequently obliged to be changed. The night we arrived, the Master of the Ceremonies was robbed of all his cloaths and some money; and the following night, Mr Miller, who came with us, lost out of his drawers 6 pair of new silk stockings. Are these not proofs of the bad government of this country? And how shocking is the contrast between the regal pomp of the Vice Roy and the wretchedness of the people! Were they less oppressed, they would be more virtuous and more industrious.

The pageantry of the procession to the House of Lords, and the sort of hommage paid to the Ld.-Lieut., did not enchant me, for it exceeded even what I had expected; and the guards on horseback, the principal Officers of the Household with their wands, and the pages in their liverys, paddling on foot through the mud, with grooms of the chambers and footmen, through streets lined with soldiers, had an air of absolute monarchy, and of military force to support it, that, had I been an Irishman, I am certain I could not have endured the sight of. . . .[17]

Congress addressed itself to "the People of Ireland," an entity as vague as "the People" in whose name the Constitution would declare its identity some 12 years later. We would be foolish to imagine that many Irishmen outside the ranks of the Protestant episcopalians and Presbyterians were ready to assume themselves so addressed, much as American women, blacks, Indians, and persons of no property would have realised they had little right to see themselves in that cosy first person plural "We, the People." Yet Irish Catholics would in the future claim that it was they to whom the American address had been dedicated, much as the Constitution's "people" were presumed to have been enlarged as time elapsed. Irish nationalism as it evolved concerned itself with concepts of custody of its beliefs for future generations; the American address might not have been intended, or accepted, as being for an Irish Catholic public in its own day, but a century later there was no problem. Catholic nationalists in the 19th century wished to acquire the credential of having supported a by now highly respectable American Revolution: it made them and their relatives more acceptable immigrants to the United States, and it helped their insistence that their demands in the 19th cenutry were but the extension of the Irish Protestant Parliament's search for constitutional independence in the 18th century.[18] As more and more Irish Catholics became enfranchised British subjects or invaluable nonvoting supporters of constitutional agitation it was vital to convince Protestants in Ulster and elsewhere that the Irish nationalist cause was that enunciated in the age of the American Revolution under good Protestant auspices.[19] Simultaneously Americans with generous instincts and pride in their revolution assured themselves that their revolution had been a liberating force for the Catholics. It was no longer possible to speak of Irish liberty when what was meant was a freer hand for the Irish Protestant elite, but George Bancroft ably rang the changes between British oppression of the Irish Catholics (whose descendants, after all, usually supported his party) and Irish Protestant opposition to North's American policy. By the 20th century the myth was complete. "The Roman Catholic Irish, long abused by their conquerors, sympathized with the Americans," wrote Professor John Richard Alden in his standard account of the Revolution, published in the famous New American Nation series edited by Henry Steele Commager and Richard B. Morris.[20] "There were, in fact, encouraging signs of Irish sympathy," agreed Dr. Pauline Maier. "Dubliners instructed their parliamentary representatives to refuse any aid to Britain in its conquest of America, and went so far as to hold an extra-legal freeholders' meeting to consider the war." [21] But Dubliners, as James Joyce has reminded us, are not a conceptual monolith, and Lord Harcourt's son would agree with him.

In fact, Dr. Maier's awareness of conspiracy is the clue to which we are looking in seeing the American Revolutionary impact on Ireland. The many Irelands of 1775 agreed among themselves as to what the American Revolution was about.

It was about religion.

And they took sides accordingly, in specifically Irish terms. The friends of the American Revolution in Ireland were, in general, the severest enemies of any relaxation of penal laws against the Catholics. The conspiracy of North against American liberties had an Irish relevance, i.e., to the threat against Irish liberties. And to defenders of the Protestant cause the whole thing added up. George III and Lord North, supported by crypto-Jacobites, would be soft on the Catholics. The Quebec Act meant the end of Irish liberty, by which was meant the socioeconomic hegemony within Ireland of the Protestant episcopalian ascendancy. An anxious Protestant, writing to the extreme Whig *Hibernian Journal* in July 1775, summed up:

It is now no Secret, either in England or Ireland, that there will be another Attempt made by the Papists in the next Session of our Parliament to Take off some of our Popery Laws.[22]

Since Papists could not sit in Parliament it will be evident what depth of influence and concealment on their part is being assumed. He went on:

But I must inform my Countrymen, and they ought to know it, that their Property is here concerned as well as their Religion, and that nearly one Half of the lands of Ireland will find new Owners, if Popery shall again be prevalent among us. I know so well the Nature of this Religion, and the Bitterness of these People's Zeal against us, that it is a very Dangerous Thing to make any Alteration in these Laws, by which their Hands are tied up from Hurting us. . . .

The Quebec Act in America meant the loss of land for which the colonists had had hopes. In Ireland it looked unpleasantly like the loss of land which the colonists held. We can be certain that Lord North had no such intention, but the memory ran high that in 1689 the fugitive James II summoned a largely Catholic Parliament in Ireland which, in the words of Professor F. G. James, "meted out to Protestant rebels the same harsh treatment they had received, at least in terms of confiscation." [23] That Parliament had been milder about religion per se, but if Protestants gave their fears the emotive mortar of horror stories about the insurrection of 1641, the brick and stone of their edifice of anti-Catholic sentiment were the memories of the threat of loss of land in 1689. There was, of course, more than land involved: there was also wealth. On October 23, 1775, Charles George Agar, Bishop of Cloyne, preached a sermon on the insurrection of 1641 and its alleged Catholic massacres of Protestants before the viceroy, Lord Harcourt, who made a State visit to Christ Church Cathedral for the occasion.[24] It was a ceremonial reminder of the formal anti-Catholic constitution of the Kingdom of Ireland, and Agar on his part fought to maintain that constitution without one shadow of relaxation in its severity. He died in the following century archbishop of Dublin, earl of Normanton, and worth £400,000. He had about as much reason to question the veracity of his horror stories or vote for Catholic relief as had John D. Rockefeller to proclaim himself a Socialist.[25]

The Irish Constitution meant no rights for Catholics, and preservation of Protestant hegemony, and subordination to the Imperial Parliament, which was prepared to grant a free hand to the Irish Protestants, within limits, in return for economic hegemony. Irish Protestants understandably resented having to give away so much pottage in return for maintaining their birthright, but the Protestant Constitution was all-important in Ireland. It was clearly under attack in America, what with the Quebec Act. Irish readers noted the Congress's own reference in 1774 to its establishment of "a religion fraught with sanguinary and impious tenets." [26]

Hence "Liberty" meant "No Popery." A series of toasts of literally stupefying number drunk by the Society of Free Citizens at their quarterly dinner in that month of July 1775 takes on a very different complexion when one realises what was foremost in the drinkers' minds, other than drink: "Our

Fellow Subjects in America now suffering Persecution for attempting to assert their Rights and Liberties." "The Constitution: and Charles the First's Fate to him that violates it." "Laud's Fate to every Bishop that voted for the Establishment of Popery in Quebeck." "May we hand down to our Children, pure and untainted, the Liberty we have derived from our Ancestors." Yet there was a hint that if the Westminster Parliament and the ministry were showing a disposition to interfere with the unwritten understanding which had horse-swapped Irish Protestant ascendancy for English economic sovereignty, habitual Irish Protestant complaints about undoubted discrimination against Irish manufacturers and exports would have a sharper edge: "Prosperity to Ireland: and may it never submit to be taxed by a British Parliament." There was a readiness to see change in the Anglo-Irish relationship if never in the Protestant-Catholic one. Naturally the Ireland which was called on "never to submit," that is, was requested to show less submission, was in no way confused with the Ireland which was expected to maintain its posture of absolute submission, although later generations would seek to confuse them.[27]

John Adams had been irritated by the pusillanimity of other addresses from Congress and by constrast his and his cousin's offering to the people of Ireland tended to breathe the spirit of rebellion with which Jefferson would infuse the Declaration of Independence one year later. Indeed, the last sentence offered an imagery from which even Paine and Jefferson seem to have recoiled. Speaking of "our fellow-subjects beyond the Atlantic" they told the Irish (presumably the group primarily referred to under this head):

Of their friendly disposition, we do not yet despond; aware, as they must be, that they have nothing more to expect from the same common enemy, than the humble favour of being last devoured.[28]

To Irish Catholic revolutionary and separatist elements in 1875, 1886, or 1919, those lines must have been all the greater incentive. The so-called "Mother Country" was no more than some frightful cannibalistic ogre. Such a view conformed pleasantly with the image of Mother England presented to readers of the New York *Irish World*, of Patrick Ford's *Criminal History of the British Empire*, or of the impressive propaganda machine behind Dáil Éireann and Sinn Féin.[29] But in the ears of the Protestant Irish readers of Adams's words in 1775, they would have borne a very different connotation. The British Ministry's intent of devouring Ireland would fulfill itself by unleashing the Papist mob. Many contemporaries, and not merely those of Scotch-Irish origin, were quick to draw the parallel between the Irish Catholics and the American Indians, and Irish Protestant students of the Declaration of

Independence would have had little difficulty in ascribing to the British authorities the responsibility for unleashing the Indians on which that document insists. It is doubtful that even Sam Adams intended any such parallel. His rhetoric was inflamed, which in fact was not very wise in an Irish context: vigor of rhetoric and unreality of content were commodities of which Ireland had—and has—little lack. Both Adamses had hopes of Irish converts to American revolutionary attitudes and of Irish military or administrative diversion of British governmental avenging might.[30] But the use of the myth of Polyphemus seems simply to have emerged from that curious propensity of American literati to think of the Ulysses theme when confronting Ireland.

What the Irish Protestant readers of the *Hibernian Journal* on September 22, 1775, when the *Address* appeared, made of the passage is another matter.[31] Already it was being learned with mounting horror that Roman Catholics were enlisting under the king for the war in America.[32] Their enlistment was illegal but, despite denials, Protestants became increasingly alarmed. In fact, it is evident that many Roman Catholics were enlisted in the army destined for America. Roman Catholic peers and gentry offered bounties to recruits; the Catholics of Limerick city and county put up half a guinea per man for the first able-bodied 200 enlisting with Major Boyle Roche.[33] Kilkenny was reporting by September 6 that "so far are the common people from having the least Objection to the American Expedition (as has been lately asserted) that they have large Expectations by the forfeited Estates and cultivated Lands which may fall to them when the Troubles subside." [34] In fine, the American war offered the Catholics the prospect of sauce for the gander, and the Protestants knew it. John Ridge of Dublin wrote to Burke at the end of September: "All the Protestants, as far as I can see, especially the Presbyterians, except a few who have connexions in the army at Boston & a few military Generals are, here with us, friends to the American cause. The Roman Catholics, who receive no favours, no quarter, from their fellow subjects of a different persuasion & are indebted to Government for some lenity in the execution of the laws against them & have no liberty, . . . are ready to give their beggarly assent to Government." [35] Lord Shelburne, himself Irish-born and owner of extensive Irish estates, found little change there three years later:

I find all classes in this kingdom much more animated about America than in England. In every Protestant or Dissenters' house the established toast is success to the Americans. Among the Roman Catholics they not only talk but act very freely on the other side. They have in different parts entered into associations, and subscribed largely to levy men against America, avowing there dislike of a Constitution here or in America, of which they are not allowed to participate. On the other hand the Parliament pretend to no will but that of the Ministers.[36]

Whatever the Protestant fears of a Scottish conspiracy in the Jacobite interest manipulating George III toward a restoration of an Irish Catholic supremacy, there was little Jacobite feeling in the Irish attitude. The most one can say is that Irish Catholics have generally had some degree of affection for the English monarchy.[37] This was briefly diverted to the exiled Stuarts at the beginning of the 18th century, but it never assumed any serious dimensions and by 1775 there was no pull on Catholic loyalties.[38] The Irish Catholics would have agreed with the Namier school in denying a revolution in government policy in 1760, which offers us a nice marriage of conservative minds across the centuries. The Reverend James White, a Roman Catholic priest of Limerick, asserted that the Catholics began to pray for George III and his queen publicly in their chapels in January 1768, but that there had also been a decided Catholic cult of George II. "His Majesty . . . did not enforce the laws already made, or suffer new laws to be made against them; during his reign they enjoyed greater liberty, than for many years before." [39] By 1775 a religion naturally deferential to civil authority, an awareness of the identity of antimonarchical and anti-Catholic sentiments, and a tradition of an English restraining hand over the anti-Catholic arm of the Irish government, placed the Catholics firmly on the side of George III and Lord North. And there were decided hopes that a good Irish Catholic record during the American war as well as a poor Irish Protestant one could win benefits for the Catholics, quite apart from the profits of individual soldiers of fortune. It is not clear how far the Catholics themselves saw the parallels with Indians and Blacks which others were making in their name, but Irish journalists in British government pay had the wit to stress the dangers to the subject population in the acquisition of power by American patriots "who *nobly* take arms to *oppose* the *legal* authority of Great Britain, and to *defend* their inalienable hereditary right to enslave their fellow creatures! . . . whilst the *Shouts* of *Liberty* resound through the wide extended Continent of America, the agonizing cries of their expiring tortured Slaves ascend to the offended Majesty of Heaven." [40]

The danger point for Irish Catholic loyalties was of course 1779, when the Catholic powers of Spain and France were on the high seas and even threatening an invasion. The Reverend Arthur O'Leary, a highly appropriate Catholic apologist for the age of the Enlightenment, was concerned enough to address a pamphlet to the "Common People of Ireland," making it much clearer than Congress whom he intended under this description. But whether he wrote to keep potentially wayward Catholics in line or to remind Protestants that Catholic priests were advocating the strictest loyalty to their coreligionists is a nice point. There was also the aspect that government might, in O'Leary's eyes, do worse than take a moment to realize its good fortune in having its

Catholics so loyal. If anti-Popery laws were to be rescinded, it was clear that the impetus had to come from government. If government were ever so slightly reminded that a little amelioration might make Catholics more loyal than ever, no harm would be done. O'Leary himself would appear a more valuable subject, in addition, and he was not insensible to a little financial subvention for his efforts. He certainly found arguments which reasserted the religious nature of the struggle while disposing of the French claims to Catholic leadership: "When the French joined the Americans, it was not from love of the Presbyterian religion. If they landed here, it would not be with a design to promote the Catholic cause." Bonnie Prince Charlie had died some two months earlier, he noted, "and by his death has rid the kingdom of all fears arising from the pretensions of a family that commenced our destruction and completed our ruin." And he remarked with a bluntness that the rhetoric of the American Revolution cannot quite offset: "the common people are never interested in the change of government. They may change their masters: but they will not change their burden. The rich will be still rich. The poor will be poor. In France, they have poor of all trades and professions: it will be the same here. . . . It is then equal to a man, what religion his neighbour or king be of, provided his own conscience be pure, and his life upright." [41]

What of Gaelic-speaking Ireland? What in particular of the poets who kept up the cult of the exiled Stuarts in their verse? Robert Burns offers us a case of a Jacobite supporter of Washington;[42] what of his counterparts in Irish Gaelic folk culture? In fact, they offer little difference from the Catholic norm. The Irish Burns—and one dislikes the title because of the diminution of quality implied—was, without any question, Eoghan Ruadh Ó Súilleabháin, whose lyrics stand with the satiric epic of Brian Merriman, as the last great expression of poetic genius in the Irish language. The work of both men is curiously representative of the Europe of their day in its sophistication, in its irony, and in its love of the baroque. Merriman stands without question as a satirist, but Ó Súilleabháin deserves more consideration in this respect. Both were acid anticlericals; both were vigorous celebrants of sexuality in verse and in life; both were fascinated by the labyrinthine capabilities of subtlety of the dying tongue in which they worked; both were alienated, at times reaching levels of cosmic anger such as Bernard Bailyn saw in Tom Paine in his magnificent lecture here two years ago; both were men of bottomless humor.[43] But the surviving poetry of Ó Súilleabháin, where it follows the poetic traditions of his illustrious predecessors, has won him a name as a late follower of the exiled Stuarts. He seems far too intelligent to have been anything of the kind. These *aislingí* or dream poems of Jacobite sentiment in his hands turn into baroque finger exercises. His life belies them. He took service under

George III and served under Rodney during the later engagements of the American revolution. He even celebrated the admiral's victory in a poem as deficient in grace as his work in Irish is redolent of it. "Rodney's Glory" was recited before the kindly appreciative admiral, and one is forced to follow the somewhat sentimental reflections of Daniel Corkery on the irony of the English hero's acquaintance through this absurdity with a poet who in his own language could rival Burns or Heine:

> How may prosperity attend
> Brave Rodney and his Irishmen,
> And may he never want a friend
> While he shall reign commander;
> Success to our Irish officers,
> Seamen bold and jolly tars,
> Who like darling sons of Mars
> Take delight in the fight
> And vindicate bold England's right
> And die for Erin's glory.

Another Ireland had replied to the American revolution. We may be very safe in agreeing with Corkery, Dineen, and other commentators that the poet himself had little more incentive than an Irish desire to please in this effusion. But secret Jacobitism or Irish nationalism is as dubious as sincere loyalism. From what we know of Ó Súilleabháin we may simply say that he produced what his audience would want, and what came naturally from him. And his fellow Irish-speaking Catholics would probably have accepted his sentiments without his underlying cynicism.[44]

Dangerous though it is to declare blanket generalizations, the Irish Catholics offer no chance for reservation about their loyalty—apart from one illustrious exception—throughout the course of the war. The pressure group, the Catholic Association, were as comforting as O'Leary in the draft address to George III which they approved on July 15, 1779:

Sensible of the many blessings, which in common with the rest of our fellow subjects, we have enjoyed under the mild and free government of your majesty and your royal ancestors, and particularly grateful for the benefits conferred on us by the liberality of an enlightened legislature, during your majesty's reign; we cannot but see with abhorrence and feel with indignation the insidious and base attempts of the French and Spanish courts to disturb the peace and distract the happiness of your majesty's dominions. . . . we doubt not that, under God, your majesty will be able speedily and effectually to chastize the insolence and punish the perfidy of all your enemies. . . .[45]

And Home Secretary Lord Weymouth agreed. "The zeal which the Roman Catholics of Ireland have shewn, leaves no reason to doubt of their loyalty," he acknowledged to Harcourt's successor as viceroy, Lord Buckinghamshire, while expressing some concern about the dangers of seminarians from France and Flanders causing disaffection.[46] Buckinghamshire in answering him knew of only two such immigrants, neither likely to cause disquiet; revealingly, his means of guarding against trouble from such a quarter was to tell "some of the superiors of the Romish clergy of the intelligence I have received, and recommend to them to be particularly watchful." [47]

It is, oddly enough, the Catholic Association which tells of the only exception to the rule of Catholic loyalty. It offered money for the apprehension of a dangerous pamphleteer from whom an inflammatory advertisement spoke of efforts to inflame those of the Catholic public who read beyond his title: "The urgent necessity of an immediate repeal of the whole Penal Code, candidly considered. To which is prefixed an enquiry into the prejudices entertained against Catholicks: being an appeal to the Roman Catholicks of Ireland exciting them to a just sense of their civil and religious rights, as citizens of a free nation. The pamphlet, more innocuous than the advertisement, was never published. The author was in fact a youth of 19, but as the case of Alexander Hamilton should remind us, teenage revolution could be a feature of that age as much as of this. Mathew Carey came of the rapidly increasing Dublin Catholic middle class, but had early demonstrated his independence of a father opposed to the dangerous craft of journalism by taking service as a bookseller's apprentice and writing occasional pieces for the extreme Protestant and Whig *Hibernian Journal*, of which his master was part owner. Evidently its mixture of Irish Protestant self-assertion and Americanophile sentiment led the young Carey to apply somewhat different interpretations of "liberty" from those of normal readers. The American message had broken through the web of Irish religious sectarianism.[48]

Yet if it had, it had done so in a way which must be seen in the sectarian context. If Irish Catholics could not advance politically or in landed society, they could climb commercially as Carey's father had done through his bakery. Thomas McDaniel, or MacDonnel, to whom he was apprenticed, needed the money Carey's father could supply; there may have been other ties—Carey has a curious jeer about his change of name which may suggest a judicious conversion from Roman Catholicism, leaving with it an accessibility to pressure from the Catholic community.[49] On the face of it, young Carey might merely be an apprentice moved by the excitement of such items as the Congressional Address to the People of Ireland, published in the journal in the year he took up his apprenticeship. No doubt it did influence him, but we also have to look to a pattern of a lame, resentful boy, bitter against his master, aware of all the pro-American talk in the shop and quick to realize that Catholics could profit by this new rhetoric and Protestants forced to come to terms with its implications. Carey was a great printer, publisher, and economic thinker in later life, but he always remained ferociously defensive about the wrongs of Irish Catholics.[50] There even exists in his pro-American rhetoric a contrast which others were drawing at the treatment of the American rebels and of the Irish Catholic population. He remained suspicious of any signs of anti-Catholicism in his America as he was establishing himself there,[51] and for all of his adjustment into respectability and statesmanship remained a blend of American revolutionary influence and

> Out of Ireland have I come
> Great hatred, little room
> I carry from my mother's womb
> A fanatic heart.

In his case there were many targets against the hatred: the Catholics in Ireland who disowned and denounced him, the government which sought to prosecute him, the extreme Protestants who reviled him, the master who despised him. Well, revolutions, like everything else, have to make their impact on people and people have individual attitudes.[52] His father packed him off to Passy, where he found the world of Franklin more congenial to him. He seems to have given little encouragement to French enquiry as to others of his sentiments, thereby supporting the report to Vergennes from Franklin's secretary, Edward Bancroft, that the Irish would not help an invasion.[53] His authority must stand higher with the historian on this point than that of Bancroft, however, since Carey was not in British pay.[54] He returned to Ireland after the war, founded the *Volunteer's Journal* in 1783, continued to find Ireland cold to his views, and finally emigrated in 1784 to the United States, where he achieved so remarkable a career.[55]

In less spectacular fashion, others would support the lesson to be drawn from his case, that a major effect of the American Revolution on Ireland was to encourage the emigration of those interested in it. But it was economics rather than ideology that seems to have drawn them; nor can we dismiss that priority from Carey's case. Crèvecoeur's *Letters From an American Farmer*, printed in Dublin in 1782 and in Belfast in 1783,[56] seems to have been an event of more significance for Ireland at this point than the Declaration of Independence. The author's assimilationism, which led him to posture as an American of English extraction, suggests an ironic prelude to the assimilationism which would lead many Irish emigrants of this period to ease themselves into America with few backward glances and fewer traces. Whatever Crèvecoeur may have been taken to be—and Ireland seems to have been blissfully unaware of his own descent on her coast from a shipwreck in 1780 [57]—

he certainly was no tocsin of republican inspiration. James Magee of Belfast advertised the book with the legend: "it is now only left to us to hope, that the obvious interests and mutual wants of both countries, may in due time, and in spite of all obstacles, happily re-unite them." [58] The two countries would have been America and Britain—Irish Protestant writers easily varied between regarding themselves as Irish and as British. It is a sobering thought that to Crèvecoeur's by now thoroughly hackneyed question—"What then is the American, this new man?"—the answer from Belfast was "an Englishman."

That the American Revolution did have serious effects in Ireland has long been known, but it must be stressed how very little, at the time, these were concerned with ideology. The loyalty of the Catholics won a first installment of reward in 1778. It may be true, as Mathew Carey was afterwards to claim, that the granting of permission to Catholics to hold leases of land for 999 years and to be rid of the gavelkind which had fragmented Catholic holdings was the result of British defeat in America.[59] Henry Grattan's son and namesake would afterwards term it the "first fruits" of Saratoga.[60] But it was to North's Government that the Catholics owed what freedom they had received. The removal of troops from Ireland for service in America gave rise to the formation of Volunteers, to whose pressure Catholic relief was afterwards ascribed. But the only contribution of the Volunteers in 1778, according to Buckinghamshire, was that of reassuring the Protestants. With arms in their hands they had less reason to fear the relaxation of the penal code against Catholics. They "might, with some plausibility, have murmured, if they had not been indulged in arming for their own defence, at the moment when the legislature was holding out protection to a denomination of men, whom they so long had deemed their inveterate enemies." [61]

It quickly emerged that the American revolution, if it contributed little in ideology to Ireland, gave a new sense of priorities to Irish Protestants. Once they were armed they could see the logic of more economic power for themselves as preferential to the absolute subordination of the Catholics. Ideology did have a negative effect, as Maureen Wall has shown. Irish Protestants were ready enough to parrot American rhetoric, if only to alarm British politicians. And with frequent use of slogans about no taxation without representation to protest against the Westminster Parliament's economic legislation for Ireland, there had to be an end to Protestant attempts to penalize Catholic middle-class economic activity through the implementation of the quarterage tax.[62] Friends of the government and journalists in its pay forced acknowledgment of the wrongs of Catholics from some of the more consistent friends of America. Nevertheless, as the friends of America became, in some instances, more ready to admit the justice of some Catholic claims, it was noticeable that the enemies of the American rebels, such as Viscount Beauchamp, were still ahead of them as champions of the Catholic cause.[63] It is interesting to notice that despite American hostility to Beauchamp, Mathew Carey in his infancy as Philadelphia publisher and bookseller took the risk of putting Beauchamp's *Letter to the First Belfast Company of Volunteers* on sale. He was under few illusions as to who his coreligionists' friends were.[64]

The notable exception to the guiding rule that to be pro-American was to be anti-Catholic and *vice versa* was of course Edmund Burke, who was conspicuous for his friendship both to the Catholics and to the American rebels. But Burke has to be looked on as an emigrant, as something very close to a Catholic "passing for white" and, apart from his political and psychological alliance with the Rockingham Whigs and their ideology, ready to transfer some of the criticism of British colonial rule in Ireland which he could not state explicitly to other contexts, such as India, in which he could speak more freely. Liberated from his Irish environment, as professing Irish Catholic stay-at-homes were not, he could directly sympathize with the Americans because of the Irish experience, and thus if Professor Alden is wrong about the Irish Catholics he is right about the greatest figure to emerge from Irish Catholic roots in the 18th century. And Burke himself, far more than the Americans, persuaded some of his fellow-Whigs to a more liberal attitude. His success in Britain made his speeches and writings first-class news in Ireland, and his celebrity as well as his clarity induced its own following. Of course interest did not always mean unstinted admiration. When the Dublin *Chronicle* ran his speech of January 9, 1770, as its first and second column on the first page, it concluded quite accurately by stating: "The Adventures of a Monkey, in our next." [65]

As American events progressed Irish loyalties became increasingly mixed. The leaders of the Volunteers were in many instances vociferous spokesmen for American rebellion, but the threat of depredations from John Paul Jones or smugglers hired by Franklin was another matter,[66] and the arrival on the scene of the traditional Catholic enemies, France and Spain, meant that the Americans could no longer be clearly the Protestant cause. On the other hand, the scrupulous behavior of the Catholics, with the exception of Mathew Carey, ensured that the bogey of Popish treachery was to some degree laid; the Protestants were forced to emphasise their own loyalist credentials. The increasing evidence of economic pickings and constitutional bulwarks to be gained by shrewd deployment of Volunteer power made for even greater uncertainty. It became desirable to try to outbid the government for Catholic support, and political rivals could counter plans for reform with proposals for Catholic relief. The Catholics had learned from the events set in motion by the war to play off one section of the ruling caste against another; the Presbyterians had found the same thing in 1780 when the Test Act was repealed. Oddly enough, the survival of pathological fears of the Catholics led Protestants actually farther into alliance with them, on the principle that if Catholics are all that diabolically clever and are beginning to get power it might be better to seek their friendship. "The Roman Catholic question was our ruin," William Drennan told his sister in August 1784, speaking of the collapse of the Volunteers, "but if the reformers had not *pretended* a wish for alliance with them on the grand question, government would have anticipated the volunteers and made the Catholic Volunteers act against the Protestants." [67] At the same time once certain Protestants had forced themselves to swallow Catholic relief and cooperation with Catholics, they became ready to go further. James Napper Tandy, whom we encountered roaring loyal, Protestant, American toasts at the Society of Free Citizens, was to progress to the United Irishmen and its antisectarian program. We can perhaps acknowledge that here if not elsewhere the Revolution radicalised some Irishmen as it radicalised some Americans. But it is dangerous in the extreme to be generous about their numbers or over-optimistic about the character of that radicalization. It is important also not to confuse the impact of the American Revolution itself with those tendencies Professor Palmer has brought to our attention so ably respecting the age of the democratic revolution rather than simply the age of the American revolution.[68] It was natural, after all, that Europe should still be of greater consequence than America for Ireland. The Americans, as I have argued elsewhere, were very conscious of Irish influence, but few Irish people actually knew much of America. With Europe, on the other hand, both Protestant and Catholic Ireland had strong links and we can see the impact of the Enlightenment in the sardonic realism of Father O'Leary, or in the humanity of the Protestant Reverend William Crawford, who in 1783 published a history of Ireland at once vigorously extolling the Williamite cause and the "genuine spirit of toleration which has begun in this kingdom and is likely universally to prevail," in the light of which he denounced former injuries to the Catholics.[69] Certainly the events of the American war gave incentive for the greater display of enlightened ideas; they looked like paying off. The various religious sects continued to maneuver, and sought to outbid one another in power-hungry alliances. Ultimately, after the "blood-bath of 1798," as Maureen Wall has pointed out, one saw "the divisions between catholics and protestants in Ireland become deeper than at any time since the middle of the century." [70]

The acquisition of Irish legislative independence in 1782 was very generally ascribed to the direct influence of the American revolution. Francis Dobbs declared in a famous passage that "it was on the plains of America, that Ireland obtained her freedom." [71] "A voice from America had shouted to liberty," agreed Henry Flood.[72] A versifier offered a higher source:

> But great was the change in the year seventy-seven,
> We then were inspir'd by a spark sent from heav'n,
> We shook off our sloth, took our muskets in hand,
> And in less than six years new-modell'd our land.[73]

"The territory of America, and the velocity of her population, turned the eyes of mankind to that aera, when by a gentle effort, she should stand disengaged from the shackles of dependence," acknowledged a pamphleteer.[74] But in fact any analysis of the pamphlet literature of the period invites a strong line of distinction to be drawn between the American events which helped bring about Irish constitutional independence, and its alleged American ideological origins. America had not shown the Volunteers and their Parliamentary allies and rivals what freedom meant beyond a rhetorical expression; she had shown that Britain was weak, and could be forced to make concessions at a moment of adversity.[75] Francis Dobbs, as the nephew of North Carolina Governor Arthur Dobbs, might show signs of American libertarian influence; in any event ideology for him was rather a special matter, ultimately coming to involve concentration on the imminence of the Day of Judgment.[76] In most other instances, there is nothing that can be compared to the self-sustaining ideology Bernard Bailyn has noted.[77] Hence what Ireland got in 1782 was the advantage that a corrupt and utterly unrepresentative assembly had to be bought and bribed and could no longer be directly ordered about its business. Lacking any real ideology of liberty, the Parliament, in Palmer's phrase, "escaped reform." [78] Its extinction in 1800 disposed of one of the most self-interested assemblies in history.

What, one is tempted to say, is a nice revolution like yours doing in a nasty place like this? It is with a sense of deep admiration for the great work of R. R. Palmer—surely one of the few historians of this century who can be named alongside Macaulay and Ranke—that I assert here the necessity to see the limits of the impact of that democratic revolution he has so brilliantly scrutinized in action. Yet it does seem to me that, in a way that lay outside the scope of his enquiry, the American revolution had a series of profound effects on Ireland.

I have not so far given much attention to what was perhaps the closest connection between Ireland and America during the revolution—the Scotch-Irish. It is in general important to realize that the Irish showed little American sense. In the case of the Scotch-Irish, with their strong sense of group identity, their remarkable self-absorption, and their special experience, the connection must have been much greater. There is no point in my following inadequately the excellent work of Professor E. R. R. Green [79] on them. But a few points can be suggested. As with other parts of Ireland, the Presbyterians of the North seem to have been primarily influenced by the promise of America as a haven for emigrants. It also seems reasonable to posit the thesis that Ireland in its Scotch-Irish dimension influenced America much more at the time than America influenced the Scotch-Irish. The Scotch-Irish in America do seem to have sharpened their democratic teeth on the example of their experience in Ireland and on that of their kinsmen who remained. Blair McClenachan of Philadelphia was one of the subscribers to Crawford's *History* with its celebration of the Williamite achievement and its denunciation of the "inhuman treatment to which the [Catholic] natives were exposed from the rapacity of the English adventurers," [80] and it was McClenachan who after Jay's treaty moved "that every good citizen kick this damned treaty to hell!" [81] More remotely, it seems reasonable to say that the Scotch-Irish frontier experience in Britain and Ireland led to the development of a particular American frontier experience where Scotch-Irish influence was abroad, lending further point to Owen Lattimore's assertion that Turner should be stood on his head: [82] the American changed the frontier, rather than the reverse. Specifically, they brought the racism of the Irish frontier to bear on the Indians. Where the reverse impact becomes noticeable is in the growing Scotch-Irish cult in the late 19th century, as the Ulster Protestants found themselves growing increasingly isolated. The emigrant search for credentials led to a Scotch-Irish claim on every distinguished American on whom hands could be laid.[83] The Irish-American Catholics followed suit, and both groups in Ireland saw their own tribalism increase as a result.[84] Each claimed a place in America which granted nothing to the other, and each was hence disposed to admit nothing to the other in their view of their place in Ireland. In place of the ecumenism of the Reverend William Crawford and of Mathew Carey's interest in Protestant media and readership, there came endless streams of self-gratifying and self-serving propaganda. The American Revolution told the Scotch-Irish that they were the makers of liberty; it followed that their concept of liberty was no more open to question than had been that of Sir Edward Newenham.[85] The Irish Catholic reached the same route through a larger variety of self-absorbed reflections, if only because the reality behind Irish Catholic claims of participation in the American Revolution was so thin, despite desperate circumlocutions of late 19th-century Irish Catholic apologetics.[86]

As a certain American political party has pointed out, the American Revolution has to be considered as an event in the history of republicanism as well as in that of democracy.[87] Its influence on Ireland was naturally somewhat affected

in the former respect by the fact that the first impact of American republicanism was not until the era of the French Revolution. But it is possible to
discern behind the overlay of French influence an increasing American basic
layer. The persons affected, the United Irishmen of the 1790's, were few in
number, but their subsequent influence on the development of Irish nationalism was to be profound. Their readiness to turn to France for aid and inspiration was in part derived from the American alliance with France during the
struggle for independence.[88] Thomas Paine played his part in giving them an
Anglophone introduction to the French Revolution.[89] The very respectability
of the America to which Irishmen were going gave the idea of a republic a
respectability which the bizarre tidings from France could never do alone.
Few cases are as clear as that of Lawrence O'Connor, a schoolmaster hanged
at Naas in 1795 for administering oaths to "the present United States of France
and Ireland." [90] The republicanism of later generations was to go back, self-
consciously, to that of the United Irishmen, as well as being renewed by the
continued existence of the American republic whose place in shaping Fenianism
and its successor movements should require no comment.[91]

How far the development of Irish democracy advanced as a result of the
impact of the American Revolution is far less clear. It is not sensible to speak
of its development until the point when mass agitation entered Irish politics,
and that took place with Daniel O'Connell in the 1820's. O'Connell owed
much to Burke, and while he was more complex and less consistent in his
reaction to the French Revolution over the years than was his great precursor
as the major Irish influence on the British Parliament, his sense of democracy
seems to have derived from the safe revolution as much as from the dangerous
one. O'Connell took pride in being compared to Washington, and seems to
have seen himself as another leader drawing strength from dependence on a
large mass of his fellow countrymen. Certainly the type of democracy which
O'Connell preached and practiced had a confidence in itself that a mere
evolution from the British system could not have possessed. It outran its
American antecedents to some degree; O'Connell secured mass participation
on a level which the Americans, proportionately speaking, had yet to obtain.[92]
He could produce 60,000 signatures to an antislavery address, a matter on
which, with all due respect to the Irish, very few were likely to exert themselves
without his intervention.[93] Equally, it was more limited than the American
form. It was not a republican democracy: partly with an awareness, which
his successors regrettably lacked, that Ireland had to cater for many political
faiths, including Irish nationalism, O'Connell made quite a cult of the British
monarchy, even noisily toasting the fecundity of Queen Victoria.[94]

But the most serious consequence of the American Revolution for Ireland was the legitimacy which it gave to physical force. George Washington and his associates had taken up arms. Even the nonviolent O'Connell could not ignore that side of his exemplar. "He was driven into the field and obliged to take up arms," he said but added, "I know a trick worth two of that." [95] But his more romantic young followers, the Young Irelanders, drenched the pages of their periodical the *Nation* with bloodthirsty poetry equating Irish manhood with martial achievements. Michael Doheny, afterwards an insurgent in 1848, an emigrant to the United States, and one of the founders of Fenianism, wrote for the Young Ireland "Library of Ireland" *The History of the American Revolution*, which was published in 1847. In his introduction he commented:

The American conflict was truly a guerrilla warfare, and its success was principally owing to the skill and intrepidity with which those posts were disputed.

It is quite possible this may be dangerous ground, yet I cannot help saying, that defensible positions scattered through the country, and the ability and skill necessary for their maintenance, are the last and surest safeguards of a population struggling for liberty. And it is fit that all men should know their value. They may have had superior advantages in America, where vast forests intervened, and the march of armies was so difficult except on the principal lines of road. But in every country they are available in a greater or less degree. In Ireland they are eminently so. Except along the coast it would be utterly impossible to preserve a communication between an invading army and its stores, with a population so numerous that at an hour's warning 20,000 men could be concentrated on any one point along the line.

To know the advantages, whether military, commercial or social, which his country presents, is the duty of every upright citizen. If a jealous law brooks with impatience and suspicion his examination of these things—his inquiry how far they may be turned to account—thereby it stands self-condemned. And wherever his apprehension so far prevails as to induce the neglect of what it is becoming in a free man to know, the citizen is a slave, and the government despotism. I do not think so meanly of my country or so harshly of its government. I believe it to be quite compatible with its repose as well as permanent security, that the Irish people should thoroughly understand and know how to make use of their country's capacity for a military struggle.[96]

The year previous to this, Young Ireland had broken from Daniel O'Connell on the specific issue of the right to use violence. Thomas Francis Meagher proclaimed "Be it for the defence, or be it for the assertion, of a nation's liberty, I look upon the sword as a sacred weapon. . . . Abhor the sword and stigmatise the sword? No, my lord, for at its blow a giant nation sprang up from the waters of the Atlantic, and by its redeeming magic the fettered colonies became a daring free republic." [97] He also cited the example of the Bavarians, the Tyrolese, the Belgians (all conveniently Catholics), and the biblical heroine Judith. But the stuffing of the argument was in the American example. For all of their fellow-Catholicism, the Belgians, Bavarians, and Tyrolese were a little remote, and Judith was positively unwise, given the

Irish peasant suspicion of anyone quoting the Bible save a priest. Yet George Washington could not be quarreled with. Denounce Washington and you denounce the source of whatever funds were coming into peasants' houses in famine-striken Ireland from the Eldorado which the United States seemed.

Irish nationalist militarism has never looked back from this incident. John Mitchel's venomous attacks on O'Connell's nonviolence swept all before them. Irish popular songs were drenched with celebrations of bloodletting. The American Fourth of July oratory sparked off a response among Irish immigrants, and they in turn influenced their relatives. It became the great Irish virtue to assert that they were, in the words of Joseph I. C. Clarke, "The Fighting Race":

> "When Michael, the Irish Archangel, stands,
>   The angel with the sword,
> And the battle-dead from a hundred lands
>   Are ranged in one big horde,
> Our line, that for Gabriel's trumpet waits,
>   Will stretch three deep that day,
> From Jehoshaphat to the Golden Gates—
>   Kelly and Burke and Shea."
> "Well, here's thank God for the race and the sod!"
> Said Kelly and Burke and Shea.[98]

Even nonviolent movements after this kept their followers happy to the strains of some versification about bloodletting or martyrdom. T. D. Sullivan denounced the Fenians but all nationalist Ireland rang to his insistence that:

> Whether on the gallows high
> Or the battlefield we die
>   Oh, what matter when for Erin dear we fall.[99]

Parnell's followers sang it, and if the constitutionalism of his movement was superseded after 1918 by a crusade of violence, the Parnellites had laid the trap for themselves by perpetuating the popular culture of violence.[100] Ireland finally won the status of the Irish Free State after a conflict in which violence was celebrated in popular song and rhetoric as never before, and if those who accepted the Anglo-Irish Treaty then found themselves engulfed in civil war with their former comrades who refused to accept the settlement, in denouncing them they denounced the creed through which they themselves had been brought to power. Its effect would be that for some republicans constitutionalism and democracy could never be allowed to triumph over the ideal of force, and for the party which is now Ireland's largest the same rhetoric was seasonally employed to give an additional legitimacy to what Sean Lemass, afterwards premier, and leader of the party, termed "a slightly constitutional party." [101] A national anthem was adopted hailing the Irish as "children of a fighting race";[102] a national mythology was handed out to schoolchildren glorifying nationalist appeals to violence. With what results, we know.

Yet I cannot leave the American Revolution without noticing one final legacy to Ireland. You may remember that Hope remained as the last creature to emerge from Pandora's Box. In 1796, the 21-year-old Daniel O'Connell noted in his journal:

I have read since Tuesday Boswell's *Johnson* . . . Adams's *History of Republics*, Preface and 28 pages of account of the author's life; Watson's *Chemical Essays* . . . Mr Adams was born at Massachusetts October 29th, 1735. He is by profession a lawyer.[103]

O'Connell was more interested in Boswell and Watson at that moment, yet it is hard to resist the conclusion that Adams left some mark on his mind. *A Defence of the Constitutions of Government of the United States of America* opens with an examination of the horrors of slaughter and bloodshed which classical times produced by what Adams termed "want of an equilibrium." He posed the problem of creating a constitution which would contain liberty and yet be immune from bloody dissension and civil strife. And he did so in terms which still ring eloquently today as a revelation of his profound abhorrence of bloodshed and the destruction of human life.[104] It seems to me that Adams's conviction of the need to create a peaceful state is something which deserves greater celebration than it has yet achieved. In his case at least, zeal for peace has to be seen as one effect of the American Revolution whose strife had torn from him his dearest friend. And of course, he put his principles into practice when he split his party and destroyed his chances for reelection by his refusal to win cheap laurels by leading the country to war with France. His pride in that refusal is justly famous.[105] And Daniel O'Connell, who had read those opening passages, was to do precisely the same thing, when at Clontarf in 1843 he canceled his monster meeting rather than let his enraptured followers face the guns of British warships in Dublin Bay. It was not the only connection between their families: John Quincy Adams defended O'Connell's attack on the slaveholding American minister Stevenson. Whether O'Connell thought of the fate of his Massachusetts lawyer when he took his own decision we cannot tell. That Adams's words lingered consciously or otherwise to deepen his commitment to peace I would believe. And in a world saturated by violence, its advocates and its images, it is good to remember this final impact of the American Revolution on Ireland, that of the American Revolutionary leader who knew Ireland best upon the Irish national leader who brought to political consciousness the people of his own country, and to know that both of them had the sublime courage to prevent their followers going to die for liberty.[106]

Notes

[1] It is with great pleasure that I record my thanks initially to the Library of Congress, whose kindness to me from my early days as a graduate student gave me the courage to begin messing about in this field, and whose generosity continued so magnificently through this lecture, on which my last work was done with the resources of the Library itself. My gratitude is also due to the National Library of Ireland (especially to Patrick Henchy and Alf Mac Lochlainn), to the National Library of Scotland, to the Library of the University of Edinburgh, to the Massachusetts Historical Society, and to the Department of Archives, University College, Dublin.

This paper has benefited enormously from a (very) critical reading from my former colleague in graduate school, Lynn Parsons. My wife, Bonnie Lee Dudley Edwards, criticized and inspired design and execution while the paper was in preparation. Conversation with the following scholars opened up several fascinating lines of investigation and saved me from many errors: my father, R. Dudley Edwards; my mother, Síle Ní Shúilleabháin; George A. Shepperson; H. T. Dickinson; H. F. Kearney; Peter Marshall; Andrew Hook; Thomas P. O'Neill; John A. Woods; Conor Cruise O'Brien; Lyman Butterfield; Thomas N. Brown; Rhodri Jeffreys-Jones; Gordon Wood; David N. Doyle; N. T. Phillipson; and my students at Edinburgh University, notably the North American Studies seminar. My father has been most generous with assistance in making Dublin source material available to me. Martin Dowle rescued the paper from several blunders at the proof stage. It seems a poor recompense to all of them to utter a mere word of thanks (and of course exculpation).

I should also say that over the years I have learned very much from certain scholars in this period and three of the major authorities have been exceptionally kind to me along the road. I have normally not cited the work of R. B. McDowell, *Irish Public Opinion 1760–1800* (London: Faber and Faber, 1944), or of Maurice R. O'Connell, *Irish Politics and Social Conflict in the Age of the American Revolution* (Philadelphia: University of Pennsylvania Press, 1965), simply because virtually every footnote would demand mention of them. They have borne the heat of the day in pioneer work; I have only gathered a few grains in the evening. I cannot begin to express my debt to the late Maureen Wall, the only historian who was able to draw together all the diverse elements of 18th-century Ireland, who could move from the world of Namier to the world of Corkery and make each far more real for her having been there. It was my very great privilege to have been taught by her, and delighted by her, from the time I was about eight years of age. I dedicate this essay to her memory: a poor substitute for what we have lost by her passing.

Do sgaoil gach scoil toisc an bháis seo.

[2] Herbert Butterfield, "Eighteenth-Century Ireland," in T. W. Moody, ed., "Thirty Years' Work in Irish History (I)," *Irish Historical Studies* 15 (September 1967): 381–82.

[3] I have examined this in detail in "The American Image of Ireland: A Study of its Early Phases," *Perspectives in American History* 4 (1970): 214–41. I shall have to make reference several times to this work for convenience; I apologise for the vulgarity of doing so.

[4] [Allan Ramsay, the younger], *Thoughts on the Origins and Nature of Government Occasioned by the late Disputes between Great Britain and her American Colonies* (London: T. Becket and P. A. de Hondt, 1769), p. 51. For statements of the traditional view of the influence of the

American Revolution on Ireland, see Sir Reginald Coupland, *The American Revolution and the British Empire* (London: Longmans, Green and Co. 1930), pp. 85–159, which begins ". . . in no part of the British Empire were the effects of the American Revolution more immediate, more direct, or more far-reaching"; Michael Kraus, "America and the Irish Revolutionary Movement in the Eighteenth Century," in Richard B. Morris, ed., *The Era of the American Revolution* (New York, 1939), 332–48; and Lawrence Henry Gipson, *The British Empire Before the American Revolution*, vol. 13 (New York: A. A. Knopf, 1967), pp. 3–31 ("Of all the parts of the empire that did not revolt in 1775, perhaps the closest in sympathy with the revolutionary movement in North America was Ireland" are the first words).

[5] Dudley Edwards, "American Image of Ireland," p. 229, n. 41, makes the case for John Adams's authorship. However, the opinion of Lyman Butterfield on the question of style must be regarded as decisive, so I withdraw John's penmanship and argue for his inspiration. We are in agreement that the other committee members, William Livingston and James Duane, can be discounted.

[6] Americans may not realise just how brilliant, and how original, John Adams's understanding of Irish history in *Novanglus* is. Dudley Edwards, "American Image of Ireland," pp. 215–18, says something of Sam Adams's achievement in mendacity on Irish questions.

[7] I owe this idea to H. F. Kearney, whose study of the origins of modern sectarianism in Ulster is awaited with impatience. The Phillips thesis was enunciated in "The Central Theme of Southern History," *American Historical Review* 34 (October 1928): 30–43.

[8] "The Lord Chancellor Bowes and the Chief Justice Robinson both distinctly laid down from the bench that 'the law does not suppose any such person to exist as an Irish Roman Catholic.'" W. E. H. Lecky, *A History of Ireland in the Eighteenth Century*, rev. ed., 5 vols. (New York: D. Appleton and Co., 1893), 1:146. Michael Davitt (1846–1906) is a famous example of left-wing Irish nationalism and labor leadership; his *The Boer Fight for Freedom* (New York: Funk and Wagnalls Co., 1902), is distinguished by its utter indifference to the blacks.

[9] Washington to Newenham, June 22, 1792, in George Washington, *The Writings of George Washington*, ed. John C. Fitzpatrick, 39 vols. (1931–44; reprint ed., Westport, Conn.: Greenwood Press, 1970), 32:73.

[10] Washington to Newenham, October 20, 1927, ibid., 190.

[11] Captain Benjamin Chapman, in a letter from America to an Irish friend, made unkind references to congressional inconsistency on this issue: "In their Address to the People of Canada," he wrote on June 21, 1775, "after inviting them to join their illegal Opposition and Combination, they flatter them with the Enjoyment and Prosperity of a Religion, which, in their Address to the People of Great Britain, they themselves say is frought with the most *impious and sanguinary Terms.*" *Faulkner's Journal* printed the letter, and hence it was—rather oddly, given the paper's pro-American attitude—picked up by the *Hibernian Journal*, August 4/6, 1775. The complaint was fair enough: compare the "Memorial to the Inhabitants of the Colonies," the "Letter to the Inhabitants of the Province of Quebec," and the "Address to the People of Great-Britain from the Delegates appointed by the several English Colonies," in *Extracts From the Votes and Proceedings of the American Continental Congress Held at Philadelphia on the Fifth of September 1774* (Philadelphia, 1774).

[12] *Dublin Gazette*, September 7/9, 1775. A circular letter excommunicating Whiteboys was shortly thereafter sent by the Roman Catholic Bishop of Ossory to his clergy and read, at his command, by every one of them from their altars on three successive Sundays in what he insisted had to be "an audible Voice." This offers a reasonable paradigm of social relations between the state authorities and the lords spiritual of the outlawed Roman Catholic Church. The slight suggestion that priests might in one or two cases be sympathetic enough to the Whiteboys to mumble their doom unless otherwise ordered is also symptomatic of the nature of the time. (*Dublin Gazette*, September 28/30, 1775.)

[13] *Dublin Gazette*, September 2/5, 1775.

[14] *Hibernian Journal*, July 14/17, 1775.

[15] *Dublin Gazette*, August 17/19, 1775. The proclamation was reprinted in successive issues for several weeks thereafter.

[16] *Dublin Gazette*, August 19/22, 1775.

[17] George Simon Viscount Nuneham to Mr. Whitehead, November[?] 1773, in Edward William Harcourt, ed., *The Harcourt Papers*, vol. 3 (Oxford: Printed for private circulation by J. Parker and Co., 1880), pp. 116–18.

[18] Wesley Frank Craven, *The Legend of the Founding Fathers* (New York: New York University, 1956) pp. 158–59.

[19] "A Member of the Irish Press," ed., *History and Proceedings of the '82 Club*, vol. 1 (Dublin, 1845) conveys a fair impression of this kind of thing. See Kevin B. Nowlan, "The Meaning of Repeal," in James Hogan, ed., *Historical Studies III.* (Cork and Cambridge, 1965).

[20] George Bancroft, *History of the United States, From the Discovery of the American Continent*, 10 vols. (Boston: Little, Brown and Co., 1834–75), 5:59–77; 8:168. John R. Alden, *The American Revolution, 1775–1783* (New York: Harper, 1954), p. 61. It should be said of Bancroft that the overblown rhetoric of the Irish House of Commons was never transformed into so exotic a *soufflé* by any other writer. One might think the Irish "patriots" did their thing in the expectation of his subsequent scrutiny, as in a sense of course they did:

> Still less did the ministry possess the hearts of the people of Ireland; though it controlled a majority of her legislature, and sought to allay discontent by concessions in favor of her commerce and manufactures. . . . "If we give our consent," objected Ponsonby, in the debate on the twenty fifth of November, "we shall take part against America, contrary to justice, to prudence, and to humanity." "The war is unjust," said Fitzgibbons, "and Ireland has no reason to be a party therein." Sir Edward Newenham could not agree to send more troops to butcher men who were fighting for their liberty; and he reprobated the introduction of foreign mercenaries as equally militating against true reason and sound policy. "If men must be sent to America," cried George Ogle, "send there foreign mercenaries, not the brave sons of Ireland." Hussey Burg condemned the American war as "a violation of the law of nations, the law of the land, the law of humanity, the law of nature; he would not vote a single sword without an address recommending conciliatory measures; the ministry, if victorious, would only

establish a right to the harvest when they had burned the grain."
(Bancroft, *History of the United States*, 8:168–69.)

It would be heartless to interrupt such a narrative by pedantic *sics* but perhaps the reader unhappily unacquainted with the immortal names in this passage needs to be reminded that the usual forms of two of them are *Fitzgibbon* and *Hussey Burgh*.

[21] Pauline Maier, *From Resistance to Revolution—Colonial Radicals and the Development of American Opposition to Britain, 1765–1776* (New York: Knopf, 1972), p. 255. It is obvious that Dr. Maier's remark is in theory correct: Catholics were not possessed of the vote and so it could be argued that the passage could stand. But it really does symbolize the kind of history which equates a country with its ruling elite and the book in general, while very valuable, presumes Ireland to be that which the Americans treated it as being—a small group of Protestants.

[22] "A Protestant" to the Conductors of *Hibernian Journal*, printed in the issue of July 12/14, 1775. The time of year was of course appropriate for such reflections.

[23] Francis G. James, *Ireland in the Empire, 1688–1770: A History of Ireland From the William-ite Wars to the Eve of the American Revolution* (Cambridge: Harvard University Press, 1973).

[24] *Dublin Gazette*, October 21/24, 1775.

[25] The *DNB* rather oddly ignores Agar, but some account may be obtained from the *G.E.C. Complete Peerage*; and see Lecky, *History of Ireland*, 5:303 and n. for a suggestive little anecdote.

[26] U.S. Continental Congress, "An Address to the People of Great-Britain . . . ," in *Extracts From the Votes and Proceedings*, pp. 2–3. And see n. 11, above.

[27] *Hibernian Journal*, July 17–19, 1775. James Napper Tandy, president, and they dined at the King's Arms, in Smock-Alley.

[28] U.S. Continental Congress, *An Address of the Twelve United Colonies of North America by their Representatives in Congress, to the People of Ireland* (Philadelphia: W. and T. Bradford, 1775), p. 10.

[29] Thomas N. Brown, *Irish-American Nationalism 1870–1890* (Philadelphia: Lippincott, 1966) is the standard work on Ford and the *Irish World*, but it is impossible to get the full flavor of it without looking over its files for an issue or two, notably that produced for July 4, 1876. Despite its obsessively horrific Anglophobia, the newspaper well merited its high circu-lation and status as a major labor newspaper and played an important part in the radical labor politics of the 1880's. *The Criminal History of the British Empire* was originally published in installments in the journal in 1881 and was reprinted as a book by the *Irish World* (New York, 1915) after Ford's death. The date of the reprint is important. Ford was somewhat respectabil-ized by Gladstone's declaration for home rule ("conversion" is surely the wrong word there), but the *Address* was suitably trotted out in his *The Irish Question as viewed by one hundred eminent statesmen of England, Ireland and America* (New York: Ford's National Library, 1886), and as he had been supporting physical force as against constitutionalism but two years before that, some of his constant readers would have had little difficulty in taking a fairly exotic interpretation of the passage. The *Address* was reprinted yet again in *Ireland's Claim for Recognition as a Sovereign Independent State Presented Officially to the Government of the United States by Eamon de Valera President of the Irish Republic* (Washington, 1920), pp. 110–14. I am deeply grateful to Thomas P. O'Neill of University College, Galway, for a gift of this rare pamphlet.

[30] Dudley Edwards, "American Image of Ireland," pp. 215–32.

[31] *Hibernian Journal*, September 20/22, 1775, where it covered the first three of the four columns of the first page.

[32] Maurice R. O'Connell, *Irish Politics and Social Conflict in the Age of the American Revolution* (Philadelphia: University of Pennsylvania Press, 1965), pp. 33–35.

[33] *Dublin Gazette*, September 2/5, 1775.

[34] Ibid., September 7/9, 1775.

[35] Ridge to Burke September 25, 1775, quoted in Gipson, *British Empire*, 13:30, and see n. 92 on that page.

[36] Shelburne to Price, September 5, 1779, printed in Lord Edmond Fitzmaurice, *Life of William, Earl of Shelburne, afterwards first Marquess of Lansdowne* ... (London: Macmillan and Co., 1876), 3:57. I am grateful to Conor Cruise O'Brien for this reference.

[37] A study of Irish monarchism is very much overdue. The recent spate of letters to the *Irish Times* attacking Maeve Binchy for her somewhat unkind report of Princess Anne's wedding suggests that the feeling has survived independence, an impression supported by much additional evidence.

[38] Any examination of Gaelic poetry, street ballads, or other forms of popular culture seems to support this. Such Jacobite comment that survives seems purely formal; Burns, by contrast, seems much livelier in his assertions of the Jacobite cause.

[39] If White's manuscript on the history of Limerick has survived or was ever printed, it is unknown to me. J. Ferrar, *The History of Limerick; Eccelesiastical, Civil and Military* ... (Limerick: A. Watson & Co., 1887), quotes from p. 193 of the manuscript on his p. 360. White (1715–68) wrote annals of Limerick whence the first printed history was taken, and also a short description of the county and city. He had been educated at Salamanca. It is singular how much of our information on Catholic loyalism emanates from Limerick, whose siege was not then a century old.

[40] Britannicus to the Printer, &c., *Dublin Gazette*, August 10/12, 1775. Britannicus might or might not have been from the larger island, but even if he were not Irish it is significant that he was thought worth bringing before the attention of the Irish. Allan Ramsay the younger signed several pieces attacking the colonies under the name of Britannicus but it may not be his. He was somewhat ill at this time and embarked for Paris to recruit his health. The styles of his work and this letter have irony and indignation in common, but this letter is more heavy handed than his work. It deserves some attention as a fine antislavery Loyalist argument. On the parallel with the Indians, see Lecky, *History of Ireland*, 1:227, 241, where Berkeley is one commentator making the analogy; also Howard Mumford Jones, *O Strange New World* (New York: Viking Press, 1964), pp. 167–73, showing the antiquity of the association.

[41] Arthur O'Leary, "An Address to the Common People of Ireland ... in July 1779" in his *Miscellaneous Tracts* (Dublin: J. Chambers, 1781), pp. 167–87. Rev. Thomas R. England, *The Life of the Reverend Arthur O'Leary* (London, 1822), pp. 79–81.

[42] A reading of Burns' poetry supplies one of the most interesting bodies of documentary material available to us in this era. The cult of Washington itself, so differently expressed by Burns and Byron, to name but two, suggests that this could well prove a point of important investigation. Burns' most obvious expression of his feelings is in his own poem to Washington, Byron's in his *Ode to Napoleon*, which R. T. Savage has edited and will, I hope, publish.

[43] Although Merriman has survived largely through one poem, it has been translated several times (as "The Midnight Court"), whereas Ó Súilleabháin is largely available only to readers of Gaelic. His work is well represented in any satisfactory anthology of Gaelic poetry for use in schools or otherwise.

[44] Daniel Corkery, *The Hidden Ireland: A Study of Gaelic Munster in the Eighteenth Century* (Dublin: M. H. Gill and Son, 1925), pp. 208–10, reprints the whole poem. The book is still highly suggestive, given our limited knowledge of Gaelic Ireland, but must be used with extreme caution as much because of the author's innocent romanticism as because of his somewhat ruthless efforts at thought control. See also Padraig Ua Duinnin, *Beatha Eoghain Ruaidh Uí Súilleabháin* (Dublin, n.d.), pp. 20–22, 42 (which last is in English), and the same author's *Amhráin Eoghain Ruaidh Uí Shúilleabháin*. (The English translations of these titles are "The Life of Red Eugene O'Sullivan" and "Songs of Red Eugene O'Sullivan," respectively. The poet's name is often anglicized as Owen, but inaccurately. He is the original of "Red Hanrahan" in Yeats' poetry. I owe all of this material to my mother, although the views on the poems are mine.)

[45] R. Dudley Edwards, ed., "The Minute Book of the Catholic Committee (1770–93)," *Archivium Hibernicum* 9 (1942):39–42.

[46] Weymouth to Buckinghamshire, August 4, 1779, printed in Henry Grattan, *Memoirs of the Life and Times of the Rt. Hon. Henry Grattan*, 5 vols. (London: H. Colburn, 1839–46), 1:369–70. Young Grattan assumes this letter is proof of the ministry's involvement in the anti-Catholic scare mentality; but in fact the text is against him.

[47] Buckinghamshire to Weymouth, August 19, 1779, in Grattan, *Memoirs*, 1:370–71.

[48] Dudley Edwards, "Minute Book of the Catholic Committee" pp. 60–64. The dating here—November 1781—is at variance with the dates supplied by Carey and followed by other chroniclers of the incident—November 1779. In other respects Carey's recollection is surprisingly accurate, and his statement of the title leads one to wonder whether he had retained souvenir sheets of the portion of the pamphlet printed. See his "Autobiography: Letter I," *New England Magazine* 5 (November 1833), 404–8. Edward C. Carter II, "Mathew Carey in Ireland, 1760–1784," *Catholic Historical Review* 51 (January 1966):503–27, is useful but contains some odd statements such as that McDonnell was a Catholic and that "there is no mention of the motion of the Committee" in my father's edition of the minute book.

[49] On the background to this see Maureen Wall, "The Rise of a Catholic Middle Class in Eighteenth-century Ireland," *Irish Historical Studies* 11, no. 42 (September 1958): 91–115. Carey's jibe about his master is in his "Autobiography," p. 406: "McDaniel, who, during the period of my apprenticeship, changed it to McDonnel, as a more respectable name." Of course, McDaniel might have been a Jew, or a Protestantized Jew: that would explain change of name, readiness to accept a Catholic apprentice as well as publish an extreme Protestant newspaper, and Mathew Carey's charitable remark.

[50] His *Vindiciae Hibernicae* (Philadelphia, 1837) is an extraordinary ragbag of scholarship and bad temper, execrably arranged.

[51] His bitter feud with Colonel Oswald, culminating in a duel, offers a useful illustration of this. See their exchange in the *Pennsylvania Evening Herald*, January 14, 1786, and Carey's satiric verse *The Plagi-Scurilliad* (Philadelphia, 1786), a copy of which is in the Massachusetts Historical Society.

[52] The quotation from Yeats is employed by T. N. Brown in *Irish-American Nationalism, 1870–1890* (Philadelphia: Lippincott, 1966) with great effect.

[53] Carey maintains ("Autobiography," p. 409) that "I was utterly unable to give any information on the subject, as I had lived in a state of total seclusion from public affairs, of which I knew little or nothing." Dr. Carter is suspicious of this, very rightly. The idea of a lively young printer's apprentice luxuriating in ignorance to this extent is absurd, especially considering who the apprentice was. It seems much more likely that Carey did tell Lafayette or whomever he talked to that the Catholics were progovernment but that he did not then wish to injure the image of Irish Catholicism in America and therefore concealed this in writing his autobiography.

[54] Dudley Edwards, "American Image of Ireland," pp. 238–39, and works therein cited.

[55] Brian Inglis, *The Freedom of the Press in Ireland, 1784–1841* (London: Faber and Faber, 1954), pp. 25–34. Inglis is very helpful, but it is curious that he describes the official administration, or Dublin Castle, publication, the *Dublin Gazette*, as "not in the strict sense a newspaper" (ibid., p. 37), whereas readers of these footnotes will have noticed my obligations to it. The answer may be that while in the early stages of the American conflict the *Gazette* was a very lively journal, no more impaired by its sponsorship than other journals equally committed to different interests were impaired by theirs, the war turned it into a tediously official handout. So that the impoverishment of the government press may be looked to as a further impact of the American revolution on Ireland.

[56] J. Hector St. John [i.e., Michel-Guillaume de Crèvecoeur], *Letters From an American Farmer* was printed in 256 pages by John Exshaw, of Dublin. The Belfast edition, printed by James Magee at the Bible and Crown, 9, Bridge Street, Belfast, contained 208 pages.

[57] J. Hector St. John de Crèvecoeur [i.e., Michel-Guillaume de Crèvecour], *Letters From an American Farmer* (London: J. M. Dent & Co., 1912), introduction by Warren Barton Blake, p. xviii.

[58] Magee advertisement, in "St. John," *Letters* (Belfast, 1783).

[59] Carey, *Vindiciae Hiberniae*, pp. 393–94.

[60] Grattan, *Memoirs*, 1:287.

[61] Buckinghamshire to Weymouth, May 24, 1779 in Grattan, *Memoirs*, 1:347–49.

[62] Maureen MacGeehin (afterwards Maureen Wall), "The Catholics of the Towns and the Quarterage Dispute in Eighteenth-Century Ireland," *Irish Historical Studies* 8 (September 1952):113–14.

[63] *A Letter to Lord Viscount Beauchamp upon the subject of his letter to the first Belfast company of Volunteers, in the province of Ulster* (London: Printed for J. Debrett, 1783).

[64] *Miscellaneous Pamphlets, Chiefly on American Affairs Sold by Mathew Carey* (Philadelphia: Mathew Carey, 1776–88). The collection also included the pamphlet of Carey's fellow-Irishman Aedanus Burke, *Address to the Freemen of South Carolina* (by Cassius, 1783) and Mirabeau's self-signed adaptation of Aedanus Burke's attack on the Cincinnati, translated and ascribed to him.

[65] Dublin *Chronicle*, January 25/27, 1770.

[66] The smugglers would have been another group of Irishmen who had a very clear awareness of one impact of the American Revolution. See the account of them in William Bell Clark, *Ben Franklin's Privateers: A Naval Epic of the American Revolution* (Baton Rouge, La.: Louisiana State University Press, 1956).

[67] William Drennan to Mrs. M. McTier, about Autumn, from Newry to Belfast, in David A. Chart, ed., *The Drennan Letters* . . . (Belfast: His Majesty's Stationery Office, 1931), p. 24.

[68] This note was in fact prepared after hearing R. R. Palmer's lecture, which preceded it in this volume; his remarks on the Enlightenment as conditioner of European attitudes at the time of the American Revolution are very helpful in assisting me on this point.

[69] William Crawford, *A History of Ireland From the Earliest Period, to the Present Time in a Series of Letters, Addressed to William Hamilton Esq.* (Strabane: J. Bellew, 1783), 1:vii. Lecky, *History of Ireland*, 2:505, sees the significance of the work though perhaps he is a little unkind about its historical worth.

[70] Maureen Wall, "The United Irish Movement," in J. L. McCracken, ed., *Historical Studies* 5 (London, 1965), pp. 135–36.

[71] Francis Dobbs, *A History of Irish Affairs, From the 12th of October 1779, to the 15th September, 1782, the Day of Lord Temple's Arrival* (Dublin, 1782), pp. 14–35, incorporating his *Letter to Lord North*.

[72] Lecky, *History of Ireland*.

[73] *Ireland's Story; or, A Comparative View of Ireland, in the Year 1776 and 1783* (Newry [1783]), p. 3.

[74] *A View of the Present State of Ireland* . . . (London: R. Faulder, 1780), p. 7.

[75] I base this on a reading of a wide cross section of pamphlet literature on commercial and constitutional questions during the period 1775–83.

[76] *Dictionary of National Biography*, s. v. "Dobbs, Francis."

[77] Notably in Bernard Bailyn, *The Ideological Origins of the American Revolution* (Cambridge: Belknap Press of Harvard University Press, 1967).

[78] Robert R. Palmer, *The Age of the Democratic Revolution: A Political History of Europe and America, 1760–1800*, 2 vols. (Princeton: Princeton University Press, 1959), vol. 1, chap. 10.

[79] E. R. R. Green, "The Scotch-Irish and the Coming of the Revolution in North Carolina," *Irish Historical Studies* 7 (1950): 77–86; "Scotch-Irish Emigration, an Imperial Problem," *Western Pennsylvania Historical Magazine* 35 (1952): 193–209; "The 'Strange Humours' that drove the Scotch-Irish to America, 1729," *William and Mary Quarterly*, ser. 3, 17 (1960): 183–99; *Essays in Scotch-Irish History* (London, 1969).

[80] Crawford, *History*, 1:vii.

[81] *United States Gazette*, August 27, 1795, quoted by Reinhard Cassirer, "United Irishmen in Democratic America," *Ireland To-Day* 3 (1938):133

[82] Owen Lattimore, "The Frontier in World History," *Studies in Frontier Culture* (London: Oxford University Press, 1962).

[83] See the publications of the Scotch-Irish Historical Society in the United States of the late 19th century, or those of the Northern Ireland tourist offices.

[84] See the *Journal of the American-Irish Historical Society*.

[85] George Dangerfield, *The Strange Death of Liberal England* (London: Constable, 1936) is unkind but not inaccurate on this mentality. See also my own work *The Sins of Our Fathers: Roots of Conflict in Northern Ireland* (Dublin: Gill and Macmillan, 1970), chapters 2 and 3.

[86] Conor Cruise O'Brien, *States of Ireland* (London: Hutchinson, 1972) is very helpful here.

[87] I draw these views from the debate on convention rules at the Republican National Convention, Miami Beach, August 1972, particularly the remarks of Congressman (now President) Gerald Ford.

[88] Palmer, *Age of the Democratic Revolution*, vol. 2, is an excellent starting point on this matter.

[89] The reception of Paine in Ireland has been overestimated by Ray B. Browne in "The Burke-Paine Controversy in Eighteenth-century Irish Popular Songs," in *The Celtic Cross: Studies in Irish Culture and Literature*, ed. Ray B. Browne, William John Roscelli, and Richard Loftus (West Lafayette, Ind.: Purdue University Studies, 1964), but his sources are impressive if not as representative as he believes.

[90] Rev. John Brady, "Laurence O'Connor: A Meath Schoolmaster," *Irish Ecclesiastical Record* 49 (January-June, 1937):284. I am grateful to T. P. O'Neill for supplying me with this article.

[91] The *Irish People* (Dublin), April 16, 1864, gives a good example of this chain of ideological descent.

[92] A comparative study of O'Connellite and Jacksonian democracy, stressing interactions, is very much needed.

[93] This question is cleared up, together with many others, in Dr. Douglas Cameron Riach's Ph.D. dissertation, "Ireland and the Campaign Against American Slavery, 1830–1860" (University of Edinburgh, 1976), especially at pp. 162–68. It was a privilege to have supervised this thesis.

[94] Speech of Daniel O'Connell in *History and Proceedings of the '82 Club*, p. 15.

[95] Malcolm J. Brown, *The Politics of Irish Literature: From Thomas Davis to W. B. Yeats* (London: Allen and Unwin, 1972), p. 70.

[96] Page vii.

[97] Brown, *Politics of Irish Literature*, p. 93. Charles Gavan Duffy, *Four Years of Irish History: A Sequel to "Young Ireland"* (London: Cassell Petler, Galpin & Co., 1883).

[98] Quoted, most conveniently, in Frank O'Connor, pseud. (Michael O'Donovan), ed., *A Book of Ireland* (London: Collins, 1957), p. 61.

[99] Brown, *Politics of Irish Literature*, pp. 212–13.

[100] Richard Barry O'Brien, *The Life of Charles Stewart Parnell, 1846-1891*, 2 vols. (London: Smith, Elder & Co., 1899)—especially vol. 1—is quite suggestive on these points.

[101] Conor Cruise O'Brien, in the *Irish Times*, March 27, 1975.

[102] The full text is even more depressing.

[103] Daniel O'Connell, "Journal," in Arthur Houston, *Daniel O'Connell: His Early Life, and Journal, 1795 to 1802* (London: Sir I. Pitman & Sons, 1906), pp. 143–44, 146.

[104] John Adams, *The Defence*, in *The Works of John Adams . . .* , ed. Charles Francis Adams (Boston: Little, Brown and Co., 1850–56), vol. 4.

[105] Notably in his self-written inscription for his tombstone.

[106] I owe the inspiration of these last lines to their converse, the close of G. K. Chesterton, *A Short History of England* (London: Chatto & Windus, 1917).

Owen Dudley Edwards has been lecturer in history at the University of Edinburgh since 1968. Previously he has taught at the University of Oregon and the University of Aberdeen. He has written for numerous journals and newspapers on both sides of the Atlantic on historical and political affairs and writes regularly for the Irish Times. *His publications include* The Sins of Our Fathers: Roots of Conflict in Northern Ireland *(1970)*, The Mind of an Activist: James Connolly *(1971)*, and *(with Gwynfor Evans and Hugh MacDiarmid)* Celtic Nationalism *(1968)*, as well as *"The American Image of Ireland: A Study of Its Early Phases"* (Perspectives in American History *4, 1970); he has coedited* James Connolly: Selected Political Writings *(1973)* with Bernard Ransom and *1916: The Easter Rising *(1968)* with Fergus Pyle. He also edited *Conor Cruise O'Brien Introduces Ireland *(1969). His latest book, *P. G. Wodehouse: A Critical and Historical Essay, *is in press. He was visiting lecturer in history, California State University at San Francisco, 1972–73, and visiting associate professor of history, University of South Carolina, 1973. He is married and has three children.*

The Impact of the American Revolution on Germany–A Comment

ERICH ANGERMANN

DESPITE the enormous flood of German references to the American Revolution and the Constitution of 1787, recently uncovered by one of my students, Horst Dippel,[1] there is little ground for assuming that the American Revolution had any strong impact on Germany at all. R. R. Palmer's statement, applied over a decade ago to Germany before 1800, holds true for the whole of German history up to now: "The Germans neither rejected revolution in the abstract, nor accepted it in its actual manifestations." [2] A vision of abstract "liberty" in the strain of Enlightenment ideology helped radicals to conceal their lack of truly revolutionary vigor and drove conservatives into relentless opposition to what they chose to call "Western" influences.

The impact of the American Revolution on German political thought was of course outdone by that of the French Revolution—so much so that, as far as revolutionary principles are concerned, the two forces became almost indistinguishable. It does not follow, though, that the image of the American Revolution suffered from the German repudiation of the French invaders in all instances. On the contrary, as the example of Edmund Burke and his German interpreter Friedrich Gentz suggests, the American Revolution might well serve as a foil for the excesses of the French Revolution—and this was strongly felt well into the era of German "Vormärz" in the 1830's and 1840's.[3]

The moving force of the American Revolution, as it was seen in Germany, was of course the idea of "liberty." German lumières and romantics, like their counterparts all over Europe, were not found wanting in willingness to worship a visionary liberty even though—or perhaps because—it was so remote from their daily lives as to lack all tangible reality. Possibly it was this enthusiasm for a lofty but somewhat evasive ideal which prevented, at least in the early decades, so many admirers of the American Revolution from understanding the more down-to-earth constitutional devices designed by the Founding Fathers for the protection of liberty. There was, indeed, a certain predisposition in the Holy Roman Empire for the acceptance of two of the basic concepts of the American Revolution—the sovereignty of the people and federalism.[4] Yet, both carried an entirely different meaning in the context of strikingly different political settings: "Sovereignty of the people," in the constitutional context of the Holy Roman Empire, was devoid of democratic implications in any modern sense. The term "federalism" was understood to mean the absence of a consolidated national government in a confederation of states. It was, however, not felt to be at variance with a hegemonial powerstructure and to require an essential equality of the constitutent member states. This attitude was taken over by the German Confederation (Deutscher Bund) from the Holy Roman Empire.

Abstract ideas about liberty and romantic visions of an irresistible, self-feeding revolutionary process were by and by complemented with more accurate knowledge about political institutions and constitutional proceedings of the United States. Sometimes this familiarity was meticulous and pedantic— it was in fact a German scholar, Robert Mohl, who produced the first comprehensive compendium of the federal constitutional law of the United States.[5] I have elsewhere tried to explain how and why such prodigious theoretical knowledge of things American did not lead to a true understanding of American political life in Germany, how in particular German Liberals failed to comprehend the interaction of democracy and federalism in the American system, and how they mistook their own effort in 1848–49 to establish a constitutional German Empire under the hegemony of Prussia to be an emulation of the American experiment.[6] I do not want to dwell any longer on that subject. I should like to suggest, however, that the felicitous outcome of the American Revolution appears to have been due to the unfailing leadership of a group of responsible men whose actions were rooted at least to some extent in a democratic consensus about a satisfactory political order, much more than to any sophisticated constitutional devices. Needless to say, it would have proved even more difficult to supply equally efficient leadership than to transfer and adapt a constitutional system from one country to another—and to so different a political society as Germany for that matter.

Nevertheless, there can be no doubt that even in the concept of German unity developed in the 1860's and translated into political practice by Bismarck the impact of American federalism was not altogether lost, even though the widespread German disapproval of democracy was to increase rather than give way in the period to come.[7] Even if a strong interest in American achievements prevailed in both pre- and post-World War I Germany,[8] any significant impact of either the constitutional pattern or the political ideas brought forward by the American Revolution was scarcely imaginable. It was not until after World War II that American constitutional principles, now in an entirely different political setting, exerted an unmistakable impact on the creation of a new German constitution, both in terms of democracy and federalism and their interaction. Even then, however, the hegemonial tradition prevailed over the American concept of federalism. And certain unitary undertones in today's German political scene would seem to indicate a reversal at least of the federalist trend rather than a stronger impact of the message of the American Revolution.

Notes

[1] Horst Dippel, "Deutschland und die amerikanische Revolution; Sozialgeschichtliche Untersuchung zum politischen Bewusstsein im ausgehenden 18. Jahrhundert" (Ph.D. diss., University of Cologne, 1972). In spite of certain shortcomings, especially on the interpretive side, this study is particularly useful and includes a truly formidable bibliography. Based on a vast amount of source materials largely unknown to other authors, it supersedes to some extent most of the previous literature. An English version will be published in 1976 by the University of North Carolina Press and Franz Steiner Verlag as a joint project of the Institute of Early American History and Culture at Williamsburg and the Institut für Europäische Geschichte Mainz.

[2] Robert R. Palmer, *The Age of the Democratic Revolution . . .* , 2 vols. (Princeton: Princeton University Press, 1959–64), 2:425.

[3] Friedrich Gentz, "Der Ursprung und die Grundsätze der Amerikanischen Revoluzion, verglichen mit dem Ursprunge und den Grundsätzen der Französischen," *Historisches Journal* 2 (Berlin, 1800):3–140; John Quincy Adams, trans., *The Origin and Principles of the American Revolution, Compared With the Origin and Principles of the French Revolution* (Philadelphia: Asbury Dickins, 1800).

[4] Friedrich Hermann Schubert, "Volkssouveränität und Heiliges Römisches Reich," *Historische Zeitschrift* 213 (1971):91–122; in general, for the last decades of the empire, Karl Otmar Frhr. v. Aretin, *Heiliges Römisches Reich, 1776–1806: Reichsverfassung und Staatssouveränität* (Wiesbaden: F. Steiner, 1967). The structural differences between the United States and the Holy Roman Empire as well as its successors are aptly pointed out by Robert C. Binkley, "The Holy Roman Empire Versus the United States: Patterns for Constitution-Making in Central Europe," in Conyers Read, ed., *The Constitution Reconsidered*, rev. ed. (New York: Harper & Row, 1968), pp. 271–84.

[5] Robert Mohl, *Das Bundes-Staatsrecht der Vereinigten Staaten von Nord-Amerika* (Stuttgart-Tübingen, 1824); and Erich Angermann, *Robert von Mohl, 1799–1875: Leben und Werk eines altliberalen Staatsgelehrten* (Neuwied: H. Luchterhand, 1962).

[6] Cf. Erich Angermann, "Early German Constitutionalism and the American Model," *Proceedings of the Sixteenth International Congress of Historical Sciences* (San Francisco, 1975).

[7] Cf. Rudolf Ullner, *Die Idee des Föderalismus im Jahrzehnt der deutschen Einigungskriege, dargestellt unter besonderer Berücksichtigung des Modells der amerikanischen Verfassung für das deutsche politische Denken* (Lübeck: Matthiesen, 1965).

[8] Cf. Peter Berg, *Deutschland und Amerika, 1918–1929: Über das deutsche Amerikabild der zwanziger Jahre* (Lübeck: Matthiesen, 1963).

Erich Angermann is professor of history and director of the Institute of Anglo-American History at the University of Cologne. His recent publications on the United States include Die Vereinigten Staaten von Amerika *(1966, rev. ed. in preparation), a history of the United States since 1917; he is editor and coauthor of two collections of essays on the American Revolution to be published in 1976 as well as the two-volume* Handbuch der Amerikanischen Geschichte, *the first volume of which is due for publication in 1977.*

The Impact of the American
Revolution on Japan

NAGAYO HOMMA

I SHOULD LIKE to take this opportunity to point to some ironies about the impact of the American Revolution upon constitution-making in modern Japan. Japan was isolating itself from the rest of the world·at the time of the Revolution, so obviously we cannot talk about the immediate response of the Japanese people to the American Revolution when it took place 200 years ago. But the spirit or idea of the Revolution as expressed through the Declaration of Independence and the federal Constitution had very much to do with the constitutional history of Japan.

Japan has had two constitutions in modern times, the Meiji Constitution of 1889 and the New Constitution of 1947 after World War II. The new constitution was proclaimed when Japan was under American occupation, and in that constitution there are passages which are, to borrow Professor Morris' words, "close paraphrasing or direct plagiarism from the Constitution of the United States and the several American states." Nonetheless, this constitution was accepted by the Japanese people as the fundamental law of the newly reborn democratic Japan, and to this day no responsible politician or scholar, whatever his political persuasion may be, has ever called openly for a repeal or abolition of the constitution.

In the case of the Meiji Constitution (the older one) we have to focus our attention on Itō Hirobumi, one of the most important statesmen in the Meiji era of Japanese history, who was assigned the job of making a draft of the Constitution. It is well known that some of the leading thinkers and opinion-makers in the early Meiji period were heavily influenced by the spirit of the American Revolution. Fukuzawa Yukichi, founder of Keio University, translated the Declaration of Independence into Japanese at the time of the Meiji Restoration of 1868. But it was Itō and his secretaries—one of whom, Kaneko Kentaro, had studied at Harvard Law School—who actually drafted the Constitution.

Itō came to know about the U.S. Constitution for the first time in his life when he visited the United States immediately after the Meiji Restoration. In 1870 he met Secretary of State Hamilton Fish, who recommended the *Federalist Papers* to Itō as the best book from which to learn about the making of the U.S. Constitution. According to Kaneko's memoirs, Itō referred to the *Federalist Papers* again and again during the period when he and his secretaries were drafting the Japanese Constitution.

Itō must have been aware of the advice given by Gen. Ulysses Grant to the emperor when the former President of the United States visited Japan in 1879. Grant suggested that the young emperor go slowly in giving political rights to the people because those rights, once given, were very hard to withdraw later.

Eventually, however, Itō turned to Germany to learn about constitution-making, and the final product of his efforts was influenced more by German thinking than by the American precedent.

After the promulgation of the Meiji Constitution, Kaneko prepared English versions of the Constitution and Itō's *Commentaries on the Japanese Constitution* and visited the United States and Europe asking politicians and scholars for comments. In the summer of 1889 Kaneko saw Secretary of State James Blaine, who, although he had been so busy that he had not read the Japanese Constitution, made four points. First, he said that a constitution should state only the fundamental principles without going into too much detail. Second, he warned against following the British example concerning the sovereignty of the monarch. Third, he recommended that ministers should be responsible only to the emperor and not to the people. Fourth, Blaine suggested that no provision about the impeachment of ministers should be made in the Constitution. When Kaneko replied that the Japanese Constitution already met these four points, Secretary Blaine was visibly pleased.

Another interesting comment was made by Oliver Wendell Holmes, Jr., then justice of the Massachusetts supreme court, who observed that the constitutions of European countries and the United States were suitable to their respective countries but were not applicable to Japan and that the Japanese Constitution should be based upon the tradition and customs of the Japanese people.

This glance at the history of constitution-making in Japan shows that, in the case of the Meiji Constitution, we started examining the American experience intensely but ended up with a constitution which was more influenced by the German Constitution than the American. It also shows that, in the case of the New Constitution, America imposed the American model upon a defeated Japan—against Justice Holmes warnings—but it has worked admirably.

Today, in this year of the Bicentennial celebration and the final collapse of South Vietnam, Americans are being challenged, according to Prof. Stanley Hoffman of Harvard University, to accept the proposition that the American model cannot be easily exported and is not relevant to huge parts of mankind. If so, the Japanese Constitution may remain the single tangible glory of the impact of the American Revolution in Asia, despite the vast difference in the historical experience of the two countries.

Nagayo Homma is professor of English and American history at the University of Tokyo. Among his recent publications are Mass Culture in America *(1975),* Life Styles and Values: Japan and America *(1973), and* Studies on Modern America *(1971).*

The Impact of the
American Revolution on Spain

Summary of Remarks

IGNACIO RUBIO MAÑE

KING FERDINAND VI of Spain, who kept his country out of the Seven Years War, died in 1759. His successor, Charles III, renewed the Family Compact with France (August 15, 1761), as a result of which Spain drifted into the war on the side of its Bourbon neighbor. The fortunes of war were not kind to Spain: she lost Cuba and the Philippines to the British. Britain restored these possessions to Spain at the peace negotiations, in return for Spanish cession of Florida to George III. To compensate Spain for her loss, France ceded Louisiana to her, thus bringing the Spanish into contact with the British American colonies along the full length of the Mississippi.

After the war, Charles III introduced reforms in Mexico through new administrators, José de Galvez and Juan de Villalba. The reforms were unpopular and the new governors more so; they excited unrest and riots among the Mexicans and can be said to have planted the seeds of revolution against Spain.

In 1776 de Galvez, now returned to Spain, became minister of the Indies. In 1777 he sent his nephew, Bernardo de Galvez, to New Orleans as governor of Louisiana with instructions to befriend the American insurgents. Galvez's predecessor, Don Luis de Unzaga y Amezaga, had in 1776 informed the home government of the progress of the rebellion and on September 7, 1776, enclosed petitions from Congress and Gen. Charles Lee, asking that trade be opened between the United States and Spanish colonial ports. Arms were in fact sent to the Americans from Havana via New Orleans.

In 1776 Floridablanca replaced Grimaldi as Spanish foreign minister. Floridablanca was far cooler toward the American cause than Aranda, the Spanish minister at Versailles, who courted the American commissioners and encouraged one of them, Arthur Lee, to visit Spain, where he assured him he would receive assistance; however, Floridablanca rebuffed Lee.

After a series of complicated negotiations in which Britain rejected Spain's offer to mediate her quarrel with France, Spain joined her French ally in the war against the British in 1779. In the same year Bernardo de Gálvaz was transferred to Havana with orders to plan the invasion and reconquest of Florida. Gálvaz executed his assignment with signal success: Pensacola was attacked and conquered on May 9, 1781. Seventeen hundred British prisoners were taken, along with a vast quantity of arms and ammunition. On August 18, 1781, the reconquest of Florida was completed with the capture of St. Augustine.

Aranda violated his instructions to sign the Peace Treaty of 1783, thus ending Spain's participation in the War of American Independence. In the last weeks of 1783 Aranda proposed to Charles III that Spain's New World possessions be divided among three princes of the royal family, who would presumably administer them in such a way as to secure them from the contagion of republican ideas flowing from the United States. The ideas was rejected, Aranda suspected, because of Charles' difficulties with his son Ferdinand, king of the Two Sicilies.

Ignacio Rubio Mañe, the Archivist of Mexico, has written extensively on the history of Mexico and Latin America and has taught at the University of Texas. He is a member of the Pan American Institute of Geography and History.

I know I voice the view of this distinguished audience in expressing our heartfelt thanks to our participants in what to me has been an exceptionally fruitful and wide-ranging program, to the Library of Congress, to Mrs. Kegan, and to the Cafritz Foundation for making it all possible, and to the State Department for its hospitality.

If we do not know now, after these two days of learned expositions, what the American Revolution has meant to the rest of the world, then we should retreat into a sullen isolation and abandon that precious sense of mission that has, for better or worse, helped fashion our foreign policy, spurred our benevolence, and in no small part shaped our destiny.

And a closing thought: 1975 is not 1776, but perhaps as we approach our Bicentennial it would be well to bear in mind the things for which America has stood among the nations of the world, the qualities that seemed best worth emulating by other nations, the governing standards that rendered it a haven for people throughout a world aching for liberty. Perhaps we can find out just where we have taken a wrong turning, and set ourselves once more on the right path.

Library of Congress Publications
for the
Bicentennial of the American Revolution

The American Revolution: A Selected Reading List. 1968. 38 p. 80 cents. For sale by the Superintendent of Documents, U.S. Government Printing Office, Washington, D.C. 20402.

The American Revolution in Drawings and Prints; a Checklist of 1765–1790 Graphics in the Library of Congress. 1975. 455 p. $14.35. For sale by the Superintendent of Documents, U.S. Government Printing Office, Washington, D.C. 20402.

The Boston Massacre, 1770, engraved by Paul Revere. Facsim. $2. For sale by the Information Office, Library of Congress, Washington, D.C. 20540.

Creating Independence, 1763–1789: Background Reading for Young People. A Selected Annotated Bibliography. 1972. 62 p. $1.15. For sale by the Superintendent of Documents, U.S. Government Printing Office, Washington, D.C. 20402.

A Decent Respect to the Opinions of Mankind; Congressional State Papers, 1774–1776. 1975. 154 p. $5.55. For sale by the Superintendent of Documents, U.S. Government Printing Office, Washington, D.C. 20402.

The Development of a Revolutionary Mentality. Papers presented at the first Library of Congress Symposium on the American Revolution. 1972. 158 p. $3.50. For sale by the Information Office, Library of Congress, Washington, D.C. 20540.

English Defenders of American Freedoms, 1774–1778: Six Pamphlets Attacking British Policy. 1972. 231 p. $4.75. For sale by the Superintendent of Documents, U.S. Government Printing Office, Washington, D.C. 20402.

Fundamental Testaments of the American Revolution. Papers presented at the second Library of Congress Symposium on the American Revolution. 1973. 120 p. $3.50. For sale by the Information Office, Library of Congress, Washington, D.C. 20540.

Leadership in the American Revolution. Papers presented at the third Library of Congress Symposium on the American Revolution. 1974. 135 p. $4.50. For sale by the Superintendent of Documents, U.S. Government Printing Office, Washington, D.C. 20402.

Manuscript Sources in the Library of Congress for Research on the American Revolution. 1975. 371 p. $8.70. For sale by the Superintendent of Documents, U.S. Government Printing Office, Washington, D.C. 20402.

Periodical Literature on the American Revolution: Historical Research and Changing Interpretations, 1895–1970. 1971. 93 p. $1.30. For sale by the Superintendent of Documents, U.S. Government Printing Office, Washington, D.C. 20402.

To Set a Country Free. An account derived from the exhibition in the Library of Congress commemorating the 200th anniversary of American independence. 1975. 75 p. $4.50. For sale by the Information Office, Library of Congress, Washington, D.C. 20540.

Twelve Flags of the American Revolution. 1974. 13 p. $1.25. For sale by the Information Office, Library of Congress, Washington, D.C. 20540.

Two Rebuses from the American Revolution. Facsim. $2.50. For sale by the Information Office, Library of Congress, Washington, D.C. 20540.